THE EXODUS ENIGMA

THE
EXODUS
ENIGMA

IAN WILSON

Weidenfeld and Nicolson
London

For Judith, Adrian and Noel
who tramped the sites with me

Endpapers
The Sinai Desert.

Frontispiece
'One day when Moses was grown up ... he saw
an Egyptian smite one of his fellow Hebrews'
(Exodus 2:11).
Pharaoh Tuthmosis III beating Asiatics,
from the temple of Amon at Karnak.

First published in Great Britain by
George Weidenfeld and Nicolson Limited
91 Clapham High Street, London SW4 7TA

ISBN 0 297 78749 7

Designed by Joyce Chester
Picture research by Caroline Lucas

Printed and bound in Great Britain
by Butler & Tanner, London and Frome

Contents

Author's preface

THERE are some books, however conscientiously researched, where the author knows at the outset that he cannot hope to come up with all the answers. This is one of them. Whether we are Christian, Moslem, Jew or atheist, almost inevitably we have heard something about the Biblical Exodus. The stories of the ten 'plagues', the parting of the waters, the wanderings in the desert and the fierce struggle for the 'promised land' – all these are part of world folklore. Yet what actually happened? And when?

No book yet written on the subject can be described as truly definitive, and this one is no exception, but in recent years there have been some remarkable new findings and new theories expounded. So far these have been scattered in different scholarly publications, often in language nearly incomprehensible to the average layman, yet collectively they are of such interest in overturning many previous assumptions about the Exodus that it is only right that some attempt should be made to bring them together. This is the aim of my book.

No one has been more aware than I of both the fascinations and the difficulties presented by this particular task, not least because of the many loose ends and controversial issues requiring further study. In my first-ever research project, on the Turin Shroud, I learned something of how to embrace a variety of academic disciplines, but research on the Exodus has, if anything, been even more diverse, including vulcanology, the ancient geography of the Nile Delta, and some of the lesser-known aspects of modern Egyptology.

In dealing with Egyptology, as the layman swiftly learns, not least of the problems is that there is no common language in which the subject is written. A pharaoh whom one Egyptologist calls Amenhotep, another calls Amenophis. It is anyone's choice whether we say Sethos or Seti, Usertesen, Sesostris or Senwosret, Tuthmosis or Thutmose, Akhenaton, Akhnaton, or Akhenaten. The dates for pharaohs' reigns vary from one scholar to another, according to whether they favour the 'high' or 'low' chronologies. Rather than weary the reader with repeated alternatives I have as a rule of thumb adopted all name styles and datings used in John Baines and Jaromír Málek's invaluable *Atlas of Ancient Egypt* (Phaidon, 1980), while stressing that all second millennium BC dates quoted should be regarded as, at best, tentative. A summary of the main relevant pharaonic dates is provided on page 189.

There are similar problems associated with Holy Land archaeology, and even with the names we use in referring to the area itself – 'Israel', 'Canaan', 'Syria-Palestine' – which are sometimes of necessity more loosely applied than one would wish. Archaeologists often disagree among themselves on the correct terminology for some of the broad archaeological periods, for instance the 'Middle Bronze IA' used by most archaeologists is Dame Kathleen Kenyon's 'Intermediate Early Bronze–Middle Bronze', while there are numerous complex disagreements concerning the identification of individual Biblical sites. Even which Biblical translation to use presents certain problems. Although my general preference is for the *Jerusalem Bible*, its continual references to God as 'Yahweh' in its Old Testament portion jar somewhat, and mainly for this reason I have opted to quote mainly from the *New English Bible* (Oxford and Cambridge University Press, 1970).

While tending to write on controversial topics, it is also my policy to consult specialist advice at every stage, and I have been particularly grateful to those in academic disciplines who have helped in this respect. At an early stage in the course of the research I wanted to devote the book almost exclusively to the Thera eruption – which I considered quite controversial enough in its own right – and from my own city Professor Peter Warren of Bristol University's Department of Classics and Archaeology generously helped with information on the latest scholarly arguments on this particular issue. On Thera itself Professor Christos Doumas, the current excavator, granted me a long interview at the Akrotiri site, while further on-the-spot guidance was kindly provided by graduate archaeology student Emmanuel Pothos of Athens University.

When, at my publishers' insistence, the book was returned to its original Exodus theme, I recognized the need to acquaint myself better with the latest developments in Egyptology. I received up-to-date information in enthusiastic abundance from practising Egyptologist John Romer, well known for his books and his TV series, *Romer's Egypt* and *Ancient Lives*. It was John Romer who recommended me to contact and give serious attention to the claims of Hans Goedicke, whose theories are discussed at length in this book. Dr and Mrs Goedicke made my wife and me most welcome at their home in Baltimore, and I have greatly valued subsequent correspondence with and information from Dr Goedicke. Because of the contentious nature of some of his translations of Egyptian texts, I have, however, also been grateful for the caution enjoined upon me by a friend of long standing, John Ray, Herbert Thompson Reader in Egyptology at the University of Cambridge. John Ray has advised me at all stages of the book's progress, including reading the manuscript, and has thus saved me from some otherwise elementary errors. It was through him that I learned of the work of Dr John Bimson, whose hypothesis redating the Exodus and Conquest dovetails neatly with so many of the other arguments advanced in this book. It was a particular delight therefore to find that John Bimson, formerly with Sheffield University, had moved to my own city of Bristol to take up his current post as lecturer in Old Testament studies at Trinity

Theological College. He kindly made available numerous scholarly papers that would otherwise have been difficult to obtain, and, like John Ray, read and advised me on the manuscript.

Among the numerous other individuals who have helped in a variety of ways, Dr Geoffrey Allen, visiting professor of chemistry at Southampton University, deserves a special mention. Dr Allen made available facilities for the microanalysis of volcanic dust from Thera, and also provided the mathematics for the relatively elementary yet crucial calculation that the Thera eruption really *would* have been visible from the Nile Delta. Similarly, I have greatly valued the help of near neighbours Ingrid and Gerry Cox, Ingrid for her ever-open village photocopying service – used exhaustively for this book – and Gerry for making available to me his cherished library of books on Egyptology. As in the case of my previous books, the Bristol Central and Bristol University Libraries provided the bulk of my reference needs, supplemented on this occasion by the Egypt Exploration Society and the Trinity Theological College.

Finally, particular thanks are due to those responsible for steering this book to publication: to former Weidenfeld deputy chairman Michael O'Mara for so promptly commissioning the idea; to picture researcher Caroline Lucas for somehow always managing to find the usually near-unobtainable photographs which I asked for; to copy editor Ralph Hancock for his swift and eagle-eyed attention to detail; and by no means least to my general editor, Wendy Dallas, for her patience and encouragement at every stage. Firmly and politely she resisted all my pleas that I needed more time to explore the fascinating avenues the Exodus research opened up. Otherwise I might still be wandering in the wilderness.

Bristol, England   Ian Wilson
July 1985

Introduction: 'Why is this night different from all other nights?'

O N a specific night of spring each year, Jewish families wherever they may be celebrate what may well be the world's longest perpetuated commemoration ceremony. Perhaps six or seven times older than American Thanksgiving and twice as ancient as Christmas (which did not begin to be celebrated until the fourth century AD), the Jewish *seder* is an annual thanksgiving for the 'Passover' by which the ancestors of today's Jews made their exodus from slavery in Egypt.

Almost every item on the meal table will be as prescribed in ancient ritual. There will be a dish of bitter herbs – in Hebrew *marorim* – traditionally lettuce, endive, chicory and nettles but today generally grated horseradish. There will be *harosset*, a sweet paste made from grated apples, nuts, cinnamon and a few drops of wine. For bread there will be *matzot*, plate-size crisp unleavened wafers – leavened bread is banned throughout Passover week. And almost incongruously there will be a single bone, usually from the shank of a lamb, roasted, but with hardly any meat remaining on it.

As if to emphasize that this is no empty observance but a real family celebration, there is a special part to play even for the youngest person present. He or she must ask, 'Why is this night different from all other nights?' and 'Why are these special foods on the table?' This fulfils the requirement of Exodus 13:8: 'On that day you shall tell your son: This commemorates what the Lord did for me when I came out of Egypt.'

The adults must now tell the child how at a particularly pressing moment of his ancestors' history God intervened on their behalf:

A wandering Aramean was my father; and he went down into Egypt and sojourned there, few in number; and there he became a nation, great, mighty and populous. And the Egyptians treated us harshly, and afflicted us, and laid upon us hard bondage. Then we cried to the Lord the God of our fathers, and the Lord heard our voice, and saw our affliction, our toil and our oppression. And the Lord brought us out of Egypt with a mighty hand and an outstretched arm, with great terror, with signs and wonders. (Deuteronomy 26:5–8)

The significance of all the Passover foods will now be explained to the child: how the *marorim* herbs are a reminder of the bitterness of Jewish sufferings at the hands of Egyptian taskmasters; how the *harosset* paste recalls the mortar with which the Israelites bound together the mud bricks they made for the Egyptians; the bread is left unleavened because of the haste with which the Israelites had to leave Egypt; and not least, how the lamb's shankbone evokes that lamb whose blood was smeared on Israelite doorposts so that they might be 'passed over' during the terrible Egyptian 'plague of the firstborn'.

The memory of that traumatic departure from Egypt is one returned to time and again in the so-called 'Old Testament' scriptures that Jews and Christians share. In Psalm 81 God reminded the Israelites: 'I am the Lord your God who brought you up from Egypt.' The prophet Amos, acting as the mouthpiece of God, spoke in the eighth century BC of 'the whole nation which he brought up from Egypt'. (Amos 3:1) His contemporary Hosea recalled in like fashion: 'When Israel was a boy, I loved him; I called my son out of Egypt.' (Hosea 11:1)

The compulsion to commemorate the moment of salvation from Egypt has been so powerful that Jews have continued to do so despite – and sometimes during – their many more recent sufferings. In the sixteenth century the Marrano Jews of Spain and Portugal celebrated the *seder* even though the penalty was death if they were caught by or denounced to the Inquisition. During the First World War the Jews of Eastern Europe celebrated the *seder* throughout the terrible privations inflicted on them by the German–Russian hostilities. In 1940 the Jews of the Warsaw ghetto resorted to the most ingenious improvisations to celebrate the *seder* even though the only future for them was starvation and butchery by German artillery.

The ceremony was already many centuries old in the reign of the Roman Emperor Tiberius when it was so fatefully celebrated by Jesus of Nazareth and his disciples in the upstairs room in Jerusalem. Much about the ceremony suggests that it may have been instituted on the very first anniversary of the escape from Egypt, while the Israelites were wandering in the wilderness of Sinai, as described in Numbers 9.

Since history is filled with tales of mass migrations and flights from danger, there must be something very special about the Exodus story that it should form so powerful a part of the folk memory of the Jewish, Islamic and Christian religions, and in our own time provide box-office success for Hollywood film makers such as Cecil B. DeMille. Yet the story itself is too elusive and too loosely documented to be considered history. Much of both Old and New Testaments has independent confirmation from other sources, and even though the exact dates of the birth and death of Jesus are uncertain, at least we have scraps of gospels surviving from within a century of his time. We are not so fortunate in the case of the Exodus. The so-called 'Dead Sea Scroll' library found at Qumran included, along with most other books of the Old Testament, a scrap from what had once been a leather scroll of the book of Exodus. This is known in scholarly circles as $4QEx^f$, and shows that over many centuries the text has remained consistent. But although the scrap probably comes from one of the master scrolls that the Qumran community acquired at its first foundation, it dates from no earlier

Traditional celebration of the *seder*, the annual Jewish family meal commemorating the Biblical Exodus from Egypt. It is thought to be the world's oldest surviving commemorative ceremony.

than the third century BC. At least a thousand years separate it from the likely date of the original Exodus events, a time in which the original account may have been irretrievably transformed into legend.

However real Moses may have seemed to generations of Sunday School classes, outside the books of the Bible there is no even remotely contemporary independent evidence of his existence. He figures in no Egyptian document, nor in any other of the surviving archives of the ancient Near East, and the story of his birth given in the second chapter of Exodus inspires little confidence. But it so happens that Neo-Assyrian and Neo-Babylonian cuneiform tablets tell a strikingly similar story of the birth of the Akkadian king Sargon I, who reigned nearly a thousand years before the likeliest time of Moses:

Sargon birth story	*Moses birth story*
My changeling mother conceived me; in secret she bore me.	. . . a Levite woman . . . conceived and bore a son . . . she hid him for three months, but she could conceal him no longer.
She set me in a basket of rushes; with bitumen she sealed my lid. She cast me into the river, which rose not [over] me.	So she got a rush basket for him, made it watertight with clay and tar, laid him in it, and put it among the reeds by the bank of the Nile. (Exodus 2:2–3)

In view of the similarity of the two stories, is it not likely that those who composed the Biblical books, perhaps at the time of the sixth-century BC Israelite exile in Babylon, simply used the Babylonian archives as a source of inspiration for how they *thought* Moses might have been born because they had no reliable information about what actually happened? In fairness, this is the only instance of a parallel between the Moses and Sargon stories. But the many duplications and inconsistencies in the first five books of the Old Testament indicate beyond reasonable doubt that they had no tidy single authorship, as from a near eyewitness. They were assembled from a bewildering hotchpotch of sources, probably several centuries after the events they describe. For instance, throughout the first five Biblical books, and even within a single story such as that of Noah's flood, the name of God varies between 'Yahweh' (Authorized Version 'Jehovah'), explained in Exodus 3:14 as 'I am who I am', and 'Elohim' which, somewhat incongruously for people believing in a single, universal God, actually means 'gods' in the plural. Similarly, within the single Book of Exodus there are two versions of the call of Moses and the appointment of Aaron. The one in Exodus 3 and 4 portrays Moses as the chief actor, with a setting in the land of Midian, whereas the one in chapters 6 and 7 casts Aaron in the leading role with a setting in Egypt. In yet another example, in Exodus 19:11 and 18, the mountain of God is called Sinai, while in 3:1 and 17:6, and throughout Deuteronomy, it is called Horeb.

Right The oldest known manuscript portion of the Biblical book of Exodus, a tattered third-century BC fragment of the famous Dead Sea Scrolls. It is probably part of a master scroll obtained when the Qumran community was first founded. The events of the Exodus were most likely at least a thousand years old when it was written.

Below The infant Moses discovered by Pharaoh's daughter, from a fresco in the third-century AD Jewish synagogue at Dura Europos on the Euphrates. Babylonian tablets tell a very similar story of the birth of King Sargon of Akkad, who reigned some thousand years before the estimated time of Moses.

Scriptural scholars have pondered long and hard on inconsistencies such as these, and have evolved a fascinating theory to explain how at least some of the various oral and literary strands were welded together to form the first five books of the Old Testament. The author or authors responsible for the 'Yahweh' material – known in theological circles as 'J' – appear to have been working in southern Israel at about the time of Solomon: that is, around the tenth century BC.

The author or authors of the 'Elohim' material – referred to as 'E' – apparently worked in northern Israel a century or so later. The material known as 'D' – in essence, chapters 12 to 26 of the present book of Deuteronomy – seems to have been written by someone close to the court of the late seventh-century reforming king Josiah of Judah. And material of mainly ritual or ceremonial interest appears to have been added by a priest or priests at the time of the Jewish exile in Babylon in the sixth century BC.

Inevitably there are tangled arguments over the details of such a reconstruction, with understandable differences of opinion over the extent to which 'J', 'E', 'D' and 'P' may have been individual, distinctive documents. Nor is there even any general agreement on this form of reconstruction. Several modern scholars have argued that this whole concept, largely the work of German 'form criticism', has been considerably overrated.

In all this confusion, what no one would deny is that the different strands, each of which contributed colouring from its own period of development, stemmed from an undetermined period of time in which the Exodus story had no formal, written form, but was a theme of entertainment and instruction recited or sung by generations of bards attached to the Israelite tribal settlements. To those who regard the Bible as infallible, such a haphazard development may appear disquieting. For cynics it may seem to provide a reason for believing nothing that the Bible relates. Such attitudes are, however, coloured by our own era of reliance on mechanical recordings. We forget that before the days of television and radio it was a matter of course for our own grandfathers to learn by rote poems and ballads of a length that seems totally impossible to us today. Even in our own time remote communities in Ireland, Armenia, Afghanistan and elsewhere have bards who regale them with centuries-old recitations of the heroic deeds of their ancestors. Many generations of Greeks transmitted the entire *Iliad* and *Odyssey* to each other in this way, and there are still Moslems who can recite from memory the entire Koran. The Biblical scholar Johannes Pedersen has pointed out signs that at least the first fifteen chapters of the book of Exodus have been designed for recitation of this kind, perhaps specifically to be 'performed' at each annual *seder* meal to answer the youngest child's question, 'Why is this night different from all other nights?'

The obvious drawback inherent in an oral tradition of this kind is that it inevitably gives rise to well-meant 'retouchings' by more individualistic bards to give their stories greater immediacy and impact in their own time. Just as painters of the Middle Ages depicted Jesus walking through medieval streets, drinking from medieval goblets, and being abused by 'Roman' soldiers in medieval armour, so it would have been natural for the occasional Exodus bard, or those working on putting the story into writing, to colour the narrative with elements familiar enough in their own time but possibly unknown at the time of the original events.

It is undeniable that throughout the opening books of the Bible, Genesis to Numbers, such amendments have been made. For instance, Genesis 24 prominently and persistently features camels in the long story of Isaac's marriage to Rebecca, an event theoretically long before the Exodus, and therefore some time in the first half of the second millennium BC. Genesis 37:25, also referring to this same approximate time, describes a camel train bringing gum, resin and other commodities from Gilead to Egypt. Yet in the Biblical Near East the camel was quite unknown as a beast of burden virtually throughout the entire second millennium BC. Cuneiform tablets from Cappadocia and Mari make frequent mention of baggage trains of asses, but never of camels. Although the wall paintings in Egyptian tombs teem with every tiniest detail of the way of life four thousand to three thousand years ago, they fail to feature domesticated camels. Not until the time of Solomon, long after the Israelites had indisputably begun to settle in their promised land, was the camel first used as a means of transport.

There are similar, clearly anachronistic references to the Philistines. In the book of Genesis the patriarch Abraham is described as living in 'the land of the Philistines' at Beersheba, in what is today southern Israel. According to Genesis 21, Abraham makes a treaty with 'Philistine' king Abimelech from nearby Gerar. And as described in Exodus 13:17, the Israelites, while escaping from Egypt, deliberately avoid a route called 'the road towards the Philistines'. It is as if, both before and during the time of the Exodus, Philistines were already occupying the land we call Israel. Yet, as is evident from the Biblical books of Judges and Samuel, the Philistines did not begin any serious invasion until some time after the Israelites had already settled in their promised land. In this respect Egyptian records provide a most helpful cross-check, since they show the time of the main incursion by the Philistines (referred to as the *P-l-s-t*, among the so-called 'Sea Peoples'), to have been during the reign of Pharaoh Ramesses III (1194–1163 BC), well after any time when the Exodus may actually have occurred. A bard has therefore quite clearly projected political and geographical colouring of his own time into his story.

Such tinkerings might be considered mere irritations were it not for the fact that the Genesis and Exodus narratives omit any name either for the Egyptian pharaoh who confronted the Biblical Joseph or for the pharaoh who confronted the Biblical Moses. The Israelite invasion of the promised land seems to have been during the Bronze Age, since it is the Philistines who are credited with the introduction of iron (1 Samuel 13:19–22); but this merely places it before the twelfth century BC. Since the northern part of Egypt (confusingly called Lower Egypt) was occupied by Asiatics, the so-called 'Hyksos', for substantial parts of the seventeenth and sixteenth centuries BC, it is often assumed that it would have been one such Asiatic king who appointed Joseph as vizier and invited the Biblical Israelites to settle in Egypt. The pharaoh who 'knew nothing of Joseph' (Exodus 1:8) would therefore have been one of the martial New Kingdom Egyptian monarchs who threw the Hyksos out. But who? All that can be said with any reasonable certainty is that if there was an Exodus, it would most likely have occurred at some time in the period covered by the chart shown below.

The problem is compounded by the fact that it would probably be misguided to think of any specific group recognizable as the Biblical Israelites during the period before the Exodus event, whatever and whenever that was. Throughout the whole of the second millennium BC, colourful groups of nomads and semi-nomads, accompanied by large flocks of animals, drifted back and forth across the Near East. They were called a variety of names, mostly uncomplimentary, by the ostensibly more sophisticated

Canaan	BC	Egypt	Biblical events
	— 2000 —	12th Dynasty	
		MIDDLE	
	— 1900 —	Senwosret III	Time of Abraham and Patriarchs?
MIDDLE BRONZE AGE		KINGDOM	
	— 1800 —	13th Dynasty	
	— 1700 —		
	— 1600 —	15th–17th Dynasties	Time of Joseph?
Fall of Middle Bronze Age cities		HYKSOS DOMINATION	
	— 1500 —	18th Dynasty	
		Hatshepsut Tuthmosis III	
	— 1400 —	NEW	
LATE BRONZE AGE		Akhenaten	Time of Joseph?
		19th Dynasty	
	— 1300 —	Ramesses	Oppression?
		II KINGDOM	- - - - -
		Merneptah	Exodus and Conquest?
	— 1200 —	20th Dynasty	Judges?
Coming of the Philistines		Ramesses III	Coming of the Philistines
	— 1100 —	21st Dynasty	Saul King David
IRON AGE			
	1000		

Broad chronology of the second millennium BC, showing the generally understood correlations between events in Egypt and events in Canaan. There are, however, considerable scholastic disagreements on points of detail, for example on the exact dates of Egypt's pharaohs. The traditional chronology for Biblical events is shown on the right.

Above A present-day Bedouin encampment, with camels. Despite Biblical illustrations showing camels, and frequent mentions of them in the book of Genesis, it is generally recognized that camels did not appear as domesticated animals in the Near East until around 1000 BC, well after the events of the Exodus. Biblical references to camels must therefore be regarded as an anachronism, one of many clues that the books were committed to writing several centuries after the events described.

Right Man drinking from a water-skin, as depicted in the tomb of the Egyptian scribe Nakht (*c* 1420 BC) at Thebes. That the Biblical Israelites used perishable containers like this is clearly indicated by passages such as Genesis 21:14, 16 and 19, which may well account for the absence of clearly identifiable Israelite remains from the Exodus and Conquest periods.

cosmopolitan societies on whose fringes they made temporary settlements. As remarked by one pharaoh of the early second millennium BC, among words of advice to his son: 'Lo, the wretched Asiatic . . . he has been fighting since the time of Horus, he does not conquer, nor yet can be be conquered . . . Do not trouble yourself about him: he is only an Asiatic. . . .' The difficulty for archaeologists of finding any trace of these people has been cogently expressed by Biblical scholar B.K. Waltke: 'Migratory groups such as the Israelites had been would not be expected to carry large equipment or durable material objects. Their containers may well have been mainly of skin, and their place of worship was portable and temporary, a tent.'

Egyptian sources speak of one such group as *'p–r–w*, or Hapiru, who seem to have been the same as those whom Mesopotamian sources call Habiru. No one bothers to describe them but they appear as drifters on the edge of ordered society, getting themselves employed, where they sought employment at all, as anything from fruit pickers to mercenary soldiers. While etymologically there is nothing wrong in identifying 'Hapiru', 'Habiru' and 'Hebrews', such is the diffuseness of these groups that, as scriptural scholars stress, the identification cannot be pushed too far. Probably the Biblical Israelites were part of the group collectively called Habiru, but certainly not all Habiru were Biblical Israelites.

What it is important to recognize is that although these people may have lived in tents, have been despised by city dwellers, and have kept no formal records, they were not necessarily primitive: indeed they had their own rich, chronicle-preserving traditions, albeit in an oral form. If instead of bowing before images in urban temples they preferred to worship a God of the open spaces, who is to say that theirs was not the richer life? Accordingly there is nothing unreasonable in the idea that such a people may at some moment have experienced so astounding a demonstration of the power of their unseen God that they felt impelled to commit this to perpetual memory in the only form they knew: a living annual feast linked to a recitation that generation could pass to generation. Of course, in committing the memory of such an event to an oral tradition, the accent would have been on theology, on glorifying God for the intervention they attributed to him. But the very same considerations would have caused them to try to preserve the most accurate possible memory of the original event.

Even some of the most hard-line Biblical scholars are grudgingly prepared to acknowledge that something along the lines of the Exodus story could once have happened. More than fifty years ago J.W. Jack remarked: 'It is far from likely that any nation would have placed in the forefront of its records an experience of hardship and slavery in a foreign country unless this had been a real and vital part of its national life.' And as Israeli scholars are wont to comment sagely: 'If Moses didn't exist, then he must have had a brother of the same name.' But exactly what happened, and when? Is anything retrievable? These issues are the crux of the Exodus enigma.

1. *The Exodus pharaoh mystery*

URING the Gemini IV space mission of 1965 there was a strange experience for US astronaut James McDivitt. As, with fellow astronaut Edward White, he looked out of the orbiting satellite and down at the earth slowly spinning 115 miles below, there came into view what he at first interpreted as a giant lava flow, a triangle of darkish blue in an apparently desolate terrain leading to a brilliant blue sea.

Then McDivitt realized his error. In reality the triangle below him was the richly fertile terrain of the Nile Delta, where the river fans out on its last seventy miles before reaching the sea. A little to the east lay the Sinai desert, white sand merging into mountains as the land narrows between the gulfs of Suez and Aqaba. And just visible in the curve of the horizon glistened the Negev foothills that mark the entrance to Israel. Whether or not he was aware of it, in that single moment of time McDivitt had a God's-eye view of the entire setting of the events of the Biblical Exodus. Presumably somewhere in the dark triangle Moses must have argued with the Egyptian pharaoh. Somewhere in one of the marshier areas Moses' Hebrew refugees made their spectacular crossing of the Sea of Reeds. And presumably somewhere along the scorching Sinai wasteland those same refugees voiced their complaint that they wished they had stayed among the fleshpots of Egypt. But clear as the setting might be, the time when these events took place is much less so.

Despite the forcefulness of the pharaoh's exchanges with Moses, exactly who he was in the long and well-established list of Egypt's pharaohs has gone unrecorded. And however academic that may seem, the correct identification of that pharaoh is crucial to our understanding of the whole early part of the Old Testament. Get it right, and whatever historicity there may be to the Exodus story should begin to fall into place. Get it wrong, and what may have been the Jewish religion's most seminal event must remain lost in the realms of myth.

As has long been recognized, the Bible does contain at least one apparent clue to the date of Exodus, and thereby the Exodus pharaoh. In 1 Kings 6:1 we are told that Solomon's Temple was founded 'in the four hundred and eightieth year after the Israelites had come out of Egypt, in the fourth year of Solomon's reign over Israel'. Since Solomon's reign is reasonably reliably known to have been between 970 and 931 BC, a simple calculation sets the Exodus at around 1450 BC. This would put it within the reign of the powerful Tuthmosis III, dated, according to a well-respected chronology, between 1479 and 1425 BC.

But for understandable reasons the world of Biblical scholarship refuses to accept that the Exodus can be dated so straightforwardly, or indeed dated by any one individual item of evidence. One of the most undeniably untrustworthy features of the Old Testament is its numbers. Can we really believe that Noah lived for 950 years (Genesis 9:29), or that 3,000 Hebrews were put to death for dancing around the golden calf (Exodus 32:28)? As is obvious from both Old and New Testaments, there are certain numbers that recur time and again – particularly seven, ten, twelve, and forty. While it would be incorrect to call these magic, or holy numbers, each had a certain symbolic meaning. Possibly because there are ten fingers on a pair of human hands, the number ten seems to have been thought representative of human frailty: hence ten plagues and ten commandments. Perhaps because there are twelve months in a lunar year, the number twelve seems to have been believed to be perfect, so we have twelve tribes of Israel and twelve disciples of Jesus. Although the exact reason is unknown, the number forty seems to have been associated with individuals or whole peoples being put to the test. Accordingly we find the world flooded for forty days (Genesis 7:17), Moses obliged to spend forty days on Mount Sinai (Exodus 24:18); the Israelites wandering forty years in the wilderness (Numbers 14:34), and Jesus spending 'forty days and forty nights' in the wilderness (Matthew 4:2).

The same considerations seem to have applied even to the multiples of such numbers. Was Moses really 120 years old when he died, or did someone attribute that age to him because twelve times ten suggests perfection within the limits of human frailty? Similarly, 1 Kings 6:1's 'four hundred and eightieth year' from the Exodus to Solomon's Temple is a multiple of twelve and forty, pregnant with any amount of symbolic meaning. The Septuagint, the famous third-century BC translation of the Old Testament into Greek, offers an alternative reading of four hundred and forty years, which hardly makes Old Testament numbers any more of a basis for trust.

In the search for an essential clue to the date of the Exodus, the world of Biblical scholarship has, therefore, in the main, focused its attention on a quite different scriptural passage. According to Exodus 1:11 the Israelites '. . . were made to work in gangs with officers set over them, to break their spirit with heavy labour. This is how Pharaoh's store cities, Pithom and Ramesses, were built.'

Ramesses: in the annals of Egyptian archaeology the name resounds like a thunderclap, instantly evoking the well-known Ramesses II, who reigned from 1290 to 1224 BC according to the best available dating. Unquestionably Ramesses was a builder on a huge scale, inevitably using slave labour. With a great flair for publicity, it was he who built the famous colossal rock-cut statues of Abu Simbel, set 200 miles beyond the country's southern border to warn any potential northward-bound Nubian intruders that they should stray no further. It was his thousand-ton, sixty-foot-high statue in the

The Nile Delta, as seen from the Gemini IV space satellite in 1965. The picture shows almost the entire area in which the events of the Biblical Exodus would have taken place: in the foreground is the Delta, with the Sinai Desert in the middle distance and Israel's Negev foothills stretching to the horizon.

Ramesseum at Luxor – now ignominiously toppled by an earthquake – that inspired Shelley's famous poem 'Ozymandias'.

However, it should be realized that Ramesses was not quite as prolific as the persistence of his name on Egyptian monuments might suggest. As Egyptian guides are fond of telling their visitors, one of his less endearing habits was to efface the pharaohs' names on monuments built before his time, substituting his own name gouged so deep that no successor was likely to repeat the process. He has accordingly been dubbed 'the great chiseller'. But as is known from Egyptian literary sources, he and his father Seti I were responsible for the Egyptian capital being moved from Thebes in the south to what the texts call 'Pi-Ramesses' ('house of Ramesses') in the Delta, precisely where he would have been in uncomfortably close proximity to any Hebrews settled in that region. And since Ramesses I reigned for only one year, and Ramesses III lived at the time of the Philistine invasion, if any Ramesses was involved in the Exodus events, it would have to have been Ramesses II.

So what do we know about him? Thanks to the Egyptian practice of mummification, he is one individual from more than three thousand years ago to whom flesh can be put, in the most literal sense. Just over a century ago, a spate of ancient pharaonic items flooding on to the black market alerted the Egyptian Antiquities Service that somewhere an important tomb or tombs had been discovered by peasants. Initial attempts to find the source proved abortive, but then, owing to a quarrel, a peasant called Mohammed Abd el-Rassul agreed to co-operate with the authorities. On Wednesday 6 July 1881, assistant keeper of the Antiquities Service Emil Brugsch was led to a hollow just outside the ancient capital of Thebes. A niche pointed out by el-Rassul led into a cave, and as his eyes adjusted to candlelight Brugsch found himself among the most incredible confusion of ancient coffins, shrines, jars, statuettes and funerary linen. In the midst of these Brugsch spied mummified bodies labelled with the hieroglyphs of some of Egypt's most illustrious pharaohs. Here was Seqenenre Tao from the Seventeenth Dynasty, Ahmose, Amenophis I and the first three Tuthmosids from the Eighteenth Dynasty and, not least, from the Nineteenth Dynasty, Seti I and his son Ramesses II. The hoard was an emergency assemblage of these pharaohs' remains by priests of the Twenty-first Dynasty after a period of chaos in which the original, obviously far more magnificent tombs, had been ransacked. It had remained undiscovered until el-Rassul and his companions had stumbled upon it six years before alerting Brugsch.

Five years later, with the hoard long since safely shipped downriver to the Cairo Museum, Brugsch stood as an onlooker when his superior, the great Gaston Maspero, began the delicate task of unwrapping Ramesses II's mummy. For the benefit of an age before television cameras, Maspero provided his own first-hand impressions of that moment:

He [Ramesses] was tall (nearly six foot after embalming), well made and perfectly symmetrical. His head was elongated and small in proportion

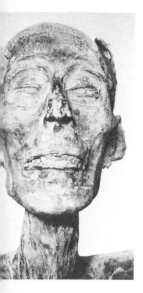

above Ramesses II's relatively well-preserved mummy, one of the cache of Egyptian royal mummies found by Emil Brugsch at Deir el-Bahri near Thebes in 1881. Although estimates of the mummy's age have varied, Ramesses is thought to have been in his nineties at the time of his death.

left Pharaoh Ramesses II (1290-24 BC), from a statue in the British Museum. He has been widely regarded as the pharaoh responsible for the oppression of the biblical Israelites.

to his body, and the top of his skull was completely bald . . . His eye-brows jutted out from a long narrow forehead. He had thick white lashes, small close-set eyes, a long thin nose, hooked like a Roman . . . hollow temples, prominent cheekbones, round protruding ears with . . . holes pierced in the lobes for ear-rings, a strong and powerful jaw, and a very high chin. His mouth was wide open and had thick fleshy lips. . . . His mask gave us a good idea of his facial expression when he was alive; he had unintelligent features which bordered on the animal, but they were coupled with a proud and determined air of sovereign majesty. . . .

Subsequent medical examinations have shown that Ramesses died in advanced old age – probably, as Egyptian literary sources indicate, well into his nineties. X-radiographs of his bones reveal that in his last years he suffered from arthritis of the right hip, which would have caused him to walk with a painful limp. Like several other pharaohs, he had serious problems with his teeth, the bone near the roots being badly pitted with abscesses. These would have made his breath most unpleasant. So was this the face that looked on Moses?

Many have certainly thought so, but the more cautious have recognized some difficulties. Although the Exodus text does not require it, it has often been assumed that the Egyptian pharaoh himself must have been drowned when his army pursuing the escaping Hebrews was swept away by the miraculous wave described in Exodus 14. To believe that the invalid nonogenarian Ramesses II personally took part, presumably shouting encouragement to his troops from a heaving war-chariot, more than strains credulity; and there has been no evidence to suggest that he died from anything other than sheer old age.

To overcome this difficulty it has sometimes been suggested that it was not Ramesses but his son Merneptah (estimated reign 1224–1214 BC) who died in the so-called 'Miracle of the Sea'. Prolific in everything, Ramesses is credited with having fathered over a hundred children, and whatever the truth of this, he outlived so many that Merneptah was actually thirteenth in the original order of succession. Like that of his father, Merneptah's mummy has survived, though from a separate hoard found in 1898 by the French Egyptologist Victor Loret. Medical examination has shown him to have been bald and overweight, the latter evident from thick overlapping folds of skin still visible despite the reducing effect of the embalming process. But in the early years of this century there was a flurry of excitement when Merneptah's skin was observed to be blotched with whitish deposits, as if from dried salt water. Surely this must be evidence that he had died from drowning, attributable to nothing other than the Bible's famous miracle?

Unfortunately for any enthusiasm that might have been generated, further study revealed a more prosaic explanation. Such encrustations are to be found on most Egyptian mummified remains, and simply derive from the natron salts used to dehydrate the body as part of the mummification process. Merneptah was seventy at his death, and the calcareous state of his aorta, sent to London for specialist examination, has suggested that he probably died of heart trouble.

In fact, quite aside from any considerations of the 'Miracle of the Sea' incident, of all pharaonic candidates for involvement in the Exodus story, Merneptah is among the most unlikely. In 1895 the great Egyptologist Sir Flinders Petrie discovered a stele or tablet from Merneptah's reign with a particularly pertinent inscription:

> The princes are prostrate, saying: 'Mercy!'
> Not one raises his head among the Nine Bows.
> Desolation is for Tehenu, Hatti is pacified;
> Plundered is the Canaan with every evil;
> Carried off is Askalon; seized upon is Gezer;
> Yanoam is made as that which does not exist;
> *Israel is laid waste, his seed is not*;
> Palestine is become a widow for Egypt!
> All lands together, they are pacified.
> Everyone who was restless has been bound by [Merneptah].

As Egyptologist John A. Wilson of Chicago has remarked, there is little doubt that the message of this stele is largely a boast, along the same lines as the propaganda of Ramesses II. The last battle fought with Hatti, the Hittite empire, was that of Kadesh, back in Ramesses II's fifth year. Although Ramesses filled some twenty temple walls in claiming it as a great victory, the extant peace treaties between the two countries reveal it to have been a draw, and neither Ramesses nor Merneptah ventured to do more than preserve this status quo.

The real interest of the stele is its reference to Israel, the first in all history. Although, in contrast to every other name mentioned, this is given the hieroglyphic symbol determining it as a people rather than a territory, the context makes clear that this is a people already so settled somewhere in Palestine that Merneptah, fictionalizing though he undoubtedly was, felt obliged to single them out for special mention. Since Merneptah reigned for only ten years, even if the Exodus had happened in his first year there would have been no time for anything even remotely resembling the purported forty years of Israelite wanderings in the wilderness.

The Merneptah stele provides, then, what historians call a *terminus ante quem* – an end point – requiring that whatever the date of the Exodus it must have been before Merneptah. We are therefore thrown back to Ramesses II and his 'store cities' Ramesses and Pithom. What, outside the Bible, do we know of them?

It has long been known that Ramesses II's Pi-Ramesses would have been in the Nile Delta, discouraging any serious efforts to discover it. Unlike in Upper Egypt, where handsome ancient stonework can be revealed simply by brushing away the sand, in the Delta any buildings that remain from antiquity are predominantly of mud and in mud. The water table can often

Pharaoh Merneptah (1224–14 BC), from a sculpture in the Cairo Museum. Ramesses
II's thirteenth son, Merneptah, was already middle-aged by the time he came to the
throne. Although it was once thought that he was the pharaoh who was drowned
pursuing the Biblical Israelites, this theory has now been abandoned.

Dating from Pharaoh
Merneptah's reign, the first
known inscription referring
to Israel, on a stela from
the destroyed temple of
Merneptah on Luxor's west
bank. Among other claims
relating to an Asiatic
campaign, the inscription
boasts 'Israel is laid waste,
his seed is not' (see detail,
right). This is clearly an
exaggeration (although
there is some evidence that
Merneptah did conduct an
Asiatic campaign), but the
inscription is important in
establishing that by the time
of Merneptah's reign the
Israelites must already have
been established in their
'promised land'.

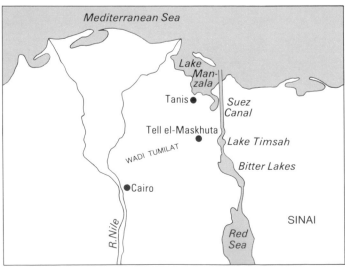

Above The huge, bleak site of Tanis, in the northern part of the Nile Delta. Because so many Ramesses II monuments have been discovered here, it has been widely identified as Biblical Ramesses. But it is now certain that the Ramessid monuments were transported from elsewhere, and that Tanis was not even founded until some two centuries after Ramesses II's time.

Left The Nile Delta today, showing sites thought to have been Biblical 'Pithom' (Tell el-Maskhuta), and 'Ramesses' (Tanis). Recent findings show these identifications to have been misguided.

be a mere foot below the surface, making the task of excavation unpleasant, scientifically difficult and, from the layman's viewpoint, fairly unrewarding. In the early years of this century the great Sir Flinders Petrie made a few cursory soundings at a site called Tell el-Retabeh, one of the tells or mounds in a depression known as the Wadi Tumilat. The find of an unusually-worded Ramesses II inscription prompted him to suggest that it might have been the Biblical Pi-Ramesses, but the idea attracted little support.

Then in 1929 Strasbourg University Egyptologist Pierre Montet began the first of more than twenty years of excavations at a vast coastal site known to the Greeks as Tanis, a barren and desolate mound set in monotonously flat surroundings. Sir Flinders Petrie had picked at it in the mid-1880s, but it was Montet who started to get excited about it. He found it to be an enormous jumble of monuments, the vast majority incised with the all-too-familiar cartouche of Ramesses II – except that these seemed to be genuinely his. Of particular interest was a temple inscription with Ramesses' name linked to what seemed to be the city name Ramesses and a whole pantheon of gods:

> Ramesses beloved of Pre of Ramesses,
> Ramesses beloved of Set of Ramesses,
> Ramesses beloved of Amun of Ramesses . . .

With the exception of Thebes, down in the south of the country, there was nowhere in Egypt with as many Ramesses II monuments as Tanis. Almost equally significant was what the site did not contain. There was nothing from the Eighteenth Dynasty, the one immediately preceding the time of Ramesses II and his father Seti I. The obvious deduction was that Tanis, alias Pi-Ramesses, was an original creation of Ramesses II, thus matching perfectly the Exodus 1:11 information that Ramesses was a city the Biblical Hebrews had to build for their pharaoh. When Montet published his arguments, not only did scholar after scholar begin to accept them, they interpreted them as proof positive that Ramesses II, and certainly no earlier monarch, must have been pharaoh of the Exodus. As pointed out in 1962 by American Biblical scholar G. Ernest Wright, 'We now know that if there is any historical value at all to the store-city tradition in Exodus . . . then Israelites must have been in Egypt at least during the early part of the reign of Ramesses II.' Four years later, laying stress on how Tanis was an original Ramesses II creation, the British Egyptologist K.A. Kitchen remarked: '. . . the Exodus can hardly be dated to the preceding Eighteenth Dynasty as was once thought by some scholars.' So prevalent has the idea been that, to this day, in most textbooks and Biblical atlases Tanis is shown as Biblical Ramesses and, in direct consequence, Ramesses II identified as the most likely pharaoh of the Exodus.

Yet it is now known with great certainty that Tanis was neither the Biblical nor Egyptian Pi-Ramesses, nor was Ramesses II responsible for building anything at that particular location. More recent careful study of the site's stratifications has revealed not only nothing of the Eighteenth Dynasty, but nothing of Ramesses' own Nineteenth either; nothing in fact until the Twenty-first Dynasty, some two centuries *after* his time. The explanation for the prevalence of so many Ramesses II building blocks and so much of his statuary is that in the Twenty-first Dynasty, roughly contemporary with Israel's kings Saul and David, these were transported from the real Pi-Ramesses several miles away. As evidence for this operation, and the crudity with which it was carried out, several of the monuments have missing bases, and one pharaonic statue, which lost its toes during the removals, had these replaced with ones of lime-coated mud. The reason for the removals appears to have been a silting up of the original Pi-Ramesses, so that by the Twenty-first Dynasty it could no longer function as an Egyptian capital.

So where was the real Pi-Ramesses? We will identify this in a later chapter, but in the meantime the fact that Tanis was *not* this city removes at a stroke the force of the very reasons advanced for Ramesses II being pharaoh of the Exodus – the absence at this site of any pre-Ramessid strata.

If the muddles over the Pi-Ramesses site have added only confusion to the Exodus enigma, little more light has been thrown by the quest for the city Exodus 1:11 calls Pithom. A consensus of Egyptologists has equated it with a Delta city the Egyptians knew as Per-Atum; and interestingly there survives from Merneptah's reign a text, intended for classroom use, which provides a rare mention of this Per-Atum. It takes the form of the sort of report a frontier official might send back to his pharaoh: 'Another communication to my [lord], to [wit: We] have finished letting the "Shosu" tribes of Edom pass the fortress [of] Merneptah . . . which is [in] Tjeku, to the pools of Per-Atum of Merneptah . . . to keep them alive and to keep their cattle alive.' This clearly shows that the Per-Atum/Pithom region of the eastern Delta was regarded as valuable pasturage for nomadic groups and their flocks: the Shosu, like the Habiru, are frequently mentioned as pastoral nomads. This particular incursion into Egypt obviously recalls that of Joseph's family described in Genesis 46:6: 'They took the herds and the stock which they had acquired in Canaan and came to Egypt, Jacob and all his descendants with him . . .'

But where was Per-Atum/Pithom? Egyptian texts suggest that it was somewhere in the watery depression today known as the Wadi Tumilat, an east–west channel providing a southerly route to the Sinai peninsula. In 1883 the Swiss philologist Eduard Naville thought he had found it at a tell called el-Maskhuta, towards the eastern edge of the Wadi Tumilat. As at Tanis, there was a jumble of inscriptions and ruins, including a Ramesses II red sandstone fragment with the regional name Tjeku, just as on the Merneptah 'Per-Atum' document. Another inscription, although of the third century BC, referred three times to Per-Atum. Naville found the ruins of large storehouses, which he took to be responsible for the 'store city' description of Pithom given in Exodus 1:11. The mud brick from which these storehouses were constructed even seemed to correspond with the variety 'without straw' described in Exodus 5:6. But very recently Tell el-Maskhuta has been re-excavated by University of Toronto Egyptologist John S. Holladay in association with the American Research Centre in Egypt (familiarly known as ARCE). As a result, Naville's conclusions, like those of Montet, have been completely overthrown. Although Tell el-Maskhuta had some simple Asiatic settlement during the second part of the Middle Bronze Age, that is, around 1600 BC, it subsequently went unoccupied until the Saite and Early Persian periods of Egyptian history, c609 to 486 BC. In other words it was unoccupied throughout the entire period in which the Biblical Exodus can conceivably have occurred. Wherever Biblical Pithom/Egyptian Per-Atum may have been, it certainly was not at Tell el-Maskhuta.

So far, therefore, the Exodus 1:11 reference to Pithom and Ramesses has scarcely been a helpful clue as to which pharaoh confronted Moses. But as has already been remarked, no one piece of evidence can hope to determine the date of the Exodus.

Another consideration is what archaeology can tell us of the subsequent Biblical event, the conquest of Canaan. It was in the course of this event that Jericho's famous walls are said to have taken their mysterious tumble. Jericho is another site that has been the subject of exhaustive archaeological excavations, so what clues to the Exodus date has it provided?

2. *When did the walls tumble down?*

I N looking to the Israelite conquest of Canaan for clues to the date of the Exodus, one factor needs to be borne in mind. According to the Biblical account, the actual entry to the promised land, beginning with the conquest of Jericho, was not until forty years after the original Hebrew refugees had left Egypt. As already noted, no great reliance can be placed on the accuracy of Biblical numbers; yet there seems little reason for anyone to have invented a story of a prolonged wandering unless something of the kind had actually occurred.

If we expect excavations in Israel to reveal clear evidence of an explicitly Israelite incursion of this kind, and at some well-defined archaeological period, we are bound for disappointment. Although the Biblical book of Joshua, like Exodus a blend of different literary strands, is a model of detail on the various battles and stratagems, trying to equate this with what can be gleaned from archaeology and Near Eastern historical records presents an enigma no smaller than that of the Exodus itself.

In this context the apparent Israelite capture of Jericho, purportedly a major coup and told in lavish detail in Joshua 6, provides a prototype for the rest. Despite popular impressions, the Jericho of the second millennium BC was neither a particularly big nor a particularly important town. Tucked away in the Jordan rift valley, it lay in something of a backwater for anyone making a direct entrance to Canaan from Egypt, and the Egyptians seem hardly ever to have taken an interest in it. Only if someone was trying to get into Canaan from the east – Biblically, the precise route taken by the Israelites – would Jericho have been a natural target. The reason for this lies in a freak of geography. Set in otherwise arid terrain 900 feet below sea level on the fringes of the Dead Sea, Jericho has a prolific spring, the Ain es-Sultan, which provides it with such lush vegetation that it has attracted human settlement for most of the last nine thousand years. Furthermore, it provides a natural garrison point for anyone trying to prevent invasion into Canaan from east of the Jordan. From this point of view, the book of Joshua's sequence of events relating to Jericho make perfect strategic sense – as has been recognized by some present-day Israeli generals – and deserves to be respected for that.

It is when anyone tries to look for evidence of the Joshua event amid the heavily scarred mound of ruins accumulated during thousands of years of settlement that the going becomes tough. Perhaps the most important

The mound of Jericho, as seen from the air. Although the site can be confidently identified as the one referrred to in the Bible story of Joshua's conquest, it is far from certain that Jericho had any walls at the time Joshua is traditionally thought to have lived.

feature for the layman to appreciate is that unlike Egypt, but in common with virtually every other Palestinian or Canaanite site of the second millennium BC period, Jericho is dumb. While most sites in Egypt bear a wealth of inscriptions and pictorial representations which act as at least a reasonable guide to history, the archaeology of Palestine, inclusive of Jericho, is characteristically dependent on little more than what fallible archaeologists have tried to deduce from jumbles of building foundations and broken pottery.

It would be quite wrong to decry the often extremely valuable deductions archaeologists can and do make from such ostensibly nondescript materials. As first realized by Sir Flinders Petrie, pottery, like clothes, has had fashions which vary from century to century. But unlike clothes, pottery does not decay, and once broken is generally considered too worthless for anyone to try to remove. In the different habitation levels on an archaeological site sudden changes in the type of pottery can therefore be important indicators of the settlement's changes of fortune. Radical differences, perhaps accompanied by signs of burning in the previous level, are likely to denote an invasion by warlike newcomers, and to the experienced archaeologist the characteristics of the newer pottery can often indicate exactly who those newcomers were.

Valuable as the method is, it also has considerable limitations. While it may be possible to determine that a particular site suffered three successive waves of invasion by named invaders, in the absence of any written material or inscription the original historical name of that site may remain completely unknown. There are relatively few second-millennium BC sites in Israel that have been identified with certainty. The method is also dependent on each new group using a new, distinctive pottery rather than, say, some nondescript hand-made ware, or wooden platters and wineskins. Another source of confusion can be the importing of pottery from another source. The calibre of the excavators who uncover and interpret such evidence is also a crucial factor. As may be expected, the Holy Land attracted a variety of amateur enthusiasts early on, who may have gone through the motions of working on Petrie principles but had standards far short of today's predominantly Israeli professionals. Even today the arguments of highly competent archaeologists between themselves attest to how much such a method still leaves to be desired.

In this context, the history of excavations at Jericho again serves as a model for much of the rest. Because of the Ain es-Sultan spring, it does happen to be one of the sites where identification is reasonably certain, and was recognized as such by the first archaeological visitor, Captain Charles Warren of the Palestine Exploration Fund in 1867. Between 1907 and 1909 Professors Ernst Sellin and Karl Watzinger directed a German–Austrian excavation at the site, and were the first to claim they had discovered the famous walls of Jericho – two concentric mud-brick rings of fortification, the outer one of which, they concluded, 'fell about 1200 BC and therefore must be the city wall which Joshua destroyed'. In the 1930s along came

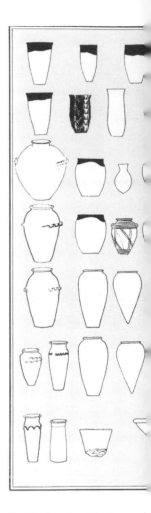

Sir Flinders Petrie's diagram of the chronological sequence of varieties of pottery he found at archaeological sites. Often archaeologists can now 'read' something of the history of a site prior to excavation, simply by studying the different varieties of pottery fragments littering the surface.

a British expedition under the leadership of Professor John Garstang. Although Garstang identified four successive building stages at Jericho, he, like Sellin and Watzinger, focused his attention on the two concentric rings, concluding, because of surrounding evidence of destruction, that it must have been the inner, later one which was the object of Joshua's attack:

> The space between the two walls is filled with fragments and rubble. There are clear traces of a tremendous fire, compact masses of blackened bricks, cracked stones, charred wood and ashes. Along the walls the houses have been burned to the ground and their roofs have crashed on top of them.

Noting that the stones of the outer wall had fallen outwards and those of the inner wall inwards, and also that the walls appeared to have been cracked by some extraneous force, Garstang concluded that what had caused them to tumble was an earthquake – not uncommon in the rift valley in which Jericho is situated – and it was this which gave Joshua's Israelites their apparently heaven-sent opportunity to make their dramatic capture. In Garstang's judgment, all this occurred about 1400 BC; although on the basis of the same evidence Jesuit Father Hugues Vincent argued for an alternative date of 1250 to 1200 BC.

Then in 1952 there arrived at Jericho the formidable British archaeologist Dr Kathleen Kenyon (later Dame Kathleen). With the benefit of joint British, American and Canadian sponsorship she spent six years at the site, cutting a deep slice into the mound in order to be able to study all the different levels right back to c9000 BC, by which she established Jericho as probably the oldest township in the world.

For us the real revelation from Kathleen Kenyon's careful trenching is how badly Garstang and his predecessors misinterpreted their evidence – by making the normal archaeological assumption that upper levels are likely to be the more recent. As she was able to demonstrate, erosion had created a misleading picture of the different levels, with the result that the wall chosen by Garstang in fact belonged to the Early Bronze Age, c2300 BC, and was the last of no fewer than seventeen successive collapses and rebuildings that had occurred during the previous seven hundred years. Jericho was then taken over by squatter nomads, followed by a period as an unwalled village settlement, after which, c1900 BC, it was rebuilt as a prosperous walled Middle Bronze Age town, and about a century later given even more impressive fortifications with a castle-like rampart. Then, as at many other Middle Bronze Age centres, there came savage destruction. According to Kathleen Kenyon's own reporting:

> All the Middle Bronze Age buildings were violently destroyed by fire. . . . That the destruction extended right up the slopes of the mound is shown by the fact that the tops of the wall-stumps are covered by a layer about a metre thick of washed debris, coloured brown, black and red and by the burnt material it contains; this material is clearly derived from burnt buildings farther up the mound.

Right Dr Kathleen Kenyon, excavator of Jericho 1952–8, who re-evaluated the findings of the previous excavator, Professer Garstang.

Below Houses of Middle Bronze Age Jericho, revealed during Kathleen Kenyon's excavations. Behind the banded marker is a cutaway section showing the layer of burnt debris from the Middle Bronze Age destruction, and beyond can be seen the crude foundations of virtually the only known Late Bronze Age dwelling found at Jericho.

Although this might conceivably sound like the work of Joshua and his fellow Israelites, right up to the end of her life this was not Kathleen Kenyon's view. For her this was one of a series of destructions of Canaanite cities at the end of the Middle Bronze Age which she and most of today's archaeologists attribute to the Egyptians. Historically (as indicated by the chronology, page 16), in about the mid-sixteenth century BC the Egyptians succeeded in expelling the Hyksos who had taken over the control of Egypt. Following up their advantage, the Egyptians launched an attack against some of the places to which the Hyksos had fled in Canaan, in turn pacifying the country to such an extent that it essentially became a province of a new Egyptian empire. All this happened between c1550 and 1450 BC; whereas for Kathleen Kenyon, if Joshua existed at all, he would have made his incursion much later, some time about the thirteenth century and the reign of Ramesses II, well into the Late Bronze Age.

Although Kathleen Kenyon never concerned herself much about the problem, here her findings raised particularly severe difficulties for anyone trying to equate archaeology and the Biblical record. For unlike Middle Bronze Age Jericho, prosperous and with castle-like ramparts, Late Bronze Age Jericho seems to have been all but invisible. There were certainly no walls, and the only significant settlement found by Kathleen Kenyon consisted of some foundation stones of a room, 'a small irregular area of contemporary floor', a mud oven and a single dipper juglet. As she wrote in 1957, 'The evidence seems to me to be that the small fragment of a building which we have found is part of the kitchen of a Canaanite woman, who may have dropped the juglet beside the oven and fled at the sound of the trumpets of Joshua's men.'

So was this all that the Joshua 'conquest' amounted to – a mere walk-over at an undefended ghost town? The problem has given rise to a variety of explanations. Since the Jericho site undoubtedly has suffered serious erosion, it has been suggested that what could have been a substantial walled Late Bronze Age settlement has simply been washed away. To this Kathleen Kenyon has responded:

> This is theoretically quite possible, but there is clear evidence against it. When layers are washed off the top of a mound, they must be washed somewhere. Broken mud brick could to some extent be blown away in a wind, but not heavier objects and in particular the all-important potsherds. These should be found in the wash at the foot of the slopes. The thirteenth-century potsherds simply do not exist anywhere on the site.

Another suggestion, the brainchild of German scriptural scholar Martin Noth, has been that when the Israelites, on entering Canaan, came across impressive Middle Bronze Age ruins such as those at Jericho, they simply invented an invading folk hero, Joshua, to account for them. To this, too, Kathleen Kenyon has brought a cogent objection:

> I find it difficult to believe that the early Israelites would have recognized this mound as a ruin, the product of human activity. It would not have

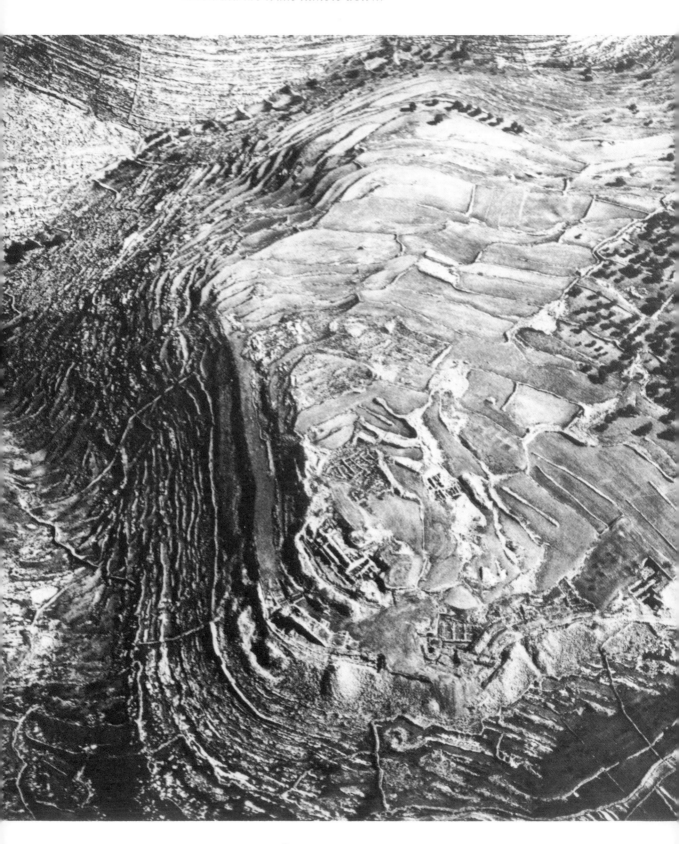

taken many decades for rain and wind to have reduced the destroyed mud-brick buildings to the mound of earth one sees today, and there would be no need to explain it.

Reinforcing Kathleen Kenyon's view is the fact that many early nineteenth-century travellers thought the *tells* of the Near East to be natural mounds until archaeology began to prove otherwise.

So if there is any truth to the Joshua story, what did happen, and when? Compounding the problem is the fact that Jericho is not an isolated case. According to the seventh and eighth chapters of the Book of Joshua, after his success at Jericho Joshua advanced into the hill country towards the north-east, where lay Ai, apparently a relatively small Canaanite city (Joshua 7:3), but with its own king (Joshua 8:14). The story of how an inadequate contingent of Joshua's men were first repulsed (Joshua 7:2–5), then via a skilful feint how they bloodily captured Ai, burned it to the ground 'and left it the desolate ruined mound it remains to this day' (Joshua 8:23–9), is accorded more or less equal importance to the victory at Jericho. The detail in both stories far exceeds that of Joshua and his companions' subsequent victories.

Ai is identified in Joshua 7:2 as 'east of Bethel', and since there has been a good consensus of agreement that Biblical Bethel was present-day Beitin, some twelve miles north of Jerusalem, Biblical Ai has been confidently identified as a substantial tell, appropriately entitled et-Tell ('the ruin'), less than two miles east of Bethel. There was a small Rothschild expedition to this site during the 1930s, led by Madame Judith Marquet-Krause, but the definitive one was that conducted between 1964 and 1972 by Dr Joseph A. Callaway of the Southern Baptist Theological Seminary, Louisville, Kentucky. From the so-called Bible belt of the USA, Callaway is one excavator who would have been delighted to offer corroboration of the Joshua story if any such had been forthcoming; but it has not. Callaway found that Ai, like Jericho, was a major fortified city in the Early Bronze Age, and that it suffered a series of destructions and rebuildings culminating in a particularly savage and decisive attack around 2400 BC. But then, unlike Jericho which had a major rebuilding in the Middle Bronze Age, Ai (or at least et-Tell), stayed abandoned and desolate for some 1,200 years. It was desultorily reoccupied in about 1200 BC by no more than a small group of squatter nomads who, without even any walls, could have offered scant resistance to the sort of invading army attributed to Joshua. Yet again the book of Joshua would seem to be a work of fiction.

If, in fact, it is assumed (as it usually is) that Joshua and his companions' attack occurred at any time during the Late Bronze Age/Ramesses II/ approximately thirteenth century BC period, there exists the same incompatibility between the Biblical and the archaeological evidence. According to Numbers 21:1–3 and Judges 1:17, before their success at Jericho the Israelites had been attacked by expeditions from two major Canaanite cities of the Negev, Arad (which had a king), and Zephath. Apparently the

The mound of Et-Tell, seen from the air. Although long thought to have been Biblical Ai (Joshua 7 and 8), Dr Joseph Callaway's recent excavations have revealed the site to have been unoccupied throughout the period to which the Israelite Conquest is attributed.

Site	Biblical account	Archaeological evidence	Agreement
Jericho (Tell-es Sultan)	Major, strongly fortified city captured and burnt by Joshua (Joshua 6:1-24)	Neither walls nor evidence of significant settlement in the Late Bronze Age	No
Ai (et-Tell?)	Major, strongly fortified city captured, burnt and made a permanent ruin (Joshua 8:19-28)	No evidence of fortification or occupation in the Late Bronze Age	No
Bethel (Beitin?)	Captured by the tribe of Joseph; inhabitants slaughtered (Judges 1:22-26)	At Beitin evidence of a 'tremendous conflagration' at Late Bronze Age level	Possible
Hazor (Tell-el Qedah)	A royal city captured and burnt by Joshua, but subsequently reoccupied by the enemy (Joshua 11:10-12)	A Late Bronze Age destruction level found, but no evidence of subsequent reoccupation	No
Debir (Tell Beit Mirsim)	A royal city captured and its inhabitants slaughtered (Joshua 10:39; Judges 1:11)	A Late Bronze Age destruction level identified	Yes
Lachish (Tell ed-Duweir)	Captured and the inhabitants slaughtered (Joshua 10:31-32)	Destruction accompanied by great conflagration dateable to reign of Ramesses II	Faintly possible
Hebron	An Anakim city captured and its inhabitants slaughtered (Joshua 10:36-37)	No evidence of Late Bronze Age occupation	No
Hormah (Tel Masos or Khirbet el Meshâsh)	A Canaanite city (Zephath) captured and renamed by the tribe of Judah (Judges 1:17; Numbers 14:21)	No evidence of existence in Late Bronze Age	No
Dan (Tell Dan)	Formerly known as Laish, captured and burnt by Danite tribe, inhabitants killed, then town rebuilt for Danite occupation (Judges 18:27)	Evidence of slight cultural change in Late Bronze Age, but no fire	No
Gibeon	Population enslaved, but city apparently preserved (Joshua 9:10)	No evidence of significant occupation in Late Bronze Age	No
Arad (Tel Malhata)	Arad's king defeated in battle shortly before main Israelite invasion (Numbers 21:2-3)	No evidence of existence in Late Bronze Age	No

If the Israelite conquest of Canaan is dated to the Late Bronze Age, the Bible and archaeology do not agree.

Israelites defeated both, Zephath subsequently being renamed Hormah ('Destruction'). Archaeologically it has been established that there indeed were such cities commanding the eastern approaches to the Negev, Arad having been identified as Tel Malhata, and Zephath/Hormah as Tel Masos. But the archaeological record also indicates that both were destroyed at the end of the Middle Bronze Age, and there is no evidence of subsequent occupation throughout the Late Bronze Age. According to Joshua 10:36-7 and also Judges 1:10 Hebron, in the hill country to the west of the Dead Sea, was a royal city whose king, and entire 'Anakim' population, Joshua and the Israelites slaughtered shortly after their success at Ai. Yet as recent excavations have revealed, although Hebron was a 'populous' and well-fortified city up to the end of the Middle Bronze Age, there was subsequently no discernible occupation until comparatively late in the Iron Age, that is, around the time of the Israelite kings Saul and David. According to the ninth chapter of the book of Joshua the inhabitants of Gibeon, a 'great city' west of Jericho, became so alarmed at the Israelite slaughterings that they negotiated a peace treaty by pretending to be poor travellers from outside Canaan. Apparently on discovering the trick Joshua treated the inhabitants as slaves, but at least honoured the treaty by preserving their lives (Joshua 9:26, 27). Yet, after extensive excavations at Gibeon during the early 1960s, the site director, the notable scholar J.B. Pritchard, was obliged to conclude:

> There was no extensive city on the tell from the end of Middle Bronze until the beginning of the twelfth century. . . . There can be no doubt, on the basis of the best evidence available, that there was no city of any importance at the time of Joshua.

The picture is, in fact, such a consistent one that it is best illustrated by a chart (see opposite). There are exceptions, notably Debir, and also Bethel and Lachish, where compatibility is possible, although recent excavations at Lachish have shown its destruction to have been during the twelfth century, in the reign of Ramesses III, and almost certainly the work of the Philistines. The notable Israeli archaeologist Yigael Yadin, who died in 1984, found a Late Bronze Age date for Joshua compatible with his excavations at the impressive fortress site of Hazor. However, even Hazor presents a compatibility problem, since Yadin has ascribed to Joshua the last of three Late Bronze Age destructions at the site (after which there was apparently only a semi-nomadic settlement), leaving no room for the information in Judges 4 that a Jabin of Hazor and his General, Sisera, some long time afterwards harassed the Israelites for a period of twenty years.

Overall, the only reasonable assessment of any attempt to set the so-called Israelite 'Conquest' within the normal Late Bronze Age period ascribed to it is that somewhere the subject is badly astray: either the Biblical accounts are very seriously wrong, or there is some fundamental error in current archaeological thinking. One further example of this concerns the so-called 'Judges' period – that is, the period of the Israelites' history from their settlement in the promised land to their facing a new enemy in the

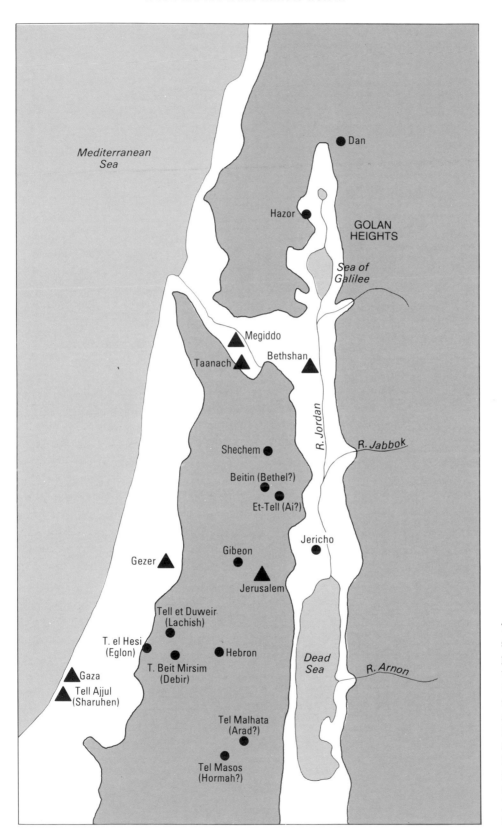

The land of the Bible, showing some of the principal sites associated with the Israelite 'conquest' (marked with a dot), and those which the Bible acknowledges the tribes failed to take (marked with a pyramid). In general Israelite successes were in the hill country and against the smaller towns. Jerusalem did not fall until the time of David.

form of the Philistines. According to the book of Judges this included the following episodes:

	Years
Oppression of Israel by Cushan-rishathaim (Judges 3:8)	8
Period of peace under Othniel (Judges 3:11)	40
Oppression by Eglon (Judges 3:14)	18
Period of peace under Ehud (Judges 3:30)	80
Oppression by Jabin (Judges 4:3)	20
Period of peace under Deborah and Barak (Judges 5:31)	40
Oppression by Midian (Judges 6:1)	7
Period of peace under Gideon (Judges 8:28)	40
Reign of Abimelech (Judges 9:22)	3
Judgeship of Tola (Judges 10:2)	23
Judgeship of Jair (Judges 10:3)	22
Oppression by Ammonites (Judges 10:8)	18
Judgeship of Jephthah (Judges 12:7)	6
Judgeship of Ibzan (Judges 12:9)	7
Judgeship of Elon (Judges 12:11)	10
Judgeship of Abdon (Judges 12:14)	8
Coming of the Philistines	
	total 350 years

As noted in the Introduction, the coming of the Philistines is known for certain to have been early in the reign of Pharaoh Ramesses III (c1194–1163 BC). So theoretically we should be looking for the Israelite invasion to have occurred, not at any time in the Late Bronze Age/thirteenth century BC, but much more like the end of the Middle Bronze Age/sixteenth century BC. Although Biblical numbers must be treated with scepticism, even the most hard-headed reading of the book of Judges suggests that there was a substantial period between the Israelite and Philistine incursions into Canaan, whereas the interval between the reigns of Ramesses II and Ramesses III was a mere thirty years.

So what are we to believe? That there was so little historical substance to the Biblical descriptions of the Exodus and conquest that generations of Jewish commemorations of the Passover have been a waste of time? Or that the whole subject needs the most careful reappraisal, step by step, with nothing taken for granted?

During the last few years there has been a quiet but important discovery, hitherto virtually unnoticed by the general public: the correct identification of the *real* Biblical Ramesses. And it is to this first, solid piece of new knowledge that we will now turn.

3. *The real Biblical 'Ramesses'*

ALTHOUGH three and a half thousand years is but a blink in the timespan of the earth, if Gemini IV's astronauts had been able to look back that far in time over the Nile Delta, they would have noted some striking differences in the appearance of the region between then and now. Obviously man has made his mark in the form of the Suez Canal, but nature's changes have been even more substantial. Today, twelve miles north of Cairo, the Nile forks into two branches only, the Rosetta turning towards the west, and the Damietta veering to the east. But even in the time of the fifth-century BC Greek historian Herodotus the Nile's final dispersion was much more complex:

> The Nile divides [Egypt] . . . flowing . . . as far as Cercasorus in a single stream, and below that city splitting into three branches, of which one trends eastward and is known as the mouth of Pelusium, and another trends westward and is called the mouth of Canopus. There remains the third branch which, coming down from the southward to the tip of the Delta, flows straight on and cuts it in two on its course to the sea. This branch, issuing at what is called the mouth of Sebennytus, is neither the least in volume, nor the least famous of the three. In addition there are two other mouths, the Saitic and Mendesian, which split off from the Sebennytic and so run into the sea. The Bolbitine and Bucolic mouths are not natural branches but excavated channels.

It is quite certain that Herodotus was telling the truth about these extra branches because not only are they attested by other sources, but in recent years aerial photography has helped in revealing the faint traces of the original beds along which they flowed. Herodotus' description 'one trends eastward and is known as the mouth of Pelusium' corresponds perfectly with one specifically eastward course which can be traced as having had its exit at the old Roman coastal town of Pelusium, the ruins of which are today three miles inland because of silting. Just how much this silting has changed the appearance of the Delta can be gauged from the fact that a thirty-foot depth of silt has accumulated during the past six thousand years. There were also serious subsidences in the coastal area during the first millennium AD. Deep core samples taken in areas subsequently given over to swampy water and salt have revealed pollens indicative not only of abundant reeds, bulrushes, ferns, asphodel and lotus, but also characteristically dry-ground flora such as tamarisk and acacia.

The lesson of these findings is that, quite aside from human activity, in about the second millennium BC the Delta seems to have been distinctly different in appearance from its rather featureless character today. Unlike the predominantly agricultural Upper Egypt to the south, the Delta was mainly pastoral, offering lush grazing to large herds of cattle, sheep, goats and any number of pigs. But there were also cities, as is quite obvious from Egyptian records, and it is only because of silt accumulations and the use of perishable, reusable mud brick as building material that today's Delta lacks the impressive ancient monuments so abundant in the south.

So where among these cities was Pi-Ramesses, alias the Biblical Ramesses? Although this is seldom realized by Biblical scholars, there have in fact been preserved from non-Biblical sources some remarkably detailed descriptions of this city, helpful from the point of view of establishing an exact location. One of the so-called Anastasi Egyptian papyri from the British Museum sycophantically praises Pharaoh Merneptah for apparently having built 'Per-Ramesses-meri-Amun', then goes on to describe it as: '. . . the forefront of every foreign land, the end of Egypt, the [city] beauteous of balconies, radiant with halls of lapis lazuli and turquoise. The marshalling places of your chariotry. The mustering place of your army, the mooring place of your ships' troops.' Another in the same collection gives it the name 'Great of Victories', locates it between Egypt and Syria, and specifies temples of different gods at each point of the compass, the one for Seth being to the south. It is described as being 'full of food and victuals'. The latter theme is one taken up in elaborate detail in a third Egyptian document, an essay written by a pupil, Pai-Bes, for his teacher Amen-em Opet:

> . . . I have arrived at Per-Ramesses-meri-Amun and found it in [extremely] good condition. A fine district whose like exists not, having the layout of Thebes. . . . The residence pleasant to live in: its countryside is full of everything good, and it has food and victuals every day. Its ponds have fishes, its pools have birds. Its gardens are verdant with herbage. . . . Its granaries are full of barley and emmer [a species of wheat]: they draw near to the sky. Onions and leeks . . . lettuce of the grove; pomegranates, apples and olives; figs of the orchard, and the mellow wine of Kankemet surpassing honey. . . . Red *wd* fish of the lake of the Residence [that live] on lotus flowers; *bdin* fish of the *Hr* [canal?] waters . . . Its ships sail forth and moor [so that] food and victuals are in it every day . . . The papyrus marshes come to it with papyrus reeds and the Waters of Horus with rushes.

Although, even with due allowance for landscape changes, these descriptions are difficult to equate with Tanis, they do not of themselves provide any more help in locating Pi-Ramesses other than to place it between Egypt and Syria, and at the 'edge of Egypt' it must have been towards the north-eastern corner of the Delta. But as it happens, a much neglected

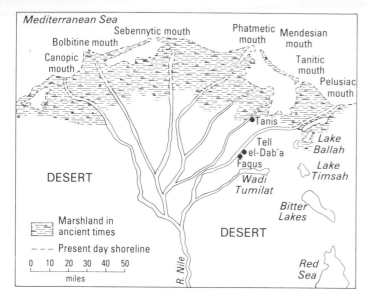

The Nile Delta, showing ancient river mouths as described by Herodotus and others, together with the likely extent of marshland in Biblical times, based on the researches of U.S. geographer Professor Karl Butzer. Broadly the Nile branches have become fewer in number and moved westwards as silt has built up over thousands of years; and much of what is dry land today was formerly sea or marsh. Although a great deal is still conjectural, and the exact topography changed from one period to another, an appreciation of these geographical changes is important to a correct understanding of the terrain in Biblical times.

fourth-century AD travelogue by the sharp-eyed French abbess Egeria pin-points it almost exactly. Although even by Egeria's time, sixteen hundred years ago, Ramesses was obviously already seriously ruined, someone appears to have told her that this was the original Biblical site. According to her account:

> But from the town of Arabia [Faqus] it is four miles to Ramesses. We, in order to arrive at Arabia, our stopping place, had to pass through the midst of Ramesses, which town of Ramesses is now fields, so much so that it does not possess a single habitation. It is true that it is visible, since it was both huge in circuit and had many buildings, for its ruins, however tumbledown they may be, appear endless even to this day.

Fortunately Faqus/Arabia is still extant today, some twenty miles south of Tanis. It is in a region full of fields, corresponding to the abundantly fertile terrain in which Pi-Ramesses was said to have been situated; but rather more pertinent is what has been found four or five miles to its north.

Two of the thousands of decorated faience tiles found at Qantir, some fifteen miles south of Tanis in the Nile's eastern delta. Inscriptions on the tiles showed them to have been from a major palace of Ramesses II and his father Seti I. So was this the site of the real Biblical Ramesses?

In 1929 an Egyptian archaeologist, Mahmoud Hamza, was excavating the southern portion of a modern village called Qantir when he came upon thousands upon thousands of beautiful faience tiles. Hamza and others retrieved so many of these that today the Paris Louvre has a reconstructed doorway of them, New York's Metropolitan Museum has a reconstructed royal 'window of appearance', and there are further assemblages in Munich and the Cairo Museum. Nothing quite like them has been found anywhere else in the Delta, and it is quite clear that they must have come from some very important and beautiful palace, the original outlines of which Hamza was able to trace amid the muddy fields. Was this the Pi-Ramesses palace 'beauteous of balconies, radiant with halls of lapis lazuli and turquoise', as described in the Anastasi text? Was this the true site of the Biblical Ramesses?

Hamza and one or two others certainly thought so. The same area, surveyed more than a hundred years ago by the great pioneer Egyptologist F.Ll. Griffith, had been described as virtually one vast mound of ancient ruins. Now, from all around Qantir, there began to be found a variety of remains with Ramessid connections. At Tell el-Shafei just to the north there came to light the base of what must originally have been a thirty-foot-high Ramesses II statue that probably formed part of the entrance to a large temple. Aerial photography revealed that the old Pelusiac branch of the Nile ran through this particular area, giving it potentially the facilities for shipping described in the Anastasi and Pai-Bes texts. Along what had been the favoured eastern bank emerged miscellaneous remains of what had once been luxury homes owned by important officials of the Ramessid period, among these the stone lintel of what was obviously once the stately mansion owned by Ramesses II's vizier Paser. It was also logical that Biblical Goshen, the territory in which the Israelites are said to have settled in Egypt, should have been close to the Faqus, or Arabia, mentioned by Egeria. The Septuagint, the Greek translation of the Old Testament made in the third century

Part of the base of what was originally a thirty-foot-high statue of Ramesses II, found at Tell Abu el-Shafei, just north of Qantir. The statue probably stood at the entrance of a large temple.

BC, in Genesis 46:34 specifically refers to Goshen as 'Gesem Arabias', Gesem/*gsm* being the ancient Egyptian equivalent of Hebrew Goshen, and Arabias linking it with Faqus, known to have been the capital of Egypt's 'Arabian' district in ancient times.

But none of this could be considered proof, nor was it considered particularly seriously by scholars until, in 1966, an Austrian archaeological team, under the direction of the young and enthusiastic Egyptological specialist Dr Manfred Bietak, began long-term excavations four miles north of Faqus at a carefully selected site called Tell el-Dab'a. Bietak knew that this site had an earlier name, Tell el-Birka, 'the mound of the lake', apparently deriving from an ancient lake, readily identifiable with a dried-up deep depression just to the north. Old maps revealed that this lake seemed once to have been joined up by an artificial waterway to the old Pelusiac branch of the Nile, which in ancient times circled the whole area. Was the Birka lake the same as the 'lake of the Residence' mentioned in schoolboy Pai-Bes's description of Pi-Ramesses? Was the encircling river joined up to this lake the same as that which brought Ramesses II's troop ships to moor at Pi-Ramesses, and gave the town its success as a commercial port? Although an effort of the imagination was needed to construct the appearance of this terrain in ancient times, at least it seemed to match the consistent early descriptions of Pi-Ramesses as being surrounded by water, as in Pai-Bes's enthusiastic report of the region's many varieties of fish.

Accordingly Bietak and his team began slow, patient and unobtrusive excavation of the 1,500-foot-diameter Tell el-Dab'a mound. Because of the mud and the likely difficulty of interpreting what they found, they used an excavation method more typical of European archaeology – the division of the site into a grid of ten-metre-square sections, the sides of which were left unexcavated as permanent points of reference. By 1979 Bietak had uncovered sufficient to make a major presentation of his findings to the British Academy in London – though these were sadly never given the attention they deserved because in terms of material remains they are unprepossessing. Quarrying, plundering and land reclamation, combined with the impermanence of the original building materials, have all so eroded the ancient remains that after thirteen years' work Bietak had little more to show than a few graves, a few scarabs, some unspectacular-looking pottery, and some uninspiring building foundations, hardly sufficient to cause much public excitement.

It became increasingly clear that part of Bietak's problem was that he had begun at what was only a fringe of the original town. So in 1979 and 1980 he opened up a new set of trenches in agricultural land four hundred yards to the west. A whole further aspect of the site was revealed. Some five hundred years before the time of Ramesses II this had been a carefully laid-out city of some importance during the time of Egypt's Middle Kingdom, a century or so prior to Egypt's takeover by the Hyksos. Readily discernible were the foundations of an imposing 450-foot-long palace, with a huge court lined by columns, that had probably served as a royal summer residence. Colourful Kamares-type pottery from Crete and a cylinder seal from northern Syria were discovered, suggesting that a Middle Kingdom Egyptian king had received deputations from foreign countries here, deputations that had presumably sailed directly upriver from the Mediterranean.

So far Dr Bietak has yet to publish a report on all his findings – indeed his researches have almost certainly many years yet to run – but from those he has published, and from the earlier work of Mahmoud Hamza at nearby Qantir, and a variety of other investigations in the locality, something of the scale and long history of this site can be built up.

The earliest level of occupation identified by Dr Bietak appears to have been about 2000 BC by a people whose method of house construction suggests they were Asiatic. This is consistent with the phase of Egyptian history known as the First Intermediate Period, in which widespread disruption was caused by bands of 'Amu', or Asiatics, from Syria-Palestine. Records show that order was re-established by strong government on the part of the kings of Egypt's Middle Kingdom, and it is to these that can be attributed the columned palace west of the Tell el-Dab'a mound, as well as a variety of other buildings and monuments that seem to have surrounded the Birka lake. One of these, a temple of the Egyptian king Amenemhet I (*c*1991–1962 BC), was found to contain a tablet specifically referring to the 'Temple of Amenemhet in [at] the water of the town' – independent corroboration of the town's abundance of water.

The next phase would appear to have been a new or renewed incursion by peoples whose way of life suggests an origin in northern Palestine and coastal Lebanon, particularly the flourishing commercial port of Byblos. This would have been around the late eighteenth or early seventeenth century BC. A vigorous copper industry was set up, and numerous moulds, crucibles and jets of clay came to light in the area of the Middle Kingdom palace.

Soon afterwards better quality Egyptian houses and even villas began to be built in the palace/main town environs. In the Tell el-Dab'a quarter to the east there were shops and wine stores, and utensils decorated with fish were found, attesting to the wealth of fish described by Pai-Bes. From the burials of this time it would appear that the Egyptians and the Syro-Palestinian immigrants lived amicably side by side.

But then there is evidence of a wave of quite new insurgents, pure Asiatics, obviously having strong cultural links with the Syro-Palestinians of the previous period, but with a markedly more barbarous appearance, evident even from their skulls, as Bietak observed. As indicated by the bronze battleaxes and daggers buried with male skeletons, these were predominantly warriors. They appear to have had local rulers, as suggested by elaborate diadems found with the occasional skeleton (New York Metropolitan Museum's Salhiya treasure probably belonged to one such as these) and some even seem to have insisted on taking the occasional servant with them to the grave. As another form of accompaniment for the afterlife, they seem sometimes to have had pairs of donkeys killed and buried at the tomb

Period (BC)	Site levels		Findings
First Intermediate Period (pre 1990)	e		A planned, carefully laid out settlement of Egyptian design in area west of Tell el Dab'a
12th Dynasty (c1990–1787)	d2 d1		Rectangular houses of a style indicative of an Asiatic immigration, but at the immediately succeeding level an imposing Egyptian palace with columned courts, store rooms, domestic quarters, etc., and evidence of trading links with Crete and N. Syria. At nearby Ezbet Rushdi a temple of Amenemhet I rebuilt by Senwosret III
13th Dynasty (c1787–1640)	H G E	c2 c1 b2	At Tell el Dab'a an initially open settlement becoming more dense, with a mixture of Egyptian and Syro-Palestinian cultural influences, particularly in respect of pottery styles and burial customs. Evidence of a flourishing copper industry developed by the newcomers
Hyksos Period (c1640–1532)	F E3 E2/1 D3 D2	b1 a2	At Tell el Dab'a evidence of insurgence by new, rich, warrior caste of Syro-Palestinians/Canaanites, and abrupt diminution of most Egyptian influence. Building of large, unequivocally Canaanite temples. Burials become purely Canaanite. But as this type of occupation becomes more dense, packed into what seem in places to have been tower-like blocks of flats (deduced from massive foundations), signs of strong Egyptian influence return, perhaps as the inhabitants acquire a taste for Egyptian-style luxuries
18th Dynasty (c1532–1307)	D1		Hiatus, and evidence of sudden abandonment and plundering of graves, attributable to Egyptian victory over Hyksos urban population, and the latter's agreed orderly withdrawal back to Canaan. Although Tell el Dab'a became largely uninhabited, a massive filling wall built across the tell during this period suggests it may have been used for some as yet undetermined military purposes. Dating from towards the end of this period, quantities of Egyptian pottery, and remains of a large temple, stores and fortifications (?)
19th Dynasty (Ramessid Period c1307–1196)	B		Evidence of some three square miles of purpose-built town, with, in Qantir area, a palace of Seti I and Ramesses II, also riverside houses of high Ramessid officials
Post 19th Dynasty	A		Continued settlement to end of 20th Dynasty, with some scanty remains from 21st Dynasty, followed by apparent abandonment until some early Ptolemaic settlement in 3rd century BC

door. Clearly these people had a different religion from that of the Egyptians; and as Bietak's excavations subsequently showed, they were unafraid to build their own temples on Egyptian soil. At Tell el-Dab'a Bietak found remains of temples of worship and mortuary temples belonging to them, one of which, some hundred feet long and sixty feet wide, proved to be the largest of any found from the Middle Bronze Age period. As was evident from many paint fragments in the vicinity, it had been painted either inside or out in azure blue. In front was a large sacred area, together with a nine-foot-wide rectangular altar, the surface of which was covered with ash and charred bones. All around this altar were deep pits filled with more ash and more charred bones, obviously from animal sacrifices. Analysis of the bones showed them to be principally of cattle and a few sheep with, interestingly, not a single pig bone among them. In the immediate surrounds Bietak found a variety of tombs, usually well provided with food for the afterlife in the form of large joints of mutton set on big plates.

It is evident from the temples' architecture, the sacrificial and burial practices, and a variety of other features, that these people were Canaanites, earlier representatives of the culture against which Joshua and his fellow Israelites would subsequently struggle in the fight for the promised land. It is also clearly correct to identify them with the hitherto mysterious Hyksos, who took control of Lower Egypt, inclusive of the Delta, around 1650 BC. According to an extract from the *History of Egypt* written in the third century BC by the Egyptian Manetho:

> Tutimaeus. In his reign, I know not why, a blast of God's displeasure broke upon us. A people of ignoble origin from the east, whose coming was unforeseen, had the audacity to invade the country, which they mastered by main force without difficulty or even a battle. Having overpowered the chiefs, they then savagely burnt the cities, razed the temples of the gods to the ground and treated the whole native population with the utmost cruelty. . . . Finally they made one of their number, named Salitis, king. He resided at Memphis, exacted tribute from Upper and Lower Egypt, and left garrisons in the places most suited for defence. . . . Having discovered in the Sethroite nome [province] a city very favourably situated on the east of the Bubastis arm of the river, called after some ancient tradition Avaris, he rebuilt and strongly fortified it with walls, and established a garrison there numbering as many as two hundred and forty thousand armed men to protect his frontier. . . . Their race bore the generic name of Hyksos, which means 'king-shepherds'. . . . Then the kings of the Thebaid and the rest of Egypt rose in revolt against the shepherds . . . the shepherds were defeated, driven out of all the rest of Egypt, and confined in a place called Avaris.

According to Manetho the Hyksos were not even able to stay in Avaris, but were obliged to agree to an evacuation: 'Upon these terms no fewer than two hundred and forty thousand entire households with their possessions left Egypt and traversed the desert to Syria.'

The phases of human settlement at Tell el Dab'a and its environs. The capital letters in the site levels column refer to Dr Bietak's excavation levels at Tell el Dab'a, the lower case letters to the levels at his most recent excavations just to the west, which appear to have been the centre of the original pre-Hyksos and Hyksos city settlements. The terms 'Egyptian', 'Canaanite' and 'Syro-Palestinian' have been used loosely to convey a broad idea of the shifting cultural influences. The overall inference from the excavations is that Hebrew infiltration into the area need not be attributed solely to the Ramessid period, but could have occurred at any time throughout the second millennium BC.

A sequence of this kind is very evident from the Tell el-Dab'a excavations. The Canaanites/Hyksos can be seen to have become progressively more numerous, their houses beginning to spill over and swamp the cemeteries surrounding the temple precincts, after which there is a remarkable termination of all the usual archaeological signs of occupation; evidence that this people suddenly disappeared from the site with an even greater abruptness than that with which they had arrived. During the subsequent Eighteenth Dynasty period, that of the militaristic Theban Egyptian pharaohs who expelled the Hyksos, the site seems to have been left largely unoccupied. Finally, in the subsequent Nineteenth Dynasty Ramessid period, there was a sudden surge of new settlement, in the form of some three square miles of new, purpose-built town, with all the houses carefully oriented north to south and east to west, as if laid out by a single planning authority. This was the period of construction of the faience-tiled palace already mentioned in the quarter now marked by the modern village of Qantir. In the north-west part of Tell el-Dab'a, on the highest ground, Bietak also found the foundations of a Ramessid temple with massive mud-brick walls in front of which were numerous stumps of ancient palm trees, 'the remains of perhaps the largest sacred grove ever found in an excavation'. As revealed by the hieroglyphic inscription on a lintel found within this temple's ruins, it was dedicated to 'Seth, great of might'. And it was one of the Anastasi papyri in the British Museum which described the city of Pi-Ramesses, 'Great of Victories', as having had just such a temple of Seth in its southern quarter, precisely the location of the Tell el-Dab'a temple in relation to the rest of the region's Ramessid remains (see reconstructed town plan, page 54).

In fact, although so much has been destroyed, and so much still needs to be excavated and better understood, there can be no reasonable doubt that the present-day Tell el-Dab'a/Qantir area was one and the same as the ancient Egyptian city of Pi-Ramesses and the Biblical Ramesses. It was from here that the original plethora of Ramessid monuments must have been removed to dreary Tanis in the Twenty-first Dynasty to create the confusion of identity that has hitherto prevailed among the archaeologists and Biblical scholars.

But what is also quite obvious from Dr Bietak's findings is that not only was this site the true Biblical Ramesses, it quite evidently had a history much earlier than the time of Ramesses II as well, and was in fact none other than the Hyksos capital, Avaris, referred to in Manetho's *History*. Dr Bietak's findings of a temple of Seth correspond perfectly to a major temple of Seth, the prime god of the Hyksos, known from the Egyptian papyrus Sallier I to have been at Avaris:

> Then king Apophis [a Hyksos king] . . . made him Seth as Lord, and he would not serve any god who was in the land except Seth. And he built a temple of good and eternal work beside the House of King Apophis . . . and he appeared every day to have sacrifices made . . . daily to Seth.

Dr Manfred Bietak of the Austrian Archaeological Institute, Cairo. His excavations at Tell el-Dab'a overturned much previous thinking concerning the site of the Israelites' sojourn in Egypt.

Canaanite temple excavated by Dr Bietak at Tell el-Dab'a, the largest so far found. Surrounding pits were filled with the bones of cattle and sheep slaughtered as sacrifices, but perhaps significantly there was not a single pig bone among them.

Burial of a pair of donkeys at the entrance to one of the 'warrior' tombs found at Tell el-Dab'a. This pair were even provided with their own drinking bowl. The burial customs from this and other phases of occupation of Tell el-Dab'a were notably different from traditional Egyptian practices.

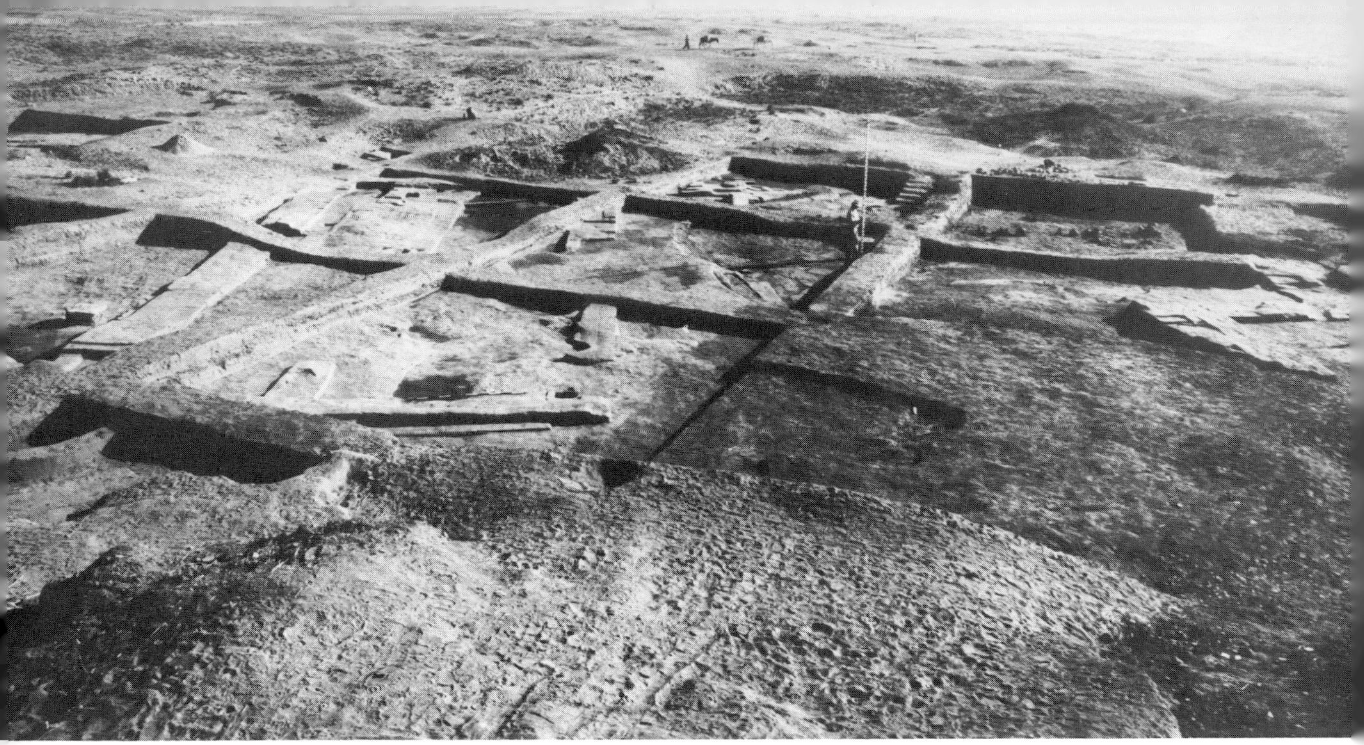

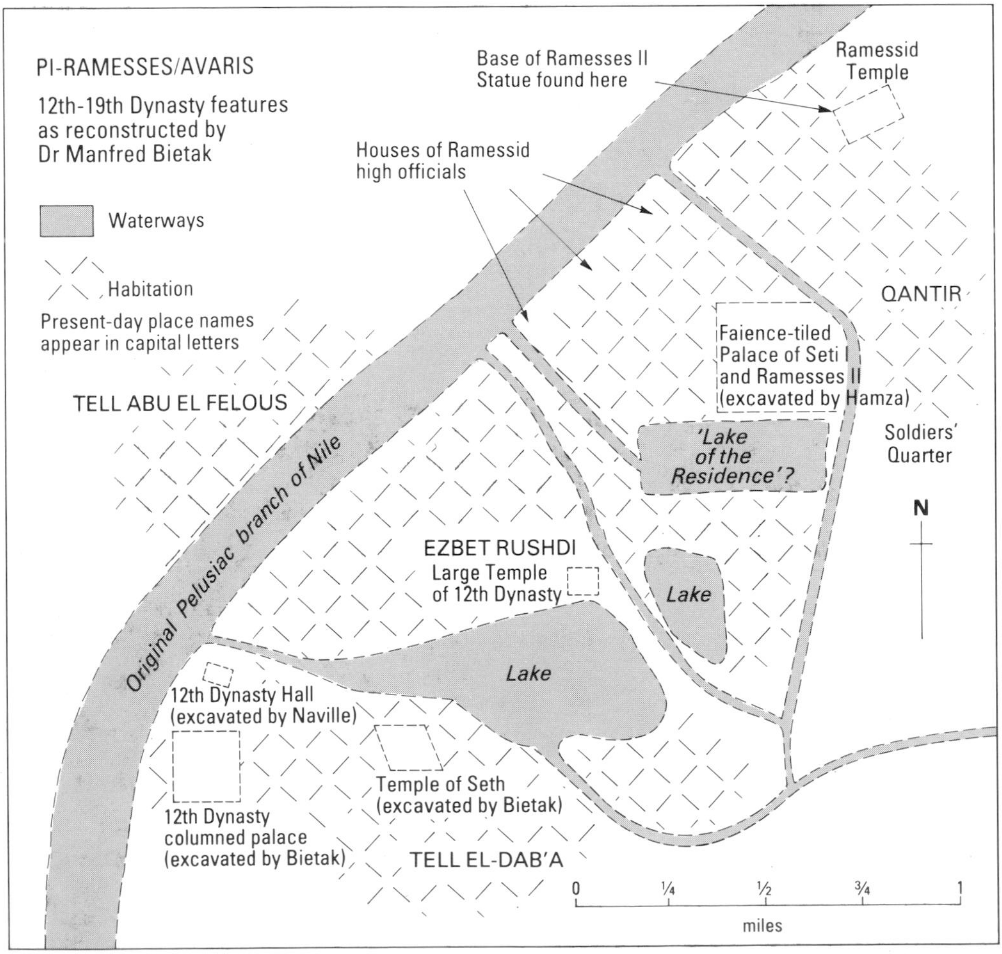
PI-RAMESSES/AVARIS
12th-19th Dynasty features as reconstructed by Dr Manfred Bietak
Waterways
Habitation
Present-day place names appear in capital letters
Base of Ramesses II Statue found here
Ramessid Temple
Houses of Ramessid high officials
QANTIR
Faience-tiled Palace of Seti I and Ramesses II (excavated by Hamza)
TELL ABU EL FELOUS
Original Pelusiac branch of Nile
'Lake of the Residence'?
Soldiers' Quarter
N
EZBET RUSHDI
Large Temple of 12th Dynasty
Lake
Lake
12th Dynasty Hall (excavated by Naville)
Temple of Seth (excavated by Bietak)
12th Dynasty columned palace (excavated by Bietak)
TELL EL-DAB'A
0
¼
½
¾
1
miles

Above Part of the Tell el-Dab'a site, showing the characteristic flatness of the Delta terrain and the grid technique of excavation employed by Bietak. Leaving the grid sides unexcavated provides a permanent check on the archaeological levels.

The Delta city of Pi-Ramesses, formerly Avaris (occupying the region of present-day Qantir and Tell el-Dab'a), based on a reconstruction by Dr Manfred Bietak. Most of the pre-Ramessid remains have been found in the environs of Tell el-Dab'a, while those from the time of Seti I and Ramesses II have come from around Qantir.

Even subsequent to the Hyksos, Ramesses II's own father Seti I must have built quite extensively on this site because the 'window of appearance' from Qantir, as reconstructed in New York's Metropolitan Museum, is undoubtedly his. In other words Pi-Ramesses was by no means a new creation of Ramesses II, such as would require much Israelite work to be done on it in his reign. He had simply once again been up to a variation on his old 'great chiseller' tricks. The Israelites could have worked at this site in any pharaoh's reign, and anyone writing about it after Ramesses II's reign would have been obliged, for recognition, to call the place 'Ramesses' just as we refer to Russia's second city as Leningrad rather than call it by its pre-Revolution name of St Petersburg.

The effect of this new information is profound. Suddenly the Biblical Israelites may geographically be set, not in some backwater 'store city', but in the environs of a vigorous metropolis which at times occupied the very centre stage of some momentous times in Egypt's history. So having identified the place, can we now identify the times in which they moved in this environment? When, and in what circumstances, may they have arrived in Egypt in the first place?

4. The coming of the Hebrews

THE importance of Dr Manfred Bietak's findings at Tell el-Dab'a is that they have provided for anyone trying to understand the Bible's historical background one key fact: the precise region in which the Biblical Hebrews or Israelites may be believed to have settled during their time in Egypt. Since everything in Hebrew tradition indicates that at this stage they dwelt in tents rather than in towns, we may anticipate that they lived with their flocks in Ramesses/Avaris's fertile environs. But it is crucial to our understanding of what followed to know when and how they came to Egypt – and who they were.

Some of the very earliest Egyptian records indicate the prickliness of the pharaohs' relations with nomads and Asiatics. From the Fourth Dynasty, in about the middle of the third millennium BC, there is a depiction of Pharaoh Khufu (Cheops) clubbing kneeling figures, accompanied by the inscription 'Khnum-Khufu, the great god. Smiting the nomads [of Asia]'. About a couple of centuries later Pharaoh Pepi I disparagingly referred to 'Sand Dwellers' against whom he campaigned – a term which, although it may have begun as a label for nomads, came to be used as a term of contempt for all Asiatics.

Then, around 2100 BC, there was a shock for all the already highly civilized urban communities of the south-eastern and eastern Mediterranean. The prosperous ports of Ugarit (Ras Shamra), Byblos (Gebal) and Gaza, together with flourishing commercial cities such as Jericho, Megiddo and Lachish, all suffered a sudden eclipse. In Mesopotamia the great Sargon I's Akkadian empire was taken over by insurgents who went on to set up their own dynasties in a different mould. Egypt's formerly prosperous Old Kingdom suddenly collapsed in a welter of confusion and anarchy that Egyptologists dispassionately call the First Intermediate Period. Conveying something of the distress of those times is a document generally thought to be contemporary, the *Admonitions of Ipuwer*, from which come the following evocative extracts: '[Men of] the Delta marshes carry shields . . . foreigners have become people everywhere. . . . Robbery is everywhere . . . the desert is [spread] throughout the land. . . . Barbarians from outside have come to Egypt. . . . No one really sails north to Byblos today.' According to Egyptian sources, the outsiders who poured into the Delta were Asiatics, generally referred to as Amu. They spoke the same West Semitic language as that of the later Biblical Israelites, and more than likely some of them were those pre-Hyksos Asiatics whose infiltration into the Delta can be seen in the earliest levels at Tell el-Dab'a, as noted in the previous chapter.

The trigger that set off these fearsome migrations seems to have been famine. A specialist in Egyptian climatology, Dr Barbara Bell, has pointed to a number of texts of the period which indicate this. When the Egyptians, after regaining control, set up a 'Wall of the Ruler' – apparently a combination of canal and earthwork wall sealing off the Delta's eastern border – its purpose was specifically described as being 'to oppose the Asiatics and to crush the Sand Crossers', and 'so that the Asiatics will not be permitted to come down into Egypt . . . in the customary manner, in order to let their beasts drink'. That 'customary manner' would appear to have been precisely that described in Genesis 12:10's laconic remark: 'There was a famine in the land, so severe that Abram went down to Egypt to live there for a while.'

Subsequently, even with a guarded frontier, there were circumstances in which some Asiatics were allowed to cross the border. The would-be immigrants might have goods or services of which the Egyptians wanted to avail themselves. Or the Egyptians might allow in a controlled number of famine victims through sheer compassion, as in the Merneptah text quoted on page 30. There were benefits in the afterlife for an Egyptian official able to claim, as did chancellor Nefer-yu: 'I gave bread to the hungry and clothes to the naked.'

In the tomb of the nineteenth-century BC nobleman Khnumhotep at Beni-Hassan, some 200 miles south of Cairo, there is a well-known painting of a group of Asiatics making just such an approach to an Egyptian border post. Five of the men carry spears, bows and throwsticks (the latter seems to have been a sort of boomerang) and they are dressed in multicoloured garments that would be strikingly evocative of Joseph's famous coat of many colours (Authorized Version, Genesis 37:3) – except that according to modern scholarly wisdom this is now thought to have been a mistranslation for 'long, sleeved robe'. Two more men lead gazelle-like animals, perhaps used for trading, while another, towards the rear of the party, holds an instrument resembling a lyre, as if his role was to entertain with ballads of the people's history while the group were on their journey. That this is a complete family mission is indicated by four women with headbands and similar multicoloured garments, and children on donkeys. According to the hieroglyphic inscription there were thirty-seven in this particular party, they were 'Amu from Shutu', thought to have been central Transjordania, and their mission was to bring into Egypt a commodity particularly highly prized by the Egyptians, stibium, a black paint used for eye make-up. The presence of two sets of bellows on top of the baggage carried by the donkeys suggests that they were also able to turn their hand to metalworking, something at which the Egyptians in general were never particularly adept.

It is of course, tempting to identify these as the ancestors of the Biblical Israelites making their way into Egypt, but this must be avoided. They should be regarded as merely among the many Asiatics who found their

A wave of Egyptian hatred towards Asiatics is clearly demonstrated by this so-called 'execration' figurine dating from the late Twelfth–Thirteenth Dynasty. For use in the performance of ritual 'magic', the figurine was inscribed with the names of Egypt's Asiatic enemies, then deliberately smashed and tossed away in the hope that a similar fate might befall those named. Egyptian 'execration' was probably prompted by the Hyksos/Canaanite infiltration.

Below Two parts of a scene showing the arrival of a group of Asiatics at an Egyptian frontier post, as depicted in the tomb of the nineteenth-century BC Egyptian nobleman Khnumhotep at Beni-Hassan. One of the Egyptian officials holds a docket with the following inscription: 'Year 6, under the majesty of the Horus . . . Kha-kheper-Re [Senwosret II]. List of the Asiatics who the son of the Count Khnumhotep brought out on account of *stibium*. Asiatics of Shutu, list thereof: thirty-seven.' The scene is frequently used to illustrate the entry of the Biblical Hebrews into Egypt.

way to the Delta, in varying circumstances, during the second millennium BC. The inhabitants of 'Shutu' are possibly the 'sons of Sheth' referred to in Numbers 24:17. They are known independently from cuneiform tablets, such as those from Mari, and seem simply to have been nomads whose prime territory was the open, non-urban areas around the Euphrates, the Syrian desert, and the central kingdom of Qatna.

Another variety of Asiatic noted by the Egyptians, at least from the Eighteenth Dynasty on, was the 'Shosu' – the name used for the tribes who were allowed in to the Delta at the time of Merneptah. This name has the broad meaning of 'shepherds', but that they were more than that is evident from a significant number of inscriptions of the New Kingdom in which they feature seemingly as mercenaries, fighting on the side of the Canaanites against the Egyptians. They then had a particular home territory, called 'Se'ir' in the great Harris papyrus of Ramesses III, which seems to have been to the south-east of Canaan, in the territories subsequently known as Ammon, Edom and Moab. Edom was certainly the place of origin of the Shosu who entered Egypt in the reign of Merneptah, and since there was clearly no love lost between Edomites and Israelites when the latter wanted to pass through Edomite territory en route to the conquest of Canaan (although a close tribal affinity is suggested by the 'your brother Israel' overture of Numbers 20:14), identity between Shosu and Biblical Israelites is again unlikely.

What of the 'Habiru' whose possible identity with the Hebrews has already been remarked on? Various references to 'Habiru', a term used interchangeably with 'Sa-Gaz', occur in cuneiform texts from the *circa* eighteenth-century BC Mesopotamian city states of Mari and Nuzi. A common feature of the Nuzi texts is for a Habiru to seek the lowest form of social status by joining a wealthy household as a slave. The tablets from Mari show them more commonly as troublesome roving marauders, ever ready to sell themselves as mercenaries on the side of Mari's enemies. According to one Mari intelligence report on enemy troop movements, 'Yapah-Adad has made ready the settlement Zallul on this side on the bank of the Euphrates river, and with two thousand troops of the Habiru of the land is dwelling in that city.'

Undeniably, as remarked in the introduction, equation of 'Habiru' and 'Hebrew' must be treated with caution, but it is worthy of note that the earlier references to Habiru do locate them in the northern reaches of the Euphrates, precisely in accordance with the patriarch Abraham's origins as described in Joshua 24:2: 'Long ago your forefathers, Terah and his sons Abraham and Nahor, lived beside the Euphrates, and they worshipped other gods.'

Furthermore, there are a variety of rather strange practices uniquely referred to in association with the patriarchs of the book of Genesis which can be traced to social customs peculiar to Mari and Nuzi. As a mark of his covenant with God, in Genesis 15 Abraham is described as having halved some animals down the middle, then 'placed each piece opposite its corresponding piece', a ritual act seemingly intended to invoke the fate of the animals upon anyone breaking the covenant. Remarkably, a nearly identical practice, the killing of an ass to bind treaties, is referred to in the tablets from Mari. Similarly, three times in the Book of Genesis (chapters 12, 20 and 26) Abraham and Isaac are represented introducing their wives as their sisters to friendly monarchs – an apparently motiveless piece of deception causing inevitable embarrassment when found out. The confusion is, however, explained by the Nuzi tablets. At Nuzi a man could impart particular sanctity to his marriage if, on marrying, he adopted his wife as his sister. A third example concerns the ostensibly modern practice of surrogacy. In Genesis the marriages of both Abraham and Jacob reach a stage of near-despair from their being childless, and in both cases their wives, suspecting it is they who are infertile, suggest that a servant girl acts as a surrogate mother. In Genesis 16:2 Abraham is told by his wife Sarai: 'Take my slave girl; perhaps I shall found a family through her.' In Genesis 30:3 Jacob is told by his wife Rachel: 'Here is my slave girl Bilhah. Lie with her, so that she may bear sons to be laid upon my knees, and through her I too may build up a family.' Such a concept is totally absent from the later scriptures, but had official blessing at Nuzi. There, if a man's wife was barren, it was her duty to find another woman to bear her husband's children, those children becoming hers as if she had borne them herself, exactly in accord with Sarai's words 'perhaps *I* shall found a family through her'. These practices strongly suggest that the Biblical Hebrews' ancestors spent some part of their wanderings on the fringes of Mari and Nuzi, at a date which may be roughly assigned to the first half of the second millennium BC.

This may give rise to a certain confidence in the antiquity of the Genesis text, but this is swiftly dashed when we turn to another part of the book that is highly relevant to the Hebrews' journey to Egypt, the story of Joseph. Far more than the rest of Genesis, indeed the rest of the early part of the Old Testament, it is a highly polished tale packed with all the elements of high drama. Jealous of their father's favouritism towards Joseph, his brothers sell him as a slave to passing traders, then return home pretending he has been killed by a wild animal. Taken to Egypt by the traders, Joseph is sold to an official called Potiphar whose wife one day tries to seduce the new young slave during her husband's absence. But when Joseph resists her wiles, she pretends he has tried to rape her, so Joseph is thrown into prison. There he has a lucky break when, hearing that the pharaoh is suffering recurring bad dreams, he interprets them correctly. Not only does he find himself released from prison, but made first minister, with the task of steering Egypt through the seven 'fat' and seven 'lean' years which the dreams have indicated. To go with his new appointment Joseph is given all the appropriate perquisites, a gold collar of office, a fast chariot with outrider, a well-born wife – Asenath, daughter of Potiphera, priest of On, and even, in order to smooth possible racial tensions, an acceptable Egyptian name, Zaphenath-paneah. At the onset of the famine that he has predicted, Joseph's brothers, unaware of his true identity, come to him pleading for food, and it is this which gives him the opportunity for a small act of revenge. By a subterfuge, he has them arrested as suspected spies, and when they are in his power he reveals that he is the brother whom they sold as a slave. Then, however, he forgives them, and invites the whole family, including his long-lost father Jacob, to come to live with him in Egypt, specifically in the Goshen area, the proximity of which to Pi-Ramesses/Avaris was noted in the previous chapter.

Often quoted as a striking Egyptian parallel to the Biblical story of Potiphar's wife's attempted seduction is the 'Tale of Two Brothers' from the Nineteenth-Dynasty Orbiney papyrus.

Orbiney papyrus	*Genesis 39*
Then she [the older brother's wife] talked with him, saying, 'There is [great] strength in you! Now I see your energies every day!' And she wanted to know him as one knows a man.	Now Joseph was handsome and good-looking, and a time came when his master's wife took notice of him . . .
Then she stood up and took hold of him and said to him, 'Come, let's spend an [hour] sleeping [together]!' . . .	. . . and said, 'Come and lie with me.'
Then the lad [became] like a leopard with [great] rage at the wicked suggestion which she had made to him. . . .	But he refused and said to her . . .
'See here . . . your husband is like a father to me. . . . What is this great crime which you have said to me?'	'Think of my master . . . he has entrusted me with all he has . . . How can I do anything so wicked . . . ?'

As the two stories go on, Potiphar's wife seizes Joseph's cloak to produce as evidence of attempted rape, while the brother's wife in the Egyptian version uses greasepaint to make it appear that she has been involved in a similar struggle. But on closer inspection there are many differences, the plot being essentially of the timeless woman's wiles variety, endlessly repeated today in TV soap operas.

A serious and penetrating analysis of the entire story, *A Study of the Biblical Story of Joseph*, was published by Toronto University Egyptologist Professor Donald Redford in 1970. As shown by Professor Redford, quite aside from late anachronistic touches, such as the inclusion of camels (see page 15), and money in what seems to have been a coin form (first used by the Lydians in the seventh century BC), the story has points of detail strongly indicative of a late composition. In Genesis 42:16 Joseph uses a particular oath, 'by the life of Pharaoh', or, more literally, 'as sure as Pharaoh lives', which, as pointed out by Redford, does not occur in this form (embodying the specific word 'pharaoh') until the eighth or seventh century BC. Even more significantly, although the Egyptian names occurring in the Joseph story – Potiphar, Asenath and Zaphenath-paneah – are all genuinely Egyptian, in the forms Potipera, 'Asenat and Zapnatpa'neah, they too are similarly late. Potipera ('He whom [the god] Re gives') occurs in only four known Egyptian contexts, three from around the seventh century BC, and one from the third century BC. The very fact that it includes the definite article dates it to the very last period of Egyptian history. Joseph's name of Zapnatpa'neah – 'God says he will live' – dates from no earlier than the beginning of the first millennium BC, contemporary with Solomon; and although 'Asenat does fare a little better, being known from the Old Kingdom, it became a popular name only during the first millennium BC.

It is possible to argue that the Joseph story is a genuinely ancient tale which someone around the seventh century BC embellished with these tell-tale points of inauthentic detail. But as the key account of how the Biblical Israelites came to settle in the Nile Delta region it scarcely inspires confidence.

However, quite aside from this, it is undeniable that from at least the nineteenth century BC onwards, Asiatic immigrants into Egypt, at least some of whom may have been the Biblical Israelites' ancestors, do begin to appear in Egyptian records, mostly as domestic servants like the Habiru of the Mari tablets. The papyrus known as the Brooklyn, from the reign of the Thirteenth-Dynasty Sebekhotpe III (about 1745 BC), contains a list of seventy-nine household slaves, forty-five of them Asiatic and among these some thirty whose names Professor William Albright of Johns Hopkins University identified as 'definitely north-west Semitic', that is, of the same language family as that of the Biblical Israelites. Recognizable among these are the Biblical Issachar and Asher, and another name nearly identical to that of the Hebrew midwife Shiphrah of Exodus 1:15.

So allowing for clumsy anachronisms, such as are found in the Joseph story, is there any way of determining when the Israelites might have made their incursion into Egypt? There is certainly no easy answer. Broadly there are three main periods to choose from, each with its opponents and proponents:

(i) the pre-Hyksos Middle Kingdom of the Twelfth and Thirteenth Dynasties, when the first Asiatics with north-west Semitic names begin to appear among Egyptian household servants;

(ii) the time of the Canaanite Hyksos, when Lower (i.e. northern) Egypt and the Delta area would have been ruled by Asiatics at least speaking the same language as that of the Biblical Israelites;

(iii) the post-Hyksos time of the New Kingdom's militaristic Eighteenth Dynasty, when many Asiatics captured in war were transported to Egypt as slaves.

Of these three, the third is the least satisfactory. There is an isolated instance of an Eighteenth-Dynasty pharaoh, the heretic Akhenaten, having appointed an Asiatic as a vizier – a possible parallel to Joseph except that

'Joseph died ... they embalmed him and laid him in his coffin in Egypt' (Genesis 50: 26). It is unlikely that early Jewish chroniclers would have related the story of their revered ancestor Joseph being buried according to the Egyptian tradition unless that was what occurred. It is also unlikely that Joseph would have received Egyptian-style burial had he lived in the Hyksos period. Accordingly there are some grounds for believing Joseph to have been a high official under native Egyptian rule.

the man's name was Tutu. But apart from this, the prevailing tendency of the Eighteenth Dynasty period was for its militaristic pharaohs to storm into Asia and haul back thousands of Semitic captives whom they would then employ as slaves. Nothing in the Biblical record suggests that the Israelites might have arrived in Egypt in such a manner, the impression being instead that they originally came with official sanction and freedom to pursue their normal way of life as shepherds. Only with the accession of 'a new king . . . who knew nothing of Joseph' (Exodus 1:8) was that freedom rudely shattered.

The second scenario, favoured by many, is that the Hebrews/Israelites entered Egypt broadly at the same time as the Hyksos. The fact that the Hyksos are known to have been Canaanites, speaking the same language as the Biblical Israelites, seems to strengthen this argument; and indisputably the name Jaqob-har is found on scarabs of the Hyksos period, strikingly evocative of the Biblical patriarch Jacob. Obviously it would have been much easier for a Semite such as the Biblical Joseph to rise to power in an Asiatic regime than in an Egyptian one; besides which, for all their fearsome reputation, the Hyksos do appear to have maintained reasonably good order. At the time when the Egyptian monarchy wanted to strike a blow for freedom, there was at least one faction of the court which counselled against this on the grounds that it might shake an apparently comfortable status quo: 'The finest of their [the Hyksos] fields are ploughed for us, our cattle are pastured in the Delta. Emmer is sent for our pigs, our cattle are not taken away . . .'

One positive indication that there were Hebrew-type people settled in the Delta at the time of the Hyksos is the abundance of joints of mutton found in the Hyksos graves at Tell el-Dab'a (i.e. Avaris/Pi-Ramesses) as offerings to the dead. The city's urban population must have had some plentiful herds of sheep (and cattle) nearby which would have needed herders, prob-ably nomads – precisely the role in which the Biblical Hebrews/Israelites are portrayed. Joseph's family is thus described in Genesis 46:32: 'Now his brothers were shepherds, men with their own flocks and herds, and they had brought with them their flocks and herds, and all that they possessed.'

But the idea that the Biblical Israelites were in the Delta at the time of the Hyksos does not require that they actually arrived at the same time – which would in fact have been unlikely, bearing in mind the antipathy between Israelite and Canaanite obvious from the Book of Joshua. Further-more, Genesis 50:26, which describes Joseph at his death as having been 'embalmed and laid in a coffin in Egypt', strongly suggests that Joseph's time as a vizier, if it can be considered at all historically reliable, was most likely at a time when the native Egyptians were in power, since mummifi-cation was neither a Canaanite nor a Hebrew practice, and it is most unlikely that anyone would have invented the story that Joseph received a non-Hebrew burial.

So were the Biblical Israelites, in so far as they were any single identifiable group, already in the Nile Delta at the time the Hyksos arrived? There is in

fact direct archaeological evidence to support such a theory. The only semblance of permanence the Biblical Israelites may have aspired to would seem
to have been in their burials, hence Abraham's insistence on purchasing a
plot at Mamre for the grave of himself and other members of his family
(Genesis 23:7-10; 25:9-10). Of special interest, therefore, is the grave of an
Asiatic woman dating, as far as can be judged, roughly from the time of
the arrival of the Hyksos, which was found at Tell el-Maskhuta in the Wadi
Tumilat area of the eastern Delta (see overleaf). The only item of pottery
found with the corpse was a hand-made jug – hence the impossibility of a
precise dating – but there was a clear indication of the woman's nomadic,
pastoralist background in two cattle skulls set at the grave door and a
whole sheep laid by her feet. More detailed inspection of the bones revealed
that hers was not a peaceful end. Clearly visible on her skull were the marks
of three savage frontal blows from an axe, two to the mouth, knocking out
some of her upper teeth, and the third, which was obviously the fatal one,
square to the middle of her forehead. Whoever was responsible for this
murder clearly killed the woman's dog during the same incident, for its
skeleton was found at her feet, the skull shattered by the same weapon that
had killed its mistress. Although it might seem difficult to determine the
perpetrator of a murder after nearly four thousand years, in fact the shape
of the injuries clearly identifies them as having been caused by a chisel-type
shaft-hole battleaxe, shaped rather like an ice-pick, and typical of the
Hyksos/Canaanites.

If this provides one possible clue that at least some of the Biblical Israelites' ancestors were already in the Delta at the time of the Hyksos' arrival,
another arises from certain background features in the Joseph story that,
despite the pertinence of Professor Donald Redford's findings, may indicate
that at least elements of the tale had a genuinely early origin.

If the Israelites arrived before the Hyksos, we are thrust back to the time
of Egypt's Middle Kingdom, that is to roughly the first three centuries of
the second millennium BC. As it happens, within this period there is one
particular reign, that of Pharaoh Senwosret/Sesostris III (c1878-1841 BC)
which at least one Biblical scholar, Dr John Bimson of Bristol's Trinity
Theological College, has proposed as the time of the Biblical Joseph.
Senwosret III's likeness is a familiar one in Egyptian art – he has three
portrait sculptures preserved in the British Museum alone – and particularly
notable are his big ears and hard, careworn face, a realism in portraiture
that is rare in pharaonic art. Could the worried countenance reflect the bad
dreams and fluctuations between famine and plenty recorded in the Joseph
story?

There is more to such an idea than meets the eye. Living as most of us
do in countries of overabundant rainfall, it is difficult for us to appreciate
just how dependent rainless Egypt was on one seemingly magical event, the
annual flooding of the Nile. Around mid-July, when the river had sunk to
its lowest, it would mysteriously well up and spill over the valley floor, then
gradually recede in about October, leaving behind a rich black soil that

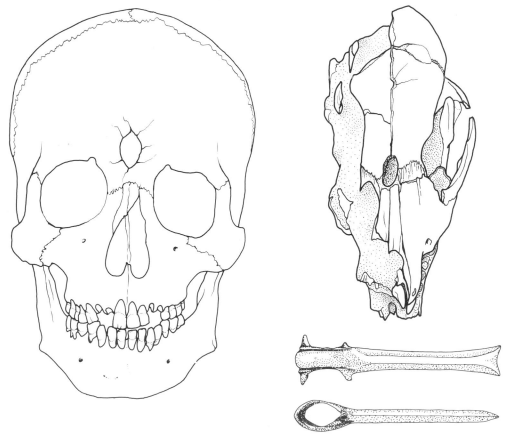

Grave L2040 from Tell el-
Maskhuta in the Wadi
Tumilat, that of a murdered
pastoralist woman buried
with a whole sheep and her
pet dog. The woman's skull
(*far left*) and that of her
dog (*left*) can be seen to
have been savagely hacked
with a chisel-type shaft-hole
cattle axe (*below*) of a type
known to have been used
by the Hyksos. This
strongly suggests discord
between the incoming
warrior Hyksos and
pastoralist Asiatics
previously settled (at least
in their own semi-nomadic
way) in the Delta region.

would, if there was enough of it, bear crops to feed an entire nation for another year. But would there be enough? No one in Egypt knew that success or failure depended on the intensity of monsoon rains far to the south in tropical Africa, but what they did know was that there was a direct relationship between the height of the floodwater, as marked on special 'Nilometers' at different points along the Nile, and the vigour or otherwise of the subsequent season's crop. If the high-water level at Aswan was six feet below normal, this could mean three-quarters of Egypt's potentially arable land going unwatered, resulting in famine unless grain stocks had been kept from previous years. And although a high-water level six feet above normal might offer the potential of extra arable land, this could be dissipated if the floodwater took too long to recede, thus reducing the amount of time for crops to grow during the remainder of the year. Since, particularly during the Old and Middle Kingdoms, it was the person of the god-pharaoh who was believed to be responsible for national fertility and good order, the pharaoh's bad dreams of famine and plenty in the Joseph story have great credibility.

But why should the story be dated to the time of Senwosret III? As climatology specialist Dr Barbara Bell has pointed out, the Nilometers have provided evidence to indicate that his reign may have suffered particularly badly from fluctuations in the Nile high-water levels. In Dr Bell's own words:

> . . . the recent discovery, at the Dal Cataract, of an inscription comme-morating a water level on 24 January 1869 BC, year 10 of Senwosret III, close to the modern high-water level, makes it reasonable to think that the Nile may have been more erratic in the reign of this king than under his predecessors.

Furthermore, it is in Senwosret's reign, and only in his reign, that we find a striking parallel to the situation in Genesis in which Joseph, having been appointed as first minister, cleverly took advantage of the famine to buy up for the pharaoh all the great Egyptian land estates: '. . . Joseph bought all the land in Egypt for Pharaoh, because the Egyptians sold all their fields, so severe was the famine; the land became Pharaoh's.' (Genesis 47:20) Before the time of Senwosret III, power in provincial Egypt had been in the hands of great nobles, very much the equivalent of the feudal barons of medieval England. They had built large and splendid tombs for themselves, and lived in great state in the nomes they administered – the Egyptian equivalent of English counties. But in Senwosret's reign all this changed. The building of the provincial tombs ceased and, as remarked by Egyptologist W.C. Hayes in his contribution to the *Cambridge Ancient History*, 'No more is heard of the "Great Chiefs" of the nomes and their local courts. Instead the provinces of Lower Egypt, Middle Egypt and Upper Egypt were administered from the Residence city by three departments of the central government.'

Could the Biblical Joseph have been administrator or vizier for Lower Egypt, based perhaps at Avaris/Pi-Ramesses, where Dr Bietak's very latest

Above Senwosret III (*c* 1878–44 BC), from a statue in the British Museum. Was he the pharaoh of Egypt's years of famine and plenty (Genesis 41–7)? There were serious fluctuations of the Nile during his reign.

Right 'During the seven years of plenty, the soil yielded generously' (Genesis 41: 48). An Egyptian harvesting scene from the Eighteenth-Dynasty tomb of Nakht at Thebes. Using a carrying-pole as a lever, the man on the right has leapt high in the air in order to apply his full weight to forcing the overflowing grain into its bin. But such crops were entirely dependent on the level of the Nile's flood each year.

findings have revealed a palace of around Senwosret III's time? While there is no direct evidence to suggest that Senwosret might have had an Asiatic vizier called Joseph, sufficiently little is known of the vizierate in Senwosret's time for this to have been perfectly possible. Furthermore, as indicated by Dr Bietak's archaeological discoveries at Tell el-Dab'a (see page 50), Senwosret's Twelfth Dynasty in the Middle Kingdom was the very time, and virtually the only time, when we find Asiatic and Egyptian living side by side in apparent harmony.

Shadowy though the evidence is, the coming of the Hebrews/Israelites to Egypt could have been as early as the nineteenth century BC, extending throughout the Hyksos period, when, while not necessarily approving the Hyksos' way of life, they may have enjoyed a ready prosperity, providing sheep and cattle for their urban overlords' food, sacrifices and grave offerings. According to Exodus 12:40, at the time of the Exodus, 'The Israelites had been settled in Egypt for four hundred and thirty years' – a substantial amount of time, not all of which can have been hardship, as confirmed by Exodus 1:7's information that in this time they '. . . were fruitful and prolific; they increased in numbers . . . so that the whole country was overrun by them'. But, if this genuinely was the case, the vicissitudes of history are such that a dramatic change of fortune was on its way.

5. 'Slaves in every kind of hard labour'

WHEN, in July 1881, Emil Brugsch discovered the mummy of Pharaoh Ramesses II, in the same cache was another royal corpse, some 300 years older than that of Ramesses, and distinguished by its particularly putrid smell. According to the label this was the body of Seqenenre Tao, one of the native Egyptian rulers forced to live far to the south in Thebes during the Hyksos period, and as was obvious even to the untutored eye, Seqenenre had met a violent end. The middle of his forehead had been smashed in by an instrument like that which had killed the nomad woman from Tell el-Maskhuta. Another blow had fractured his right eye socket, his right cheekbone and his nose. A third had been delivered behind his left ear, shattering the mastoid bone and ending in the first vertebra of the neck. Although in life he had clearly been a tall and handsome young man with black, curly hair, the set expression on Seqenenre's face showed that he had died in agony. After death he appears to have fared little better, as his body seems to have been left for some while before mummification; hence the putrid smell and signs of early decomposition.

Egyptian records are silent on how Seqenenre met his end, but almost certainly it was at the hands of the Hyksos/Canaanites. One of the few documentary sources to mention him, the British Museum's Papyrus Sallier I tells how while in Thebes he was sent an insulting message from the Hyksos king Apophis, 400 miles to the north at Avaris/Pi-Ramesses: 'Have the hippopotamus pool which is in the orient of the city done [away] with! For they do not let sleep come to me by day or by night.' Whether it was this particular goad which prompted the unfortunate Seqenenre to launch some unrecorded attack against the Hyksos we shall probably never know. Certainly the weapon that inflicted his fatal injuries was Hyksos, and no Egyptian success against the Hyksos is known from his reign.

But it was probably from setbacks such as these that the Egyptians learned the painful lesson that if they were to regain proper control of their country they had to bring themselves up to date in the rapidly developing technology of warfare. In the darkest hours of what is called the Second Intermediate Period, i.e. much of the seventeenth and early sixteenth centuries BC, the Hyksos controlled Memphis, which commanded both Upper and Lower Egypt, and they had an alliance with the Kushites of Nubia, to the south of Thebes. While the Egyptians had old-fashioned solid wood bows, and had been somewhat backward in metallurgy for the manufacture

The head of Pharaoh Seqenenre Tao II (*c* early sixteenth century BC), from his mummified remains preserved in the Cairo Museum. Seqenenre's is virtually the only known royal corpse to show signs of a violent death, which almost certainly occurred during fighting with the Hyksos.

Horses and composite bows brought as tribute, from the tomb of the vizier Rekhmire at Thebes. Although the Hyksos/Canaanites had pioneered the military use of such bows, Egypt's early Eighteenth-Dynasty warrior pharaohs achieved technical superiority in their manufacture.

of battleaxes and the like, the Hyksos had not only the much more powerful composite bow but also better made, better designed weapons of close combat and a revolutionary innovation for striking terror into enemy foot-soldiers, the horse-drawn chariot.

Somewhere in Thebes, in what no doubt was a long series of councils of war, the Egyptian monarchy devised its plans for reconquest, involving their own development and improvement on the very weaponry by which they were being held in submission. The composite bow seems to have been a difficult instrument to make, requiring, according to a Ugarit text:

> . . . [birch?] tree from Lebanon,
> . . . tendons from wild bulls,
> . . . horns from wild goats,
> Sinews from the locks of bulls.

Much greater strength was needed to draw it – reminiscent of the bow of Odysseus in Homer's *Odyssey* – and consequently thorough training was required for such a weapon to be deployed accurately by army-size units of archers.

There were also problems with horses – to the Middle Bronze Age as new and alarming as the latest missile to us. They would not have been easy to acquire from the main source of supply, which was probably north-east of Canaan. And even when some had been acquired, the art of breeding them, training them to the bit, and designing and developing chariots for them to pull, would all have had to be learned, perfected and passed on.

But somehow or other Seqenenre's successors mastered all these difficulties and trained an army of whose discipline and professionalism Egypt had never seen the like. Frustratingly, Egyptian records provide us with the most meagre information about how the war was fought. In 1954 the then Director of Fieldwork for the Egyptian Department of Antiquities, Dr Labib Habachi, found at Karnak a re-used stele with an account of how the Theban monarch Kamose fought an apparently successful series of skirmishes against the Hyksos, reaching almost as far as Avaris/Pi-Ramesses. Kamose's mother, Queen Ahhotep, seems to have distinguished herself in rallying a great deal of support, and earned the coveted military honours of three gold flies. Aside from this and the late, garbled extract from Manetho's *History of Egypt* quoted in the works of the first-century AD Jewish writer Josephus, almost all our information comes from inscriptions in the tomb of a ship's captain, Ahmose, who fought under the Pharaoh Ahmose (*c*1550–1525 BC), founder of Egypt's notable Eighteenth Dynasty. Captain Ahmose thrusts us directly into an account of the Hyksos' last stand, at their Avaris/Pi-Ramesses stronghold:

> When the town of Avaris was besieged, then I showed valour on foot in the presence of his majesty. Thereupon I was appointed to the ship *Appearing in Memphis*. Then there was fighting on the water in the canal

Pa-Djedku of Avaris. Thereupon I made a capture, and I carried away a hand [it was Egyptian custom to cut off one hand from each dead enemy warrior as proof of a kill]. . . . Then the gold of valour [the Egyptian equivalent of a military medal] was given to me. . . . Then there was fighting in the Egypt which is south of this town [Avaris]. Thereupon I carried off a man [as] living prisoner. I went down into the water – now he was taken captive on the side of the town – and crossed over the water carrying him. . . . Then Avaris was despoiled. Then I carried off spoil from there: one man, three women. . . . Then his majesty gave them to me to be slaves.

Notable from this account, as from the earlier information, is the predominance of water in the environs of ancient Avaris/Pi-Ramesses. Something of the city's importance as a commercial port at the time is evident from an Egyptian inscription recording the booty which fell to the victors: '300 *baw* ships of cedar, filled with gold and lapis lazuli, silver and turquoise and copper axes without number as well as olive oil, incense, fat, honey . . . and all their precious woods'.

Interestingly, the Egyptians' victory seems to have been so decisive in naval terms that the Hyksos were unable to use their ships to escape by sea. Yet, at least according to the late Manetho account, it fell somewhere short of a total subjugation because a treaty was agreed whereby the Hyksos were allowed: '. . . to evacuate Egypt and go whither they would be unmolested. Upon these terms no fewer than two hundred and forty thousand entire households with their possessions left Egypt and traversed the desert to Syria.' The striking feature of this episode of sixteenth-century BC history is that here we have what seems to have been a very real exodus, involving an impressive number of people, departing from a city we know to have been associated with the Biblical Israelites, and making virtually the same overland desert journey towards Canaan as that described of the Israelites. That some form of exodus on these lines occurred is abundantly evident from Dr Manfred Bietak's excavations at the Avaris/Pi-Ramesses site, which indicate an abrupt cessation of occupation immediately following the high level of population identified with the Hyksos period. When Josephus read the account of the Hyksos' departure in Manetho's *History of Egypt*, he thought it so similar to the Israelite exodus that he concluded the two events must have been one and the same. Yet, tempting though it might be for us to think likewise, in fact we have no serious justification for doing so. Those who left Avaris at this time were the urban, warrior-caste Canaanites, who had formerly toppled the native Egyptian monarchy from power in Lower and Middle Egypt. There is no reason why they should have been joined in their flight by the Delta's tent-dwelling pastoral nomads who, as we have already seen, were more than likely already in the Delta before the coming of the Hyksos. What is certain is that some Asiatics, specifically referred to as Hapiru/Habiru, and who had a rustic way of life, stayed on in the eastern Delta during the ensuing generation. This is apparent from a little-known scene among the decorations in the tomb of the noble Puyemre at Thebes, dating from the reign of Queen Hatshepsut (*c*1473-1458 BC) and her successor Tuthmosis III. This shows four men working at a winepress, carefully labelled in hieroglyphs 'straining out wine by the Hapiru' and accompanied by a second inscription telling us the scene's location, 'wine of the vineyard of Wat-Hor'. Wat-Hor means 'Way of Horus' and denotes the route leading out of Egypt eastwards from Avaris/Pi-Ramesses, the very region we have come to identify with the Biblical Israelites. Although some doubt has been expressed as to whether the inscription should be read as Hapiru, in fact identical wording has been found on another scene of the same type, from the tomb of the great herald Antef, dating from the very same period. It has to be acknowledged that these individuals are so nondescript-looking that there is nothing characteristically Semitic about their appearance; none the less, if they are Hapiru/Hebrews, these two tomb painting representations of them are the earliest known.

The departure of the Hyksos marked not only the coming to power of a spectacular new dynasty, the Eighteenth, but also a whole new phase of Egyptian history, the New Kingdom. Although earlier Egyptian monarchs are loosely referred to here as 'pharaoh', in fact it is only from the New Kingdom that Egypt's rulers are specifically described in this way. In Egyptian the term *pr-o* simply means 'great house', exactly equivalent to referring to the American presidency as 'the White House'. The most characteristic feature of the period, particularly in its earlier years, is the monarchy's new mood of aggressive militarism, as distinct from the predominant fertility-god ethos of the past. Now one pharaoh after another, even the less militaristically inclined among them, had themselves portrayed larger than life aboard a heaving war chariot, composite bow at full stretch, with wave after wave of Asiatics falling beneath the hoofs of their leaping horses. It would become a matter of pride for these pharaohs to encourage their armies to develop and maintain their fighting skills at peak efficiency. The pharaoh himself would publicly practise firing at targets for hour after hour, standing in his chariot in the hot sun. In an effort to ensure that Egypt would never again endure the humiliation of foreign domination, the Hyksos/Canaanites were pursued beyond Egypt's natural border. Inscriptions on the tomb of Captain Ahmose describe how his pharaonic master and namesake spent three years besieging a fortress city called Sharuhen, along the 'Way of the Sea' into Canaan, and probably identifiable with a site today known as Tell el-Ajjul. Pharaoh Ahmose's successors Amenophis I, Tuthmosis I and Tuthmosis II appear, although comparatively little is known of them, to have kept empire-building campaigns into Canaanite territory high on their list of priorities; it would seem that there was a need to establish a solid buffer zone between them and the rapidly developing nations, such as the Hurrians, or Mitanni, who lay further to the north and north-east.

Perhaps because the former god-like awe associated with a pharaoh inevitably lost something when his true power was seen to be invested in his

The first known artistic depiction of Habiru/Hapiru, from the fifteenth-century BC tomb of Puyemre at Thebes. The hieroglyphic inscription in the centre reads 'straining out wine by the '*prw* [Hapiru]', and the very next scene identifies the location as 'the vineyard of Wat-Hor', pin-pointing the setting as the eastern Delta. This proves that some Asiatics of humble status remained in the Delta after the Hyksos expulsion. Not surprisingly, these Hapiru look very similar to ordinary Egyptians; there would have been little racial difference between them.

generalship of an army, from the time of Tuthmosis I it became the fashion for the pharaonic tomb to be hidden from the eyes of possible looters. Tuthmosis I was the first to be secreted in Thebes' famous Valley of the Kings. Since Tuthmosis I had only a daughter, Hatshepsut, by his marriage to his 'great' or principal wife, he was somewhat unsatisfactorily succeeded by the son of a secondary marriage, Tuthmosis II, who promptly married his half-sister Hatshepsut in order to give himself greater security on the throne. But Tuthmosis II himself died before having a male heir by Hatshepsut, the succession thereby going to his very young son by a mere concubine, a boy who would become Tuthmosis III. However, at this point there now occurred a fascinating and quite unprecedented episode of Egyptian power politics, which can be traced step by step in successive Egyptian monuments. At first these show the young Tuthmosis III as the more dominant figure, with Hatshepsut diminutive behind him. The next stage was for the two monarchs to be shown side by side, as if with equal status. But within a year Tuthmosis III had simply disappeared from such representations as Hatshepsut had begun proclaiming that she was the rightful divine progeny of the god Amon-Re, and had actually been promised the throne by her father Tuthmosis I. Young Tuthmosis III was despatched from the Theban court, ostensibly for military training, leaving the stage clear for Hatshepsut to exercise the real power in the land, which she did with apparent relish.

The coup, exercized without any actual deposition of Tuthmosis III (who continued for the next twenty years to be a sort of nominal co-pharaoh), presented a variety of problems owing to the traditionalism in which Egypt was steeped. Since grammatically the word 'pharaoh' was masculine, Hatshepsut was obliged to refer to herself as 'he' in all her written, and most likely spoken, utterances. If a pharaoh was a man in speech, 'he' had to be so in dress as well, and on her monuments, and probably in life as well, Hatshepsut had herself arrayed in nothing more concealing than the royal collar and stiff knee-length kilt that was the normal male dress for the time.

But what Hatshepsut set herself to do, with the most impeccable taste, was to array all Egypt in the trappings as well as the reality of a renewed superpower. Apparently largely bypassing Hapuseneb, the titular Vizier and Chief Priest, Hatshepsut instead delegated many of her responsibilities to a commoner called Senenmut, tutor to her daughter Nefrure. With Senenmut as 'Chief Steward' of Amon, Hatshepsut tried to justify the divine birth she claimed for herself by beautifying Amon's temple at Karnak with four massive obelisks, brought all the way from Aswan on a 300-foot-long barge towed by no fewer than twenty-seven boats manned by 864 oarsmen. Nearly 200 feet tall on installation, each obelisk was originally sheathed in electrum, an alloy of silver and gold. Without doubt, however, her most perfect extant building achievement must be the mortuary temple she built for herself on the west bank of the Nile at Deir el-Bahri. Partly freestanding, partly cut into a commanding frame of cliffs, it has been described as the perfect blend of nature with the man-made. It is breathtakingly beautiful even today, and

Opposite Pharaoh Tuthmosis IV in his war-chariot, mowing down waves of Asiatics with a composite bow. This drawing is taken from reliefs on the sides of his chariot, and the image was repeated many times by the pharaohs of the New Kingdom.

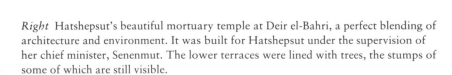

Right Hatshepsut's beautiful mortuary temple at Deir el-Bahri, a perfect blending of architecture and environment. It was built for Hatshepsut under the supervision of her chief minister, Senenmut. The lower terraces were lined with trees, the stumps of some of which are still visible.

'Keftiu' tribute bearers from Crete (dubbed 'Minoans' by Knossos excavator Sir Arthur Evans), depicted in the tomb of Senenmut at Thebes.

when it was first constructed, with trees and flowerbeds, and a 100-foot-wide approach way lined with sphinxes, it must have had an overwhelming effect.

However, such undertakings could only be given their appropriate embellishments with a variety of commodities that had to be obtained from other countries, and so it was that Hatshepsut sought to trade, rather than to wage war with, the peoples of other nations. It is in Senenmut's damaged tomb that we are able to see one of the first of what would become traditional scenes of foreign emissaries, each in their national costume, bringing to the Egyptian court the choicest items of their local produce and craftsmanship. Prominent among them are young men dressed in little more than codpieces, described in the accompanying hieroglyphs as 'Keftiu'. From the goods and pottery vessels they are carrying it is obvious that they are representatives of the civilization dubbed as 'Minoan' by Britain's Sir Arthur Evans after his discovery on Crete of the famous palace of Knossos in 1900. Crete is some 350 miles across the Mediterranean from the nearest Egyptian mainland, and it is more than that distance again up the Nile to Thebes, but so highly skilled had the 'Keftiu' become at shipbuilding and navigation that during the next fifty or so years they appear very frequently as emissaries and tribute-bearers at the Egyptian court.

The identity of the Cretan ruler with whom Hatshepsut bargained is completely undocumented, but from the dominance of women in Minoan art, and the total absence, at least during the time of Hatshepsut, of any king cult such as had been practised by most other countries, including Egypt, it is perfectly possible that this was another queen, an earthly representative of the Mother Goddess who formed the prime focus of Minoan worship. The feared Minos of Greek folklore probably arrived only with the takeover of Crete by Mycenaean Greeks a generation or so after Hatshepsut's time.

Another yet more strange trading partner of Hatshepsut's was the land the Egyptians called Punt, which was probably, judging from its produce, present-day Somalia on the Horn of Africa. An Egyptian expedition specially commissioned to make the long journey returned heavily laden with precious woods and tropical plants, among them what appear to have been myrrh trees, and animals including baboons. So vivid are the scenes of the people and animals of Punt, as depicted in the colonnades of Hatshepsut's Deir el-Bahri temple, that it seems certain that the expedition must have had its own accompanying professional artist.

The upshot of all this is that Hatshepsut, with her penchant for excellence, set Egypt on a vigorous course of self-aggrandizement that demanded maximum output from every area of life. Within a couple of generations, whenever pharaohs had a labour shortage, they would mount an expedition into Canaan and return with a fresh injection of slave labour. But under Hatshepsut and to some extent under Tuthmosis III when he succeeded her, maximum use was made of the existing labour force; a sensible scheme because for much of the year agricultural labourers were idle owing to the shortness of the growing season. Although little is known of Tuthmosis III's activities while his mother held the reins in Thebes, it is obvious from the subsequent speedy preparedness of his army after her death – within weeks he was leading it hotfoot into Canaan – that he must have devoted by far his greatest efforts to equipping and training it to a peak of professional military organization, which included the building and refurbishing of garrison headquarters, the improvement of defence lines, and the like. It is in association with Tuthmosis that we first hear of what would subsequently become the Egyptians' best-known frontier fortress, Sile or Zaru, a little to the north-east of Avaris/Pi-Ramesses and uncomfortably close to the Israelite/Habiru settlement ground of Goshen.

Such is the nature of the Delta terrain that today we can only guess at the work that might have been done and who might have done it, but it does not need much imagination to reconstruct a situation strikingly similar to that of the Israelites' 'hard labour' described in the opening chapter of the book of Exodus. The actual Hebrew words used to describe Pithom and Ramesses in this chapter are *'ārê (ham) misk^{e}nôt*, which although usually rendered 'store cities' in Exodus 1:11, in the *Jerusalem Bible* text, at least, become 'garrison cities' when they recur in an obvious military context in 1 Kings 9:19, 2 Chronicles 8:6 and 2 Chronicles 17:12. Furthermore, it is precisely in the tomb of a Tuthmosis III vizier, the great Rekhmire, that we have a scene frequently used to illustrate Exodus 1:14, describing how the Egyptians '. . . treated their Israelite slaves with ruthless severity . . . setting them to work on clay and brickmaking'.

According to a commentary on the Rekhmire scene, made in 1944 by the great British copyist of Egyptian tomb paintings, Norman de Garis Davies:

> The bricks are laid out in rows . . . and their number increases under the hands of two men, each of whom turns them out one by one from a wooden frame into which water is being worked by men whose hands and feet are visibly clotted with dirt. The workers claim our attention by their strange physiognomy and coloration.

Although in this instance Syrians and Nubians are depicted as the hardpressed brickmakers, standing over them, rods in hand, are individuals unmistakable as the taskmasters described in Exodus 1:11: 'So they [the Israelites] were made to work in gangs, with officers set over them, to break their spirit with heavy labour.' In ancient Egypt such rods doubled as symbols of authority and instruments of correction, it being a common expression that 'a young man has a back, and listens to the man who strikes it', with more extreme offenders being spoken of as 'beaten like papyrus'. As an explanation for the fact that a surprising number of bodies from Egyptian graves have been found with a broken left forearm, it has been suggested that the victim sustained the fracture when he tried to protect himself against a blow from a rod, and it may well therefore have been a surfeit of such scenes that prompted the Biblical Moses to kill the Egyptian he saw striking a Hebrew, as described in Exodus 2:11.

Pharaoh Tuthmosis III beating Asiatics, from the temple of Amon at Karnak. The Egyptians were fond of using the rod as a means of correction. According to Exodus 2:11, it was the sight of an Egyptian striking a Hebrew which prompted Moses to become a rebel against Egyptian rule.

Foreign workers brickmaking, from the tomb of Tuthmosis III's vizier Rekhmire at Thebes. Although those depicted are identified as Syrians and Nubians, the scene is sharply reminiscent of the enforced 'work on clay and brickmaking' of the Biblical Hebrews, as described in Exodus 1:14.

It is plausible, then, that the harsh oppression of Biblical Israelites, immediately preceding the Biblical Exodus, took place in the period of Hatshepsut and Tuthmosis III rather than of Ramesses II. But before we search for further evidence to support such an idea, one question, pertinent whatever the period, is worth considering: why any large tribe or group of tribes, located near Egypt's north-eastern border and suffering the sort of hardships that the Bible ascribes to the Israelites, should not simply have made their own way across the frontier. On a present-day map, if the Suez Canal is mentally removed, there seems to be sufficient open terrain for them to have been able to give the slip to, or even overpower, any roving group of border guards.

The fallacy in this argument is that it does not take into account what has been learned in recent years of the Egyptian frontier as it was in the time of the New Kingdom, and had indeed been for some centuries before. When aerial photography and on-the-spot surveying discovered the course of the old Pelusiac, or easternmost branch of the Nile, they also revealed a distinct but artificial-looking waterway running northwards from Lake Timsah, disappearing into Lake Ballah, which the Egyptians appear to have known as the 'Papyrus Swamp', and taking a dog-leg course east and then northwards to join up with the Pelusiac mouth of the Nile. The discovery began to make sense of several previously puzzling early references to the 'Wall of the Ruler' which, as mentioned in the previous chapter, served to check Asiatic incursions in the wake of the troubles of the First Intermediate Period.

At that time one pharaoh, having temporarily checked the 'Sand-Crossers' with a fortified outpost at Wat-Hor (Way of Horus), produced a still extant set of recommendations to his son Merikare in which he specifically urged the digging of a canal from Wat-Hor to Lake Timsah: 'Dig a canal until it is un(hindered); flood it half as far as Lake Timsah (Km–wr).' Although the pressure of historical circumstances seems to have prevented Merikare from carrying out his father's instructions, the task seems to have been brought to fruition in the reign of the Twelfth-Dynasty Amenemhet I, because it is from the reign of his successor that we have an account of a single individual, Sinuhe, having some difficulty in *escaping* from Egypt owing to an obstacle he calls the 'Wall of the Ruler': 'I came up to the Wall of the Ruler, made to oppose the Asiatics and crush the Sand-Crossers. I took a crouching position in a bush for fear lest watchmen upon the wall where their day's [duty] was might see me.'

While at face value this might appear to have been no more than a wall in the conventional sense, later evidence indicates otherwise. At Karnak a relief of Seti I, father of Ramesses II, shows the pharaoh returning from an expedition to Canaan, and being separated from the welcoming Egyptians by a crocodile-infested canal which can be seen to flow into the sea (denoted by sea fish). The sole route traversing the canal is a bridge commanded by the key fortress of Sile, otherwise known, like the route it controlled, as Wat-Hor. That this canal, which must surely be the one revealed by aerial

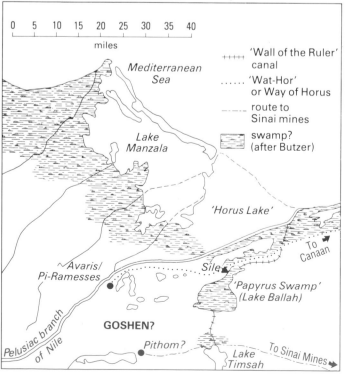

Above Pharaoh Seti I (*c* 1306–1290 BC), approaching Egypt's north-eastern frontier, from a relief in the Hypostyle Hall of Amon's temple at Karnak. The fortress commanding the single bridge across the waterway is identified as the frontier fortress of Sile, the reed-lined canal (referred to in the inscription as *Ta Denit*, 'The Dividing Waters') being thought to be part of the Eastern Canal Wall of the Ruler frontier defence system. Such a barrier would have served to keep captive peoples in as well as intruders out.

Left The likely route of the 'Wall of the Ruler' canal/earthwork, as reconstructed from information based on aerial photographs and other data. This structure, together with the swamp in the Lake Ballah region, and what the Egyptians called the 'Horus Lake' south-east of present-day Lake Manzala, enabled exit and entry into Egypt to be carefully controlled by troops stationed at the frontier fortress of Sile.

photography, existed some centuries before the time of Seti I is strongly indicated by the discovery of several Middle and early New Kingdom sites along its route. When all this evidence is put together, the only reasonable deduction is that canal and wall must have been created in one and the same operation, the latter, all trace of which has disappeared, having simply been made from the mud removed to form the canal. The reason for expending so much labour on such a construction has been admirably explained by Egyptologist W.A. Ward:

> This line of defence, once completed, would be the logical one, since it would guard the whole area from the south-eastern shore of Lake Manzala to Lake Timsah. Its northern terminus would be the land-route which entered Egypt through Way-of-Horus (Wat-Hor) and its southern terminus at the entrance to the Wadi Tumilat at Ismailia. Precisely this region was the main point of entry for nomads wishing to move out of the desert into the Delta. A fortified canal, half-filled with water, would be an ideal defensive position, easily manned by troops and mobile units on rafts or small boats patrolling the length of the canal.

While the original purpose of such a frontier had been to keep Asiatics out, it is also clear that it could serve to keep them in, just as the Berlin Wall serves the same function for the East Germans of today. More than likely such a defence line had been allowed to fall into disrepair under the Hyksos, who would have had no use for it, as a result of which it would have been high on the priorities of Tuthmosis III, or one of his immediate predecessors, to restore and indeed enhance its efficiency. It therefore scarcely strains credibility that the Habiru, whom we have already noted at work in the Wat-Hor region, may well have been dragged from their flocks to work on defences around Avaris/Pi-Ramesses.

But if the events of the Biblical Exodus are to be associated in any way with the reign of either Hatshepsut or Tuthmosis III, a significantly more substantial link is needed than anything we have discussed so far. The circumstances described in the Bible as triggering the Israelites' release were a series of cataclysms: clouds of darkness, crops ruined, animals dying, even freak waves from the sea. Is anything that might have been responsible for such catastrophes known to have occurred in the period of Hatshepsut/Tuthmosis III? Remarkably the answer is yes, and our quest for the catalyst now takes us away from Egypt, some 350 miles north-westwards across the Mediterranean to the island of the colourful 'Keftiu'.

6. Crete: a strange swath of destruction

THERE is a land called Crete in the midst of the wine-dark sea, a fair land and a rich, begirt with water, and therein are many men innumerable and ninety cities. . . . And among these cities is the mighty city Knossos. . . . (Homer: *Odyssey*, 19)

When in the year 1900 Sir Arthur Evans was unearthing the now famous throne room of Knossos' ancient palace, one of those who watched particularly intently was a twenty-nine-year-old American graduate from Boston, Massachusetts, Harriet Boyd, later to become known as Mrs Harriet Boyd Hawes. Daughter of a leather merchant, she had spent the previous four years as a graduate fellow at the American School of Classical Studies in Athens. Now, cognizant of Homer's 'ninety cities', and seeing Englishmen and Italians actually opening up 'Minoan' sites on Crete, Harriet determined to discover one herself.

The very next year Cretan peasants, newly liberated from centuries of Turkish rule, watched in astonishment as Harriet and two female companions, dressed in the ankle-length fashions of the time, quixotically made their way on muleback down a coastal hillside at Gournia, some fifty miles east of Heraklion. They were still more astonished when, after examining various oddments of broken pottery and crumbling wall, the businesslike Harriet began offering them money to dig in the hillside for her, giving them a vote on whether they would prefer to be given a basic wage, with special rewards for each object found, or to be paid slightly more for careful, methodical excavation, irrespective of however few or many objects each individual happened to come across. To Harriet's satisfaction, the men chose the latter method, but even more gratifying were the results of the very first afternoon's work. As she later recorded in her *Memoirs*:

> The men scattered over the hillside were in high spirits, for had not Lysimachus produced the first good find of the season – a perfect bronze spear point, and Michalis Paviadhakis, a curved bronze knife buried scarcely a foot below the surface? One man after another called us to see the potsherds, fragments of stone vases, etc., he had saved for our inspection. Perhaps the proudest workman was he who had laid bare a well-paved road, the threshold of a house, and a small clay gutter.

Methodical as Harriet was, she worked with a speed and vigour light-

Above Harriet Boyd amid her excavations at Gournia. She uncovered almost the entire site, and found clear evidence of a sudden cessation of occupation, accompanied by a terrible fire, at about the time of the reigns of the Hatshepsut and Tuthmosis III.

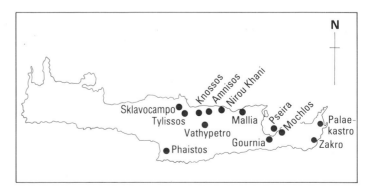

Right Crete: some of the main Minoan sites.

years removed from today's painstaking methods, and briskly reached fundamental conclusions about what she had found:

> Within three days we had opened houses, were following paved roads, and had in our possession enough vases and sherds bearing octopus, ivy-leaf, double-axe and other unmistakably Minoan designs ·as well as bronze tools, seal impressions, stone vases, etc., to make it certain that we had found what we were seeking, a Bronze Age settlement of the best period of Cretan civilization.

To this day the actual name of the town revealed by Harriet Boyd is unknown. The customary name given to the site is Gournia. Although Harriet referred to one of the buildings as a 'palace', it never had anything of the grandeur of Knossos: Minoan Gournia was a long-established, middle-of-the-road community of carpenters, coppersmiths, weavers, masons, potters, farmers and fishermen, some of whose pottery can be seen to have been identical with that of the 'Keftiu' tributaries depicted in the tomb paintings of Hatshepsut and Tuthmosis III's viziers. Clearly, then, Gournia must have been flourishing at the very time Hatshepsut and Tuthmosis III were playing their power games a few hundred miles to the south-east.

But, as Harriet Boyd also came to realize, it was at this very time that *something* brought a thousand years of previously uninterrupted settlement at Gournia to a sudden and virtually final halt. Whatever had happened had been so swift that carpenters and coppersmiths had simply dropped their precious tools on the floor, never to return for them. There was a special stone mould for casting knives and chisels which the one-time owner had valued so highly that when it broke he re-bound it with bronze strips. It lay abandoned. Whoever or whatever had been responsible for the catastrophe, its most obvious accompaniment had been a fire of extraordinary intensity. As Harriet Boyd remarked in her official report on the excavations,

> The conflagration which destroyed the town left proof of its strength in many parts of the excavation. Wooden posts and steps were entirely burned away, leaving deposits of charcoal and marks of smoke-grime; bricks were baked bright red. In a ground-floor room of the palace lay a large tree-trunk which had supported an upper floor, completely charred through, but retaining its original shape; the central hall of the palace was choked with such timbers. Limestone was calcined, steatite was reduced to crumbling fragments; in a doorway of the palace lay a shapeless lump of bronze, once the trimmings of the door. . . .

Crucial to the dating of this catastrophe was the presence of pottery showing a continuous sequence up to a type now known as Late Minoan IB, typified by lively marine motifs such as octopus, nautilus and starfish. Although, after a sizeable time lapse, someone using Late Minoan III pottery briefly reoccupied a part of the site, thereafter the ruins remained undisturbed until the coming of Harriet Boyd.

Archaeologically there was nothing unusual in a Bronze Age town being found to have been set on fire by invaders and, since Gournia had no walls, its predominantly artisan inhabitants could have put up little resistance. But then in 1906 an American who had initially worked for Harriet Boyd as a photographer, Richard Seager, began trial excavations on the now barren and uninhabited island of Pseira, a couple of miles off the coast and a little to Gournia's east. Here he found a Minoan harbour town, neatly sheltered by a tongue of land with, as at Gournia, pottery evidence of long, essentially uninterrupted occupation until a similar, sudden break in Late Minoan IB. Two years later Seager turned his attentions to Mochlos, another island three miles to the east of Pseira but much closer to the shore; indeed in antiquity it had probably been joined to the mainland by a sandspit. The Minoan port found here had had a community of craftsmen specializing in hand-crafting stone vases, but as at Gournia and Pseira their industry had come to a sudden and violent end in Late Minoan IB. A typical Mochlos house had, in Seager's words, 'perished in a great conflagration of so violent a character that almost all the objects found in it are badly charred and blackened'. And while in the previous excavations no human victims had been found, that was not the case here. According to Seager, 'In a number of places in this house were found human bones badly charred, showing that the destruction was no peaceful one, and that many of the inhabitants perished with their houses. This same fact had already been noted in other houses.'

As in the course of this century more and more Minoan sites have come to light in eastern Crete, so an almost identical picture of sudden catastrophe in Late Minoan IB has been revealed. In the early 1920s Greek archaeologist S. Xanthudides uncovered, eight miles east of Heraklion, the once magnificent stone-built villa of Nirou Khani, with flagstoned floors and forty elegantly finished rooms on the ground floor alone. Like every other site, it had been destroyed by fire. At the time disaster struck it was crammed with valuable objects, among them four superb bronze axes, the biggest so far found, and well over forty tripod-style tables, left neatly stacked against a wall. And herein lay a peculiarity. Like everywhere else on Crete, Nirou Khani had no defences. Therefore, if the place had been seized by raiders, why did they not take away with them such valuable loot? Failing this, why did not any surviving original inhabitants return at least to salvage items that the raiders had left behind?

A similar mystery emerged in the 1960s, when Greek archaeologist Professor Nicholas Platon discovered the remains of Crete's easternmost Minoan palace, with accompanying town, a short distance from the shoreline of the mountain-circled bay called Kato Zakro. Like Nirou Khani, it ended in flames. According to Platon's account,

The fire was certainly of large extent and of great intensity; it reduced everything to ashes. Fed by inflammable material such as the oil in the storerooms, it turned many stones into lime, charred completely all the wooden parts of the palace and the internal timber of the walls, burned the columns, and in some areas transformed by conflagration even the clay pots, some of which were crumbled and distorted or changed into a shapeless mass. . . .

The town suffered no less severely than the palace, yet as at Nirou Khani precious objects lay undisturbed, among them elephant tusks, bronze ingots and exquisitely made vases in the style of those depicted in the tombs of Tuthmosis III's viziers. In Platon's words,

> Most of the valuable objects were still in their original positions. Tools lay where they were being used on that day, and raw materials and unfinished artefacts were found in workshops. The finished products were still in the storerooms. In the kitchens and their annexes there were remnants of food, together with cooking utensils either in use at the time or in storage compartments.

Like all other Cretan sites of the Late Minoan IB period, Zakro had no walls with which to defend itself against marauders. But the peculiarity lay in why so many sites should have succumbed at the same time, with apparently so little resistance (bodies were found only at Mochlos), and with the hypothetical attackers apparently taking so little advantage of their marauding – failing to loot, and failing to settle in their places of conquest. Whatever had happened was so final that most of the remains were simply left for the earth to cover them. So could something other than human agency have been responsible?

For Professor Platon such an idea was not mere speculation. As he observed at Kato Zakro, in several places around the palace something very much more powerful than human agency seemed to have been at work:

> . . . huge stones, some dressed, some not, had been hurled to a distance or had fallen and shattered, blocking passages and filling open spaces. Whole sections of the upper storey had been thrown down, at many points preserving their relative continuity. Sections of the walls of the façade, carefully constructed of dressed stone, fell in a block from their bases in such a manner that the stones were spread out in a series on the floor. . . . The steps of the stairways had subsided, and in many cases were displaced from their original position. . . . Many of the pithoi [large storage jars] in the deep storerooms of the West Wing, mainly those arrayed along the west wall, had been compressed and squeezed as if pressure from some great force had been applied from east to west. A similar enormous pressure was evidenced by whole walls of dressed porous stones that had fallen from their foundations in one piece. . . .

Platon was not the first to have had such thoughts. Thirty years before, one of his fellow countrymen, Spyridon Marinatos, had been excavating yet another site of Late Minoan IB destruction, Amnisos, once the harbour town for Knossos. There, providential probing by a pig's snout had turned

Above The bay of Kato Zakro, from which 'Keftiu' merchants set out for Egypt. Like other sites in eastern Crete, it suffered sudden destruction by fire, followed by abandonment. The burnt tusks (*right*) are typical of the variety of Keftiu trading goods depicted in Egyptian tomb-paintings, and were probably awaiting shipment at the time Zakro suffered its catastrophe.

up the first signs of what was subsequently revealed as a once comfortably appointed Minoan villa, from which tattered and blackened wall paintings of lilies can be seen today in the Heraklion Museum. But as Marinatos observed, what remained of the villa's walls, particularly at the corners of rooms, had bulged outwards in an unusual way. Large upright stones appeared to have been prised out of position as if by some massive external force. Particularly instructive were the contents of a square pit in the villa's south-eastern corner. In Marinatos' words, it was 'literally full of pumice stone', and this was not of the jagged, irregular-shaped variety that might be picked up on land in the vicinity of a volcano, but 'small, rounded and polished like pebbles', indicating that it had come from the sea.

Marinatos, in his early thirties already a director of Heraklion Museum, was too astute and well-versed in the Aegean's seismic instability not to recognize there and then the likely source of the pumice. Through continuous movements of the great plates that form the earth's crust, the African continent is moving towards Europe at the rate of one inch a year, a particularly sensitive friction point being the Aegean around Crete. As a result, the region is not only prone to earthquakes, it also features the eastern Mediterranean's most active volcano, an island group called Thera (or alternatively Santorini) some sixty miles to Crete's north-east. Only seven years before Marinatos' excavations at Amnisos Thera had erupted very memorably. In an apparently related earthquake on 26 June 1926 2,000 buildings on the island had toppled in just forty-five seconds. On Crete fifty houses in the capital, Heraklion, collapsed, another 300 were badly damaged, and many surrounding villages were wrecked. On Rhodes literally thousands of houses were destroyed, some with loss of life, and the Greek islands of Karpathos and Kastellorizo were similarly affected. Mosques and houses collapsed on the Turkish mainland to the north. And far to the south-east there was widespread damage in Egypt, with the collapse of 600 houses in Cairo and Alexandria alone. To Marinatos the considerable quantities of pumice found at the Late Minoan 1B villa at Amnisos indicated that there must have been serious eruptive activity, almost inevitably from Thera, some time around the Late Minoan 1B period – that is, around the time of Hatshepsut and Tuthmosis III. But there was even more conclusive evidence that something extremely serious had happened in Minoan times on Thera itself. Overlying much of the main island and its companions was a layer of volcanic ash and pumice so deep that when vast quantities of cement were needed for the construction of Egypt's Suez Canal and Port Said harbour facilities, the contractors looked to Thera, the ash from which, when mixed with lime, produces a particularly durable and waterproof cement.

But, as the quarrying revealed, this was not ash that had accumulated over aeons of geological time. At a depth of sometimes 100 or 150 feet a soil layer was reached, indicative of a period before which the volcano had stayed quiescent for a considerable length of time. But there was not only soil. At this same level there also came to light the remains of well-built stone houses, some, where accessible, furnishing Minoan remains – although those who found them failed to record their finds too carefully. To Marinatos it seemed obvious that in the Late Minoan IB period there must have been a staggeringly large eruption of Thera, responsible not only for the ash layer on Thera itself but also for the destruction of the Minoan sites on eastern Crete sixty miles away, and perhaps untold disaster elsewhere, including Egypt. As Marinatos was aware, sea-based volcanoes such as Thera could generate huge waves moving at hundreds of miles an hour – known by the Japanese name of *tsunami*. These, he surmised, must have caused the strange dislocations of masonry at Amnisos and, as would later be discovered by Platon, at Zakro.

Marinatos put all his thinking down on paper in a cogently reasoned article for the leading archaeological journal *Antiquity*. To his delight it was accepted for publication, though with the accompaniment of a careful qualification: 'The Editors wish to point out that in their opinion the main thesis of this article requires additional support from excavation on selected sites. They hope that such excavations will in due course be carried out.' By 'selected sites' the editors chiefly meant Thera itself, where no properly documented archaeological work had yet been carried out.

But the date Marinatos' article was published was 1939, and the journal had hardly reached the academics it was intended for before they, the whole Mediterranean, and much else became swept up in the far more immediate problems of the Second World War. When the dust from this finally settled, Marinatos, a member of the Athens Academy, found himself diverted by the demands of archaeological work on the Greek mainland, at Mycenae and elsewhere. But in 1965 there took place in Bristol, England, the seventeenth Symposium of the Colston Research Society. Although this was not the sort of event likely to claim world attention, the proceedings included a scientific paper presented jointly by two geologists, Dragoslav Ninkovich and Bruce Heezen, from Columbia University, USA. Their special interest was the geology of the eastern Mediterranean seabed. Fascinated by core samples from the seabed that had been taken during 1947 and 1948 by a Swedish survey ship, the *Albatross*, Ninkovich and Heezen conducted their own survey of the same area from another ship, the *Vema*, in 1956 and 1958, and found even more intriguing results. As indicated by core after core taken across some 200,000 square miles of the eastern Mediterranean, this whole area of seabed had as part of its layers of sediment two very distinctive levels of volcanic ash.

Volcanic ash is essentially glass; and each particle has its own 'signature' in the form of a refractive index, which is unique not only to the particular volcano but also to the eruption from which it has been derived. Accordingly, as Ninkovich and Heezen established, the lower of the two ash levels was of no particular interest because it derived from an eruption which had happened some 25,000 years ago, long before settlement by civilized peoples. But the upper level was altogether more significant. Its refractive index, 1.509, exactly matched that of samples taken from the huge mounds of ash

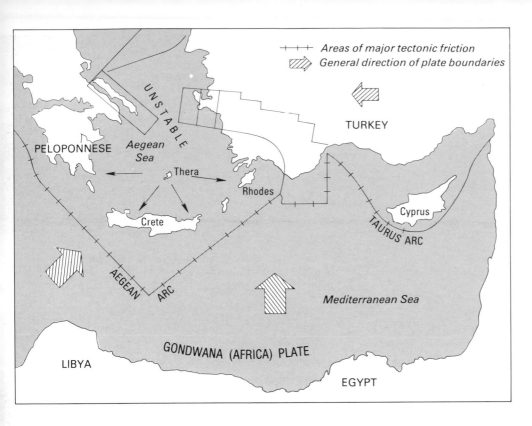

Left The seismic instability of the eastern Mediterranean. As established by the theory of plate tectonics, Africa together with part of the floor of the Mediterranean is moving north towards Europe at about an inch a year, while Turkey is moving westwards. The weak point in all these forces is in the area around Crete in the Aegean, hence its susceptibility to earthquakes and eruptions from the main regional volcano, Thera.

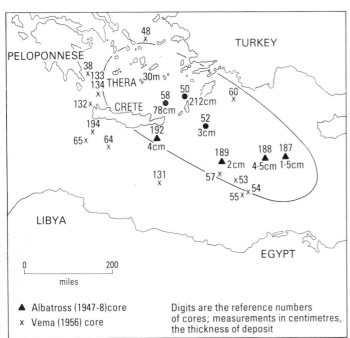

▲ Albatross (1947-8) core
× Vema (1956) core

Digits are the reference numbers of cores; measurements in centimetres, the thickness of deposit

Above Distribution of ash from the Minoan period eruption of Thera, as determined by cores from the bed of the Mediterranean sampled by the survey ships *Albatross* and *Vema* in 1947 and 1956 respectively. Note the clear indication of the ash-cloud's drift towards Egypt.

Right Part of the villa at Amnisos, showing some of the wall-blocks prised out of position. *Below* Lily frescoes from this same villa, preserved in Heraklion Museum, show clear traces of the fire associated with the abandonment of the villa.

directly overlying Thera's Minoan remains. And when the core samples containing this layer were plotted on a map, the western edge of their spread across the sea floor could be seen to bisect Crete (see lower map, page 94). The fiery ash cloud of the eruption had clearly covered precisely those eastern Cretan sites which had suffered such sudden and mysterious destruction in the Late Minoan IB period. What is more, that same ash cloud could be seen unmistakably to have drifted from Thera in a south-easterly direction, pointing ominously towards the Nile Delta area of Egypt.

Suddenly Marinatos' theory had serious scientific support. Then, within a year of Ninkovich and Heezen presenting their paper, there came to light another relevant discovery. While casually exploring a part of Thera's eastern coast an American called Edward Loring turned up a piece of black rock. It intrigued him because it seemed to have a face on it, like that of a tiny baby or a young animal – although at first Loring thought this was just the result of some chance of nature. But he happened to pass it to a Greek professor who in turn gave it to anthropological specialists. When they X-rayed it, the mystery was explained. It was the head of a monkey, semi-fossilized because it had become coated with andesite and quartzite – part of the ejecta of a volcanic eruption. The genus was identified as forming part of the sub-family Colobinae, native to the belt of tropical Africa, extending from the west across the Congo to Ethiopia. But what was such a monkey doing on Thera? The answer was to be found in some of the Minoan frescoes from Knossos, featuring near-identical monkeys. Great traders that they were, the Minoans/Keftiu brought back to Crete as pets monkeys they acquired in the course of their trading missions to Africa – perhaps even from those to Egypt, the Egyptians in their turn no doubt having acquired them from their own trade links with Punt and elsewhere to the south.

So here, frozen in volcanic death, lay a tangible victim of the catastrophe that appeared to have caused so much havoc in the eastern Mediterranean during the period known as Late Minoan IB. The monkey's skull was found to be cracked, possibly from the animal having been hit on the head by a rock ejected from the volcano, and it had then been part preserved, part cooked by hot lava.

What had happened to the monkey's owners? Marinatos needed no more prodding. In May 1967 he was on board a Thera-bound ferry, armed with a magnetometer for the detection of underground buildings, and with sponsorship from the same University Museum of Philadelphia which had funded Harriet Boyd and Richard Seager's work on Crete nearly seventy years before. The mysteries of what had happened to human life on Thera at the time of the great eruption were about to be opened up.

7. Pillar of fire

Aɴʏoɴᴇ who approaches Thera by sea is unlikely to forget the experience. Even at the height of summer the almost constant *meltemi* wind can whip the waves to a choppiness that makes one admire those Minoan mariners who braved the journey in their flimsy, high-prowed ships three and a half thousand years ago. Gradually there comes into view what at first sight seems a single, plateau-like island, roughly the size of Nassau or the Isle of Wight, with steep-sided cliffs rising sheer from the sea. As the ferry draws closer the scale of the place becomes apparent, with tiny white-washed houses perched precariously on the clifftops. If in the mind's eye there is then projected on to this scene the image of how it must have looked at the time of the great eruption, a ten-mile-wide cauldron spewing a pillar of ash and fire perhaps sixty or seventy miles heavenwards, only those lacking in imagination can fail to feel a chill in the blood.

Greater proximity does nothing to diminish this. As the ferry draws near the shore it suddenly becomes apparent that this is not a single island, but rather the fragmented remains of what *was* a single island (see map, page 99). To the west lies Aspronisi, small and uninhabited. To its north looms the jagged and larger Therasia, with the few dwellings of its hardy inhabitants clinging to the terrain like barnacles. Dominating the whole of the east and south of the island complex lies crescent-shaped Thera proper, the capital Phira and other small townships sprinkled along its cliffs, while from the midst of the bay, like two huge coke dumps, rise the 'burnt' islands of Palaea and Nea Kameni, born in 197 BC and AD 1707 respectively, and reminders that this is still the site of an active volcano.

For the entire, ostensibly peaceful bay into which the ferry has sailed is in fact nothing other than the shattered caldera or crater of the single island volcano that Minoan navigators would have known when the craftsmen of Gournia and Mochlos bustled at their trades and Hatshepsut held sway in Egypt. The 1,150-foot-high, multicoloured cliffs that one must scale to visit Thera's towns are the old volcano's one-time inner walls. These are as sheer below the water as they are above, plunging to near-thousand-foot depths that make it impossible for ships to use their anchors. And as visitors to the Kameni islands can testify, it is necessary only to scratch the surface to feel temperatures that owe nothing to the heat of the sun.

However, while tourists will freely be shown such hot spots, few if any itineraries will include the quarries just south of Phira, where to this day

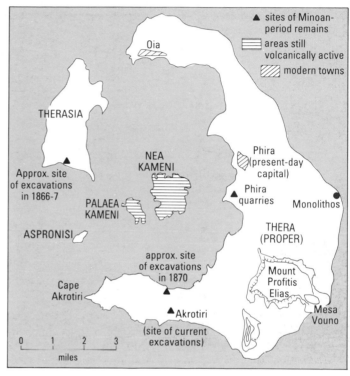

Above Thera today. A view from the capital, Phira, showing the huge bay formed by the volcanic crater, which is so deep that visiting ships are unable to drop anchor. In the centre of the bay, visible to the right of the picture, are the still active islands of Palaea and Nea Kameni, 'Old Burnt' and 'New Burnt' respectively.

Thera, showing the sites where Minoan period remains have been found (marked by pyramids), and the fragmented state of what was originally a single island.

Precariously perched on a clifftop that forms part of the rim of the old vocanic crater is the present-day Theran town of Oia.

huge volumes of ash lie waiting to be shipped as building materials all over the world. Yet here, more than anywhere else, can be gauged something of the enormity of what happened 3,500 years ago, and the order in which the events occurred. A wander down the quarry approach road discloses a 120-foot cut-away section, the top three-quarters of which consists of the fine, compacted white ash which blankets at least two-thirds of all land on Thera, Therasia and Aspronisi, even after so many millennia of *meltemi* winds, and it is the same ash that Ninkovich and Heezen found across so much of the Mediterranean seabed. Peppered among this ash, and indeed the other levels, are lumps of black basalt of varying sizes, 'bombs' spewed up from below the earth's crust.

Just below, no more than fifteen feet thick in all, lies a series of alternating layers, coarse white pumice, grey pumice, then what are usually referred to as 'coloured ribbons' of fine pink and white ash. Under these lie what can be confidently identified as the first phase of the eruption, a twelve- to fifteen-foot-thick layer of lumpy pumice, mostly greyish white, but occasionally a deep pink or brown.

But below this again is perhaps the most intriguing and telling level of all, brownish soil amid which the remains of a stone-built house are clearly visible. To this day no one has dared to excavate at this spot because of the sheer impracticability of shifting the millions of tons of constantly crumbling ash that lie above. Yet here is the most conclusive evidence that this truly massive eruption must have happened within civilized times.

From even before he set foot on Thera, Marinatos was aware that the quarries were no place for him to begin to try to uncover whatever had happened there. At a rough average, Thera's ash and pumice layer was ten times deeper than that which Vesuvius had rained on Roman Pompeii in AD 79 – evidence in itself of the quite staggering difference in scale between the two disasters. Not even Philadelphia University's generous funding could be expected to finance the shifting of so much debris. As a result, Marinatos had to seek areas of the island where, for reasons such as wind and water erosion, the thickness of cover might have been lessened.

To identify such areas Marinatos, being Greek, wisely listened to local gossip. In 1899 a German called R. Zahn had conducted some virtually unrecorded excavations, but the son of a Greek who had watched them happened to recall that Zahn had come across some remains just south of the present-day village of Akrotiri, in Thera's south-western sector. Another Greek remembered how he had been working in fields in this same region when the ground partly collapsed under his feet, revealing lumps of masonry just below the surface. When he led Marinatos to the spot, the sharp-eyed archaeologist noticed that vessels being used for animal drinking troughs were in fact ancient Minoan mortars. Obviously here was the territory to begin digging.

Marinatos promptly obtained the temporary loan of forty workmen from a Thera quarry owner, his information-gathering proving so accurate that the Philadelphia Museum's specially supplied magnetometer for detecting

A cut-away section of the Thera quarries, showing the huge depth of pumice and ash deposited by the Minoan-period eruption. Just visible at bottom left are the remains of a Minoan house.

MILL HOUSE

HOUSE OF THE LADIES

UNEXCAVATED PUMICE

UNEXCAVATED PUMICE

WEST HOUSE

Triangle Square

HOUSE DELTA

Mill House Square

Telchines Road

HOUSE 2

HOUSE BETA

HOUSE GAMMA

HOUSE 3

HOUSE 4

UNEXCAVATED PUMICE

Far left Professor Spyridon
Marinatos, the pioneer
excavator at Akrotiri,
working in one of the
Theran mills discovered
here. He died suddenly in
1974, and is buried on the
site, almost at the very spot
where he fell.

Left A simplified plan of
the Akrotiri site so far
excavated, probably just a
small fraction of the town
still awaiting recovery from
the pumice.

Minoan-period houses
engulfed by the Thera
eruption being excavated
from the pumice at
Akrotiri. Marinatos
originally planned that the
houses should remain
buried, with access gained
by tunnels cut into the
pumice, in order to avoid
erosion caused by exposure
to the air. But this proved
impractical, and the whole
site is now roofed over,
with Dexion pillars as
supports.

building remains proved unnecessary. As recalled by Emily Vermeule, research fellow at the Boston Museum of Fine Arts, who was present when the workmen's shovels made their first incursions into the pumice,

> The first afternoon we had been confident that nothing would happen for a day or two while the upper layers were thinned. By nine o'clock the next morning a workman was picking white crumbs off a wall. These were the first Thera frescoes. . . . They were still in place along one stone wall, with patches fallen in the fill, face up and face down. A few hours later we could not turn around without hitting plaster – on walls fallen from the ceiling, coated around mysterious constructions with wooden poles at the corners. Some walls had two or three layers in different color schemes. . . . A nest of wine jars and jugs and cups outside the front door took us four days to clear, and a big millstone had fallen upside down on top of another shelf-full of old Thera tableware. A stone lamp was overturned among pigs' teeth and goat bones. The flagstone floor inside the door was tilted down from the threshold at an angle of forty degrees, as though it had partly collapsed into a basement underneath. . . . The richness of the site lent it a certain madhouse quality. . . .

Although at that particular time Marinatos and his companions had available to them only six working days, it was already clear that another Pompeii had been found, but nearly twice as old. The discovery happened almost to coincide with the junta of Greek colonels appointing Marinatos Inspector General of Antiquities for all Greece and its islands, so Marinatos suddenly found himself with the power and finance at his disposal to undertake excavation at Akrotiri (the name now given to the site), on at least something of the scale the task demanded. Today, nearly twenty years later, that task is still only in its infancy.

It has become abundantly clear that Akrotiri, even as so far understood, must rank as one of the twentieth century's most significant and spectacular archaeological discoveries. Being retrieved from the pumice, inch by inch, is a complete Minoan-period town. In order to protect buildings as they are released from their volcanic shroud, the site has been given a permanent cover of prefabricated roofing with Dexion supports, so that today the visitor can stroll up a street contemporary with Egypt's Eighteenth Dynasty, viewing not mere foundations as at Gournia, nor artificial reconstructions as at Knossos, but two- and three-storey houses with at least an external appearance much as they had in their heyday. Perhaps Akrotiri's most novel and refreshing feature is that nothing yet discovered has anything to do with an élite or royal class. The houses lining the main excavated street, Telchines Street as Professor Marinatos liked to call it, were those of ordinary middle-class people, albeit ones enjoying a surprisingly high standard of living. Within the houses the only rooms with a clearly identifiable purpose happen to be water closets, functionally fitted out with small benches, below which cylindrical clay pipes were linked up to a sewage

Frescoes from some of the houses excavated at Akrotiri, indicating a high level of sophistication among the town's inhabitants. *Above* A pair of antelopes, from six that decorated the walls of a dwelling Marinatos dubbed 'house Beta'; *left* A Theran woman, possibly a priestess, from the 'House of the Ladies', the northenmost so far excavated. The woman wears the same type of topless garment depicted in frescoes and statuettes from Minoan Crete.

system which carried the effluent below properly paved streets in a manner that western Europe caught up with only a little more than a hundred years ago.

It is also evident that these Therans of three and a half thousand years ago were an artistic people. Not a house so far excavated has failed to incorporate at least one wall fresco of the kind remarked on by Emily Vermeule, and Greek restorers are doing a magnificent job piecing these together so that they can be viewed to advantage in museums. The first house on the right up Telchines Street had a whole wall of one room given over to two amorous and lively-looking antelopes, while on an adjacent wall two long-haired children were depicted sparring together, wearing little apart from the world's first known boxing gloves. The house just over to the east had a fresco of animated monkeys, perhaps the very brothers and sisters of the poor creature fossilized on the beach, while to the north, in the so-called 'House of the Ladies', the theme was one of women, apparently priestesses, paying their respects to a missing figure thought to have been the Theran Mother Goddess. Evident in the priestesses' costumes is the high state of Theran fashion of the time, brilliantly striped and flared full-length skirts and neat, half-sleeved jackets open at the front to expose the breasts fully, a style independently known from the famous 'snake goddess' of Minoan Crete. That such fashions were not peculiar to priestesses, but were everyday wear for Theran women, is demonstrated by perhaps the most fascinating fresco of all found on Thera: a Lowry-like panorama packed with details of life 3,500 years ago, forming a frieze around the walls of Akrotiri's so-called 'West House'.

The scene in question is generally referred to as the 'Ship Procession' or 'Miniature Fresco', and the fact that it is so lavish in its depiction of brightly bedecked, magnificently prowed Theran ships moving from one port to another suggests that the West House's owner was a ship's captain. Each ship in the picture has an important-looking individual seated in a box-like 'control room' at the stern, and since one of the West House's other decorations is a life-size representation of one of these 'control rooms', it seems logical to interpret this as a sign of the house-owner's pride in the high office he had achieved.

But of far greater interest is the fresco's depiction, with a wealth of accompanying detail, of two complete ports, each with its own individual landscape. There has been endless speculation concerning the likely geographical location of the port to the left. The presence of a lion chasing antelope in the undulating background, together with one or two other clues, prompted Marinatos to place it somewhere in Libya, although in fact 3,500 years ago lions were still to be found around much of the eastern Mediterranean. Since Theran trading included Canaan (as is evident from Syro-Palestinian gypsum vases and a jar found at Akrotiri) and also Egypt (indicated by three so-called 'Tell el-Yahudiyeh' juglets of Egyptian provenance found elsewhere on Thera in one of the earlier, unrecorded excavations), the river-bordered port depicted could be almost

anywhere, even Avaris/Pi-Ramesses. But as Minoan specialist Professor Peter Warren and others have pertinently pointed out, the Theran ships' use of oarsmen rather than sails, and their festival rigging, indicate that the port in question was much closer to their own home.

There has been a far greater consensus of agreement on the identity of the port on the right (see above). It is the port of arrival and apparent homecoming for the Therans, and therefore is likely to be the very same as that currently being unearthed at Akrotiri, the excavation site being but a short walk from the present-day shoreline. This view is reinforced by the striking similarity between the volcanic-looking headland featured in the fresco and the topography west of Akrotiri as it looks from the sea even to this day. The fresco suggests an area of sand immediately to the west of the town, suitable for beaching the ships; and although today this area is covered by pumice, local land-owners sinking test wells in the hope of finding water have reported finding sand at the appropriate level.

If this view is correct, the Ship Procession fresco provides us with a so far unique picture of Thera as it must have looked no more than a generation – perhaps even less – before the community's life was terminated by the disaster. All these lively people – naked servants waiting to beach the boats; pale townswomen peering over balconies, grave townsmen, some in feathery cloaks, some in plain; on the boats sweating oarsmen, with proud, kilted helmsmen at the steering oar and the occasional warrior, denoted by his boar's-tusk helmet – all would have been of the generation living on the

Top Part of the 'Ship Procession' or 'Miniature' fresco from the West House at Akrotiri, in which the home port most likely represents Minoan Akrotiri shortly before it was overwhelmed by the volcanic eruption. Note the rocky headland, and its similarity to the present-day cape west of Akrotiri (*above*).

island when it suddenly became uninhabitable. What happened to them? Only by understanding their fate and when it may have overtaken them can we begin to piece together what possibly happened elsewhere.

Frustratingly, at least as yet, the excavations on Thera provide no straightforward answer. Although as already noted the thickness of the Pompeii ash was a mere tenth of that at Thera, at Pompeii the disaster struck so quickly that hundreds were overcome in the streets, most, it would seem, asphyxiated by the ash filling the atmosphere. When this settled and solidified around them it so closely encased their bodies that plaster could be poured into the hollows, giving a perfect cast showing their original appearance. But on Thera, at least at the Akrotiri site, no human victims of the eruption have yet come to light. It is possible to argue that so little has so far been uncovered that whole gatherings of dead Therans may yet be waiting to be found. In the case of Herculanaeum, sister city to Pompeii, very few bodies were found, and it had been assumed that most of the inhabitants had managed to escape, until in February 1980 archaeologists working at the old marina uncovered dozens of bodies of people who had apparently died waiting for boats to take them to safety by sea. However, there are other indications from the Thera excavations that make any such future discovery somewhat unlikely. The houses uncovered so far have significantly lacked items of gold or silver, or of much intrinsic value, suggesting that there was some warning and the inhabitants gathered these up in anticipation of trouble. It seems that the warning took the form of earth tremors, as there are several instances of stores and utensils being found in odd places obviously thought to be proof against shock.

After that, as is quite apparent, there was a huge earthquake. At the Akrotiri excavations the signs are everywhere. In the house over the street from the West House a stone staircase can be seen to be cracked down the middle, the earth beneath having given way. Where in places a wall or storey of a house has fallen in, it is evident that the collapse must have occurred before any of the pumice fall, because there are no signs of ash underlying the rubble. It would seem likely that at this point, if not before, the main body of inhabitants, with all their most valuable possessions, made an orderly evacuation of the island, most likely on some of the very ships depicted on the Ship Procession fresco.

There seems then to have been an interval – archaeologists have reached no agreement on how long this may have been – after which some people returned to the island, apparently in an attempt to do what they could to make the town habitable once more. Unmistakable signs of the return of these people, presumably Theran workmen, include obviously shifted earth-quake debris, the rough and ready construction of a hearth outside a former wall, the conversion of a window into a doorway, and the adaptation of a couple of rooms to serve as makeshift workshops. In one place Akrotiri's excavators found a bath perched on top of a ruined building – apparently the workmen's attempt to catch rainwater for drinking. In another was a large boulder with a hole in the middle, which the Theran workmen had apparently hung on a rope to swing against unsafe masonry in the same manner as the modern demolition worker's steel ball. The suddenness with which they in their turn were interrupted in their work is evident from two buckets of fresh mortar found on an upper storey of the West House. Whoever mixed these did not stay around to use them. Something caused him and any companions to depart at speed – and it can reasonably be inferred that this was the onset of the eruption proper.

The sequence of what happened next is well enough understood from the insights of geologists and vulcanologists (see diagram, page 110). First to fall was a thin layer of pellety pumice. This would have made the whole island look as if it had received a light snowfall, but no doubt would have been quite sufficient to scare off any remaining workmen. At this point the volcano seems to have paused yet again, for this lowest layer of pumice shows signs of oxidation and pitting from rain, suggesting an interval of anything from two months to two years.

Then the volcano, at that time a cone possibly 3,000 feet high, really began to show its mettle. In the first of a series of paroxysms, tennis-ball-sized lumps of pumice were spewed out. At Akrotiri these fell up to three feet deep, and by now the ruins would have looked as if they had suffered a severe blizzard. Then came the rose-coloured pumice. No one seems yet to have properly explained why Thera has pumice of this colour but a near-identical variety formed part of the activity during the famous 1883 eruption of Krakatau. Next would have been what vulcanologists call base

Above and above right Victims of the eruption of Vesuvius in 79 BC which destroyed Pompeii. Plaster, poured into what appeared to be empty hollows in the pumice, revealed almost perfect casts of some of those overcome by the ash. But Thera's inhabitants seem to have had sufficient warning to make their escape.

A cracked and compacted staircase from 'house Delta' at Akrotiri, one of many signs that the town was badly damaged by an earthquake some as yet undetermined time before the start of the eruption proper. There are indications that some inhabitants returned to clear the damage but swiftly left a second time at the outset of renewed volcanic activity.

STAGE ONE PRE-MINOAN PERIOD	Island volcanically inactive over thousands of years. Attracts human settlement. Flourishing port develops on southern coast.	HOUSES HOUSES Monolithos Island MAJOR PORT
STAGE TWO MINOAN PERIOD	Earthquake prompts human evacuation. Vent opens and massive quantities of ash and pumice are released, covering island.	
STAGE THREE MINOAN PERIOD (contd.)	Base surges sweep away part of ash and pumice deposits, leaving hilltops uncovered. Seawater begins to flow in as vent fractures.	
STAGE FOUR MINOAN PERIOD (contd.)	Crater collapses as more ash is deposited on remaining parts of the island.	
STAGE FIVE MINOAN PERIOD (concluded)	As crater continues to disintegrate, Thera, Therasia and Aspronisi are formed. Masses of ash moved by erosion cause Monolithos Island to become part of Thera.	THERASIA THERA ASPRONISI
STAGE SIX POST MINOAN TO PRESENT DAY	Fresh volcanic activity in 197 BC and AD 1707 create islands of Palaea and Nea Kameni, which continue to grow.	THERASIA P KAMENI THERA ASPRONISI 0 2 miles

Left The main stages of the Minoan period eruption of Thera, after H. Pichler and W. L. Friedrich. Estimates of the size of the original volcanic cone vary, but it may have been as much as 3000 feet high.

The devastation at St Pierre, Martinique, after the Mount Pelée eruption of 1902.
Some thirty thousand inhabitants were killed in ninety seconds by a huge base surge
fireball. As described by official observers Drs T. Anderson and J. S. Flett, who were
at St Pierre two months later: 'the houses were burnt out, and filled with blackened
timber, ashes and mud, much of which had apparently been washed down by the
rains from the slopes behind the town. . . . The gigantic statue of the Virgin . . . had
been carried 40 feet away, and lay prone with its head pointing directly to the
crater. . . . Nothing that was combustible had been preserved. . . . Coins found in the
houses and shops were . . . most of them blackened, and often sticking together as if
they had been partially fused. The shops were empty, except those which had
contained china, glass, or iron. The china was often superficially fused, the glass in
some cases melted into lumps. The iron beams of one large building were curved
and twisted like reeds.'

surges, turbulent clouds of bedded material and hot gases sweeping outwards and downwards from the crater at speeds of more than sixty miles an hour. Such surges are called 'Pelean' after the 1902 eruption of Martinique's Mount Pelée when these were first observed, and although virtually no one survived this who was in a position to give an eyewitness account, a report to the Royal Society of London conveys something of what happened to the city in the eruption's path, the port of St Pierre:

> The mountain burst open and a great cloud appeared near its summit. It arose with a loud growling noise, and some say that in it they saw a bright red glare. Like an avalanche it poured upon the city, covering the distance in a few minutes, and enveloping all in total darkness. It passed almost as rapidly as it had come, and when the darkness lifted a little, it was seen from the ships lying in the harbour that the city was razed, and fierce fires had broken out in many places. The north end of the town was practically wiped out in an instant: nothing was left but blazing ruins; the inhabitants perished where they stood. . . . It was no earthquake that levelled the town, neither was it lightning nor the weight of ashes. All who saw the calamity and have survived agree that a mighty blast came with the cloud and mowed down everything in its path . . . the cloud was filled with hot ashes, and we have no doubt that, especially in the north end of the town, the temperature of the dust was sufficiently high to ignite combustible substances.

All but two of St Pierre's 30,000 inhabitants were killed in a matter of ninety seconds, and the port blazed uncontrollably for some thirty-six hours afterwards. In the case of Thera, according to German geologist H. Pichler and his Danish colleague W.L. Friedrich, it would have been at this stage that the original volcanic cone began to disintegrate, its walls becoming so weakened that the sea began to pour in, breaking the original single island into something approaching its present fragmented state. The amount of steam from this alone would have been enormous, and interspersed with it all would have been continuous cannonades of 'bombs' – chunks of black basalt, some of which weighed many tons and were hurled several miles.

Accompanying and succeeding all this came the longest and most impressive phase of all, the release of huge volumes of volcanic ash. In classic picture-book style a column of cloud and fire belched heavenwards. Although its exact height has inevitably gone unrecorded, it is possible to calculate that, allowing for the curvature of the earth, anything over thirty miles high would have been visible from the Nile Delta, five hundred miles across the Mediterranean (see opposite, top). Since the much smaller Bezymianny eruption of 1956 reached a recorded height of forty miles, and Krakatau's plume has been estimated at between fifty and a hundred miles high, there can be little doubt that the Thera eruption would have been visible from Egypt. And the book of Exodus speaks of just such an extraordinary 'pillar of fire and cloud' (14:24).

So there is no doubt that the eruption of Thera could have been

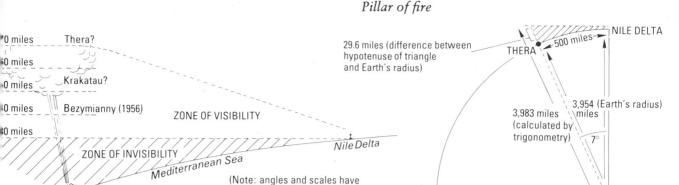

Diagram to demonstrate that the Thera eruption would have been visible from the Nile Delta. Since the earth's radius is known to be 3,954 miles, and the 500 miles distance from Thera to the Nile Delta represents 7 degrees of the earth's circumference, elementary trigonometry establishes the hypotenuse of the triangle thus formed to be 3,983 miles. Subtraction of the earth's radius establishes the zone of invisibility due to the earth's curvature to be 29.69 miles. As the comparatively minor Bezymianny eruption of 1956 has been reliably calculated to have reached forty miles, and Krakatau's plume is thought to have been upwards of fifty miles, it is clear that an eruption of the scale of Thera would have been visible without difficulty from the Delta.

responsible for considerable destruction and havoc as far afield as Crete and Egypt during the time of Hatshepsut and Tuthmosis III, but the matter is still insufficiently understood for anyone to be sure precisely how far the destruction extended, or when it happened. For while it might be tempting to believe that a base surge which rolled five miles to kill 30,000 at St Pierre might, in the case of Thera, have been able to move sixty miles across the sea to incinerate much of Late Minoan IB Crete, there is a host of very legitimate scholarly objections in the way.

Marinatos managed to attract some distinguished international academics as his supporters, among these Ireland's Professor Luce (who identified the Thera eruption with the end of Atlantis), and Britain's Sir Denys Page, Regius Professor of Greek and Master of Jesus College, Cambridge. But as Marinatos himself came to realize with each succeeding season at Akrotiri, his finds were consistently failing to support his original central thesis: that the Thera eruption had been responsible for the downfall of Late Minoan IB Crete. On Crete every one of the destroyed cities showed some signs of the pottery known as Late Minoan IB, typified by a striking marine style of decoration. But the Minoan pottery found on Thera, both at Akrotiri and wherever else odd fragments have come to light, has proved to be no later than the immediately preceding period, Late Minoan IA. Since Late Minoan IB is thought to have been in vogue for about a generation, there appear to have been twenty to thirty years between the Theran earthquake which precipitated the settlement's general abandonment and the fiery demise of Gournia, Mochlos, Pseira, Nirou Khani, Zakro and others.

Could the volcano still have been responsible for the Late Minoan IB destruction, there having perhaps been a twenty- or thirty-year gap between the precipitating earthquake and the final eruption? Yes, according to Sir Denys Page and a member of the Society of Antiquaries, James Money. On a visit to Akrotiri in 1972 Money had noticed what appeared to be a thin layer of soil between the earthquake debris and the first deposit of pumice, evidence that there had been a sufficient interval of time for soil to form. And after all, the fact that Thera had been evacuated and then returned to by the working party suggested that the volcano had taken quite a time to

Brightly decorated pots found in the excavations at Akrotiri. The fact that no Theran pottery yet found has been datable to later than Late Minoan 1A has puzzled those who believe that the Thera eruption was responsible for the desolation of Late Minoan 1B Crete.

get into its stride. But no, according to geologists and others, who insisted that to have been at all linked with the eruption the earthquake *must* have occurred a relatively short time beforehand, a matter of months rather than years. In this event Crete's Late Minoan 1B destructions could not have been caused by Thera; they must have been the work of human raiders after all.

Amid a growing swell of arguments and counter-arguments a tragedy occurred: Marinatos was suddenly struck down. In October 1974 he was standing in the excavations talking to a group of visitors, when he fell back. Those present rushed to help him, and he died in Sir Denys Page's arms. He was buried, as undoubtedly he would have wished, at the very spot where he fell. Only four years later, Sir Denys Page was also dead.

But the mystery these two distinguished men left behind remains with us still. For whatever effects the eruption of Thera may have had, and when that occurred, may well be crucial to our understanding of the timing and nature of the events of the Biblical Exodus. Every large-scale volcanic eruption in history has had surprisingly widespread effects. The question that arises in this case is: could Thera's have been responsible for the Biblical plagues?

8. Were these the plagues?

IF it is impossible to determine to the nearest year or so when the Thera volcano struck; there is none the less nothing in the general run of the current scholastic debate to suggest otherwise than that this fell some time in the reigns of Hatshepsut and/or Tuthmosis III, i.e. within a generation or so either side of the year 1450 BC. We are therefore confronted with the fact that within this period the eastern Mediterranean was the scene of its biggest natural upheaval in the span of human history. What far-flung effects may we expect to have occurred as accompaniments to this catastrophe? And could they be in any way identifiable with the Biblical descriptions of the famous Egyptian plagues – the 'thunder and hail, with fire flashing down' of Exodus 9:22-3; the 'darkness that can be felt' of Exodus 10:22; the 'water . . . changed into blood' of Exodus 7:20; the death of the livestock of Exodus 9:6; and the extraordinary behaviour of flies, frogs, locusts, etc. of Exodus 8 and 10?

For most of us the best-known volcanic eruption to have occurred in recent years is that of Mount St Helens in the north-western USA during the spring of 1980. Contrary to much popular belief (but in common with most other eruptions), this was not simply one single explosive event but a steadily progressive chain of seismic happenings of which the eruption itself formed merely a part, albeit the most spectacular part.

The first sign of possible trouble came in about the third week of March, when there were several minor earthquakes, gradually becoming more frequent. These raised the first suspicions among experts that the volcano might be about to blow, and fears were increased when occasional explosions from within were heard, accompanied by the appearance of steam vents. By the end of April, when the US Geological Survey had set up a round-the-clock watch, St Helens' north slope could be seen to have bulged more than 300 feet. Then a deceptive lull in activity caused local tensions and safety precautions to subside, with fatal consequences. At 8.32 am on the morning of 18 May, US Geological Observer David Johnston, stationed near the north summit, called excitedly over his radio: 'Vancouver! Vancouver! This is it!'

They were his last words. A blast of searing ash and gases leapt skywards with an energy equivalent to that of a ten- to fifty-megaton nuclear bomb. David Johnston and forty-six others disappeared without trace, while another twenty-five were subsequently found dead at distances up to fourteen miles from the volcanic cone. Of these latter several were still in their cars, one caught in the very act of focusing his camera to record the spectacle.

As a direct result of the blast, virtually every living thing in a 156-square-mile swath of land north-west of the volcano had met the same fate, the landscape taking on the semblance of a moonscape. Forest equivalent to a billion feet of board timber was destroyed. Animals lay roasted or asphyxiated. Tens of millions of tons of superheated mud and volcanic debris pouring into the Toutle, Cowlitz and Columbia rivers, choked the fish and boiled them alive. The same mud flows and accompanying flash floods swept away nearly twenty highway bridges, together with homes, logging equipment, and hundreds of cars.

But the volcano's effects were not merely in its immediate environs. Within a few hours its wind-borne ash cloud, between five and eight miles high, had already rolled 500 miles to the east (see inset opposite). Throughout most of eastern Washington state, northern Idaho and parts of Montana and Wyoming day was turned into night. Along some 6,000 miles of roads motorists' cars spluttered to a halt as the dust clogged their air filters. Within eight hours of the blast all rail, road and air transportation was at a standstill, even at Spokane, some 250 miles distant, and police vehicles had to be fitted with makeshift air filtration devices in order to keep moving. Radio and TV stations began issuing warnings against inhaling the dust, creating a brisk sale in surgical masks even at Missoula 400 miles to the east. Seven million hectares of previously verdant farmlands looked like a dustbowl of the 1930s, and up to 250 miles distant plants were so thickly coated with the ash that photosynthesis was halted. Nearly two hundred million dollars' worth of wheat, alfalfa and other crops lay ruined. With gradually diminishing effects the ash cloud continued over the next few days to roll steadily eastwards across the USA, reaching western Kentucky and Tennessee by the morning of Tuesday 20 May, disappearing over the Atlantic beyond Virginia later that evening. Although in the worst affected towns citizens set to with shovels and wheelbarrows to remove the ash from around their homes and streets, its grey trail was still very evident throughout the countryside of Washington, Idaho and Montana when I was there fifteen months later.

Yet by comparison with the Thera eruption, and a handful of others recorded in historical times, the Mount St Helens display of 1980 was not particularly big. Whatever the scale of comparison used – vulcanology has no equivalent to the Richter scale for earthquakes – far more massive, though still not on a par with Thera, was that of Krakatau in 1883 (see inset overleaf). Set in the sea at the western approach to the Sunda Straits which divide the Indonesian islands of Java and Sumatra, Krakatau is part of a two-thousand-mile chain of volcanoes from western Java to the easternmost part of the Lesser Sunda Islands, created by friction between two great plates of the earth's crust along this line. Until the first signs of serious activity began in May 1883, Krakatau had been thought extinct. Then in the succeeding months it became more noisy and eruptive, with earthquakes

The Mount St Helens eruption of 1980. Although it caused havoc across hundreds of miles of the American north-west, it was insignificant compared to the eruption of Thera in the Minoan period.

Inset Spread of effects of the Mount St Helens eruption of May 1980.

approx. spread
of ashcloud

CANADA

Vancouver

WASHINGTON

Seattle

MONTANA

Mount
St Helens

Spokane

Richland

Missoula

Portland Columbia River

OREGON

Billings

IDAHO

WYOMING

0   100   200
miles

ARABIA INDIA

VIETNAM

Seychelles MALAYA BORNEO PHILIPPINES

SUMATRA NEW GUINEA

6 Chagos 4 3 Sumbawa
Arch. 5 2 1 Timor
JAVA

Mauritius Rodriguez Krakatau

Réunion Alice Springs

MADAGASCAR AUSTRALIA

0 1000 2000
miles

at varying distances, culminating in a final terrifying two days on 26 and 27 August. There were four massive explosions, the sound of which travelled so far that a thousand miles away in Burma the local police began looking for a ship in distress, two thousand miles away in the Northern Territory of Australia citizens were woken in their beds by what sounded like 'the blasting of rock', and nearly three thousand miles away, on Rodriguez Island in the Indian Ocean, they thought they could hear 'the distant roar of heavy guns'.

Of the havoc which attended the explosions, the least known feature is Krakatau's demonstration of flame-throwing, perhaps of the kind that was to occur even more spectacularly in the Pelée disaster nineteen years later. At Katimbang on the Sumatran coast, twenty-five miles to the north-north-east, a Dutch government official, his wife and family and some three thousand Sumatran natives had fled to what they thought was safety on a hillside 400 feet above sea level. As the official's wife, Mrs Beyerinck, later described the scene she saw at five in the morning, 'Thousands of tongues of fire lit up the surroundings, some only small tongues, some longer. As they disappeared they left a greenish light. Others quickly filled their place. On the tops of the trees I saw flames. . . .' When the Beyerincks were eventually rescued 'in a deplorable condition . . . all covered with burns', two-thirds of the natives were in a similar state themselves, and the rest lay dead. Far worse was the death toll among hundreds of Java's coastal villages. Three of the four explosions triggered terrifying *tsunami*, giant sea waves that in the case of Krakatau reached heights of more than 100 feet, slamming on to coastal shores with such force that 165 villages were simply swept away, together with more than 35,000 human lives. Ships three thousand miles away received ash falls on their decks and encountered pumice rafts for months afterwards, while those closer had to sail through the volcano's appalling debris of ripped-up trees, human corpses, and the carcasses of tigers and other jungle animals. The sun was turned blue or green by a veil of ash, and there were lurid red sunsets that intrigued artists as far away as England.

Yet, as eruptions go, Krakatau was still relatively small, its notoriety arising largely from the fact that it was the first to be scientifically documented, principally by Britain's Royal Society and by a little-known Dutch mining engineer, Rogier Verbeek, who produced an exceptionally well-documented report in 1885. While Krakatau produced an estimated twelve cubic miles of volcanic material, twenty times greater than that of Mount St Helens, two to three times greater still was the outburst from Tambora, another Indonesian volcano some 900 miles to Krakatau's east, in 1815. As described at the time by Britain's governor on Java, Sir Stamford Raffles,

This eruption extended perceptible evidence of its existence . . . to a circumference of a thousand statute miles from its centre, by tremulous motions and the report of explosions, while within the range of its more immediate activity, embracing a space of three hundred miles around it, it produced the most astonishing effects and excited the most alarming apprehensions . . . on Java, at a distance of three hundred miles, it seemed to be awfully present. The sky was overcast at noonday with clouds of ashes; the sun was enveloped in an atmosphere whose 'palpable' density he was unable to penetrate: showers of ashes covered the houses, the streets and the fields to a depth of several inches; and amid the darkness explosions were heard at intervals, like the report of artillery or the noise of distant thunder.

Although the official death toll among those in the immediate vicinity, on the Indonesian islands was 80,000, the true figure is almost certainly unknowable because of the drastic effects the eruption had on the whole world's weather during the following year, 1816. This became known as the 'year without a summer' because of the worldwide catalogue of unseasonal temperatures and failed crops. In New England in the USA, it snowed in June. According to a Vermont local newspaper for 6 June, 'Snow and hail began to fall at about ten o'clock am. . . . Probably no one living in the country ever witnessed such weather, especially of so long continuance.' Killing frosts and resulting crop failures drove many to migrate westwards. Across the Atlantic in Europe they fared little better. Zurich's temperature records, kept since 1753, show 1816 as the coldest summer ever recorded, the result being astronomical grain prices, and the poorer citizens eating their own cats and foraging for winter sorrel and moss. Although at the time they could not know it, the cause was the shielding effect of all the dust Tambora had hurled high into the stratosphere, reflecting a high proportion of the sun's rays back into space.

While every volcanic eruption is different, there being no easy rule-of-thumb method of calculating scale by crater size, volume of ejecta, far-reaching effects, number of persons killed, or other criteria, it is only with Tambora that we have an eruption approaching in scale that of Thera *c*1450 BC. Thera may even have been substantially greater, its crater size, for instance, being twice that of Tambora. And Thera's effects may have been exacerbated by its geographical location. While Tambora's ash could be washed away by tropical rains and lost in the wide expanses of the surrounding ocean, the eastern Mediterranean is relatively arid, and on three sides surrounded by lands that were quite densely populated even three and a half millennia ago.

Interestingly, therefore, major eruptions, for all their variations, tend to exhibit certain consistent features that are vivid reminders of the Biblical plagues, particularly when we bear in mind that the stories of Exodus were part of an orally conveyed folk tradition rather than one hundred per cent accurate chronicling (see opposite).

One element common to every major eruption is a period of daytime darkness due to the passing of the ash cloud. In the course of a vivid description of the Vesuvius eruption which destroyed Pompeii and Herculaneum in AD 79 the Roman Pliny the Younger, twenty miles away at

The Biblical description of the 'plagues' compared with accounts of the far-flung effects of major volcanic eruptions.

Biblical information		Suggested volcanic interpretation
Plagues of frogs and insects (Exodus 8:2–14; 8:16–18, 21–4; 10:13–15)	'... frogs came up and covered all the land ... dense swarms of flies infested Pharaoh's house and those of his courtiers ... locusts invaded the whole land of Egypt....'	Unusual swarming of insects and other pests is commonly associated with volcanic disturbances. The accounts of the preliminaries to the 1902 Mount Pelée eruption mention plagues of stinging yellow ants, foot-long black centipedes, and deadly tropical vipers.
Rain of hail (Exodus 9:23–26)	'... hail on the land of Egypt, hail and fiery flashes through the hail, so heavy that there had been nothing like it ... it beat down every growing thing and shattered every tree.'	Both hail and showers of pellety volcanic ash are commonly associated with volcanic eruptions. Mount Pelée's activity on 4 May 1902 was described by an observer as 'like a tropical hailstorm'. Volcanic ash falls from major eruptions invariably cause widespread destruction of crops, at 200 miles distance, even in the case of the 1980 Mount St Helens eruption.
Death of livestock (Exodus 9:6)	'... all the herds of Egypt died ...'	Volcanic ash can asphyxiate animals and smother crops and vegetation, and for these reasons death of livestock is another common accompaniment of volcanic eruptions. Many animals died as a result of the eruptions of Tambora (1815), Krakatau (1883), Mount Pelée (1902) and Mount St Helens (1980).
River turned to blood (Exodus 7:20–21)	'... all the water was changed to blood. The fish died and the river stank, and the Egyptians could not drink water from the Nile. There was blood everywhere in Egypt.'	Volcanic ash may again have been responsible for the river's blood-red appearance and foul smell. Red iron oxide is often discharged in minor submarine exhalations from the Thera volcano, which kill fish as far as 20 miles distant. Mount Pelée shock waves killed marine life for miles around.
Boils and sores (Exodus 9:8–11)	'... a fine dust over the whole of Egypt ... will become festering boils on man and beast ...'	Fine dust (possibly volcanic) is specifically noted in Exodus to have been responsible for causing boils and sores, although in this instance the actual distribution of the dust is said to have been done by Moses himself. Theran volcanic dust has been specifically noted to cause skin irritations, and those affected by the Mount St Helens eruption covered their skin.
Daytime darkness (Exodus 10:21–23)	'... it became pitch dark throughout the land of Egypt for three days. Men could not see one another; for three days no-one stirred from where he was ...'	The huge ash clouds associated with major volcanic eruptions invariably cause widespread daytime darkness, as in the case of Tambora (1815), in which there was some 36 hours' darkness even at 300 miles distance, and Krakatau, in which some places were blacked out for 57 hours.
The 'Pillar of Fire' (Exodus 13:21)	'... the Lord went before them, by day a pillar of cloud ... by night a pillar of fire ...'	Quite aside from a volcanic interpretation of the plagues, it is difficult to think of better descriptions of the distant appearance of a volcanic plume than 'pillar of cloud' and 'pillar of fire'. The information that the 'pillar' was always in front of the Israelites is most likely literary licence.

Misenum, noted first 'a horrible black cloud ripped by sudden bursts of fire', then, in what should have been broad daylight, impenetrable darkness: '. . . we were enveloped in night – not a moonless one or one dimmed by cloud, but the darkness of a sealed room without lights . . . darkness and ashes, thick and heavy . . .' Sir Stamford Raffles, 300 miles away from Tambora in 1815, observed:

> An unusual thick darkness . . . all the following night and the greater part of the next day. . . . At Gresik and other districts more eastward, it was dark as night in the greater part of the 12th April, and this saturated state of the atmosphere lessened as the cloud of ashes passed along and discharged itself along the way.

In the case of Krakatau, although most of the ash cloud passed over the sea, ships like the *Berbice*, hove-to south of the Sunda Straits, reported no daylight from 6 am on the Sunday evening through to 8 am on the Tuesday morning. When, in 1980, parts of the states of Washington, Idaho and Montana were plunged into darkness by Mount St Helens, a photograph taken 130 miles from the volcano at Richland, eastern Washington, vividly conveys the ash cloud's appearance moments before it engulfed the area and made it so dark that further photography was impossible. (See page 124.)

These descriptions give a new complexion to the 'darkness that could be felt' of Exodus 10:21–3: '. . . it became pitch dark throughout the land of Egypt for three days. Men could not see one another; for three days no one stirred from where he was.' Although it has sometimes been suggested that this particular 'plague' might have been caused by a sandstorm thrown up by Egypt's almost annual *khamsin* winds, particularly common in spring-time, if it was such an ordinary event would not any Biblical bard have described it as such?

Other linked features common to the major eruptions are the noise, the destructive effects of ash fall, and the ruinous effects of ash and pumice on crops and livestock. In his account of the Vesuvius eruption Pliny the Younger described 'repeated violent shocks', 'a rain of pumice stones', and 'a rising layer of cinders and ash', causing everywhere to appear 'covered by a thick layer of ashes like an abundant snowfall'. It was necessary repeatedly to shake these ashes off 'for fear of being actually buried and crushed under their weight'. Watching Tambora, Sir Stamford Raffles noted:

> The eruptions were heard more loud and more frequent; from Cheribon eastwards the air became darkened by the quantity of falling ashes . . . in Banyuwangi, the part of the island on which the cloud of ashes spent its force . . . a large quantity of paddy was totally destroyed, and all the plantations more or less injured. One hundred and twenty-six horse and eighty-six head of cattle also perished, chiefly for want of forage, during a month from the time of the eruption.

On the *Berbice*, observing Krakatau in 1883, Captain Logan noted in his log: 'At 2 am on Monday the 27th, the ashes, three feet thick, were lying on the ship. I had continually to pull my legs out of the ashy layers to prevent them from being buried therein . . . The ashes were hot, though not perceived to be so at the moment of their falling on the skin.' Mount Pelée's activity in 1902 was described by one observer as 'like a tropical hailstorm'. The Mount St Helens ash cloud devastated crops, as has already been described, and car paintwork was blistered as far away as Wyoming. Is it mere coincidence, therefore, that in Genesis 9 we hear of a plague of 'fine dust over the whole of Egypt', producing 'festering boils on man and beast', followed by 'thunder and hail . . . so heavy that there had been nothing like it in all Egypt from the time that Egypt became a nation. Throughout Egypt the hail struck everything in the fields, both man and beast; it beat down every growing thing and shattered every tree.' Even today ash from Thera eruptions is noted for causing skin irritations.

If it might seem impossible to reconcile 'water . . . changed into blood' with phenomena from the Thera eruption, this is to reckon without one peculiarity visible today to any Thera visitor: set into one of the two Kameni islands is a bay whose water is stained a deep reddish-brown. Its temperature is bath-water warm, and at times when there have been minor eruptions (which today centre on the Kameni islands) the staining has stretched for many miles around the islands. All marine life within a twenty-five-mile radius has died when eruptions and staining of the water have occurred, apparently as a result of the presence of sulphuric acid, which, as was observed in the nineteenth century, spontaneously cleans the copper bottoms of ships. Is it possible that at the time of the main eruption, when the original island broke apart, and incalculable damage was done to the marine life, such discoloration extended as far as Egypt? Alternatively, and perhaps more plausibly, could the 'blood' simply have been caused by falls of the pink Theran ash?

There are also parallels for the plagues of frogs, lice, flies and locusts, as described in Exodus 8 and 10. In the case of Tambora Sir Stamford Raffles noted local concern that there might be excessive multiplication of insects: '. . . timely rain removed an apprehension very generally entertained, that insects would have been generated by the long continuance of the ashes at the root of plants'. And actual swarming of insects and other pests as an accompaniment to volcanic disturbance is particularly evident from accounts of Mount Pelée's eruptions both in 1902 and on an earlier occasion, in 1851. Each triggered terrifying plagues of the locality's most unpleasant insects: *fourmi-fou*, a tropical ant with a vicious, piercing bite; and *bête-à-mille-pattes*, a foot-long tropical centipede with a mouth capable of biting through shoe leather. According to Gordon Thomas and Max Morgan-Witts, in their book on the Pelée disaster, 'In 1851, when the volcano had gushed ash, the creatures . . . swept into the coastal areas, creating great havoc. In places they had destroyed whole plantations. Babies in their beds had been eaten alive.' Thousand upon thousand of these insects returned on 5 May 1902 to make a frenzied attack on the workers at sugar plantations, having been driven down the slopes of Pelée by repeated ash falls. And

above 'It beat down every growing thing' (Exodus 9:25). After the Mount St Helens eruption seven million hectares of verdant farmlands looked like a dustbowl of the 1930s, as in this scene at Spokane, 250 miles from the volcano. Nearly two hundred million dollars' worth of crops were ruined.

Left 'It became pitch dark throughout the land of Egypt for three days' (Exodus 10:22). The ash cloud from the Mount St Helens eruption seen approaching Richland, 130 miles east of the volcano.

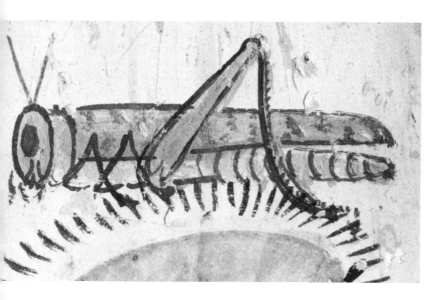

'Locusts invaded the whole land of Egypt, and settled on its territory in swarms so dense that the like of them had never been seen before.' (Exodus 10:14) *Left* A locust on a papyrus blossom, as depicted in the Eighteenth-Dynasty tomb of Haremhab at Thebes. Unusual swarming of insect and other pests have been reported in association with major eruptions such as that of Mount Pelée in 1902.

the very same day, only a few miles away, the mulatto quarter of St Pierre was the subject of a similarly concerted attack by literally hundreds of six-foot-long *fer de lance*, Martinique's deadliest snake. It is perfectly credible therefore to read in Exodus 10:14 how locusts

> ... invaded the whole land of Egypt, and settled on its territory in swarms so dense that the like of them had never been seen before, nor ever will be again. They covered the surface of the whole land ... They devoured all the vegetation and all the fruit of the trees that the hail had spared.

In fact only one of the Biblical plagues seems, at least at first sight, not to lend itself to the theory that it was caused by a volcanic eruption, that of the first-born described in Exodus 12. According to the Biblical narrative, this was the last plague, the one directly responsible for the institution of the Passover, and it is obviously illogical that any form of natural catastrophe should so specifically single out the eldest child of each family:

> ... by midnight the Lord had struck down every first-born in Egypt, from the first-born of Pharaoh on his throne to the first-born of the captive in the dungeon, and the first-born of cattle. Before night was over ... a great cry of anguish went up, because not a house in Egypt was without its dead.

But to dismiss such an account as incredible is to fail to put ourselves back into the mentality of those living in the world of 1500 BC. Faced with an unprecedented series of natural disasters, whose origins they would have had no way of understanding, what would be their natural reaction? Inevitably to interpret the events as anger on the part of the gods. How could the gods be propitiated? For the ancients there was only one obvious way: by sacrifice. But since it was commonplace for animals to be sacrificed – as is evident from, among many other indications, the Hyksos/Canaanite altars excavated at Tell el-Dab'a – it would be reasoned that the gods wanted something more: human sacrifice. And it could not be just any readily disposable human being who might happen to be around. It would have to be someone of special value to the sacrificer, his or her first-born.

Numerous passages in Genesis and Exodus make quite evident how close to the surface this thinking was in the world of the Biblical Israelites. Genesis 22 recounts the story of the patriarch Abraham coming within a hair's breadth of sacrificing his only son Isaac, and since the setting of this incident was Canaan it may be expected that human sacrifice was not unknown in the Canaanite religion of that time. There is a garbled incident in Exodus 4:23-6 in which Moses seems to be about to kill his own first-born son to propitiate God, but is prevented from doing so by his wife Zipporah substituting circumcision instead. In Exodus 22:29 God is represented as demanding: 'You shall give me your first-born sons. You shall do the same with your oxen and your sheep ... On the eighth day you shall give them to me', a striking indication that circumcision, specifically

At times of special crisis, human rather than animal sacrifice seems to have been thought necessary: dramatic evidence of this has been found in the ruins of a Minoan hilltop shrine near Arkhanes, Crete. The bones are presumed to be those of a priest and priestess killed

prescribed to be carried out on the eighth day, was intended as a substitute for sacrifice of the first-born. Excavations at Canaanite sites as far apart as Hazor and Tell el-Dab'a have revealed a disquieting frequency of infants buried in jars under house floors, possibly indicative of nothing more than high infant mortality, although archaeologists early in this century thought otherwise.

However, the most unequivocal evidence of human sacrifice, used specifically during a time of seismic disturbance, has recently come from excavations on Crete, where the religion of the second millennium BC had many affinities with that of the Canaanites. In 1979, unearthing a *c*1700 BC Minoan temple high on a hillside near Arkhanes, husband and wife archaeological team John and Efi Sakellarikis came across a group of skeletons whose attitudes and locations indicated that they had died in the course of a strange accident. One, a woman, had fallen face downwards, her legs splayed open, and her bones fractured by something heavy that seemed to have dropped from above. Another, a well-built man with a valuable ring and an important-looking seal, had fallen on his back, his arms and legs in what pathologists call the classic 'boxer' position of those who die vainly trying to fend off collapsing masonry. But most intriguing was the third skeleton, that of a youth in his late teens, lying in a foetal position on what seemed to be an ancient altar, with a still-sharp sixteen-inch bronze knife on his chest. The Sakellarikises deduced that the only reasonable interpretation was that the adults were a priest and priestess. Moments before their own deaths they had sacrificed the boy, apparently to propitiate the deity they thought responsible for earth tremors. The likelihood of this explanation is evident from the fact that the cause of the adults' deaths appears to have been a massive seismic convulsion which brought about the immediate collapse and conflagration of the building in which they were officiating, as well as palaces and other major buildings throughout Crete. A fourth occupant of the temple seems to have been killed carrying a container of the youth's blood to the temple's deity.

Was the youth the dead couple's first-born? Or the eldest son of the local king? We may never know. But if it is accepted that some time around the first half of the fifteenth century BC the effects of the Thera eruption reached the Nile Delta, an area which, as we know, probably still had a substantial element of ex-Canaanite Asiatics in its population, then in the light of the Arkhanes finds it seems reasonable to speculate that some of that population may have felt compelled to kill or have killed their own first-born in a desperate act of appeasement. It seems equally possible that another element in that population, perhaps those whom posterity would call 'Israelite', may have seen in the disasters a divinity taking their side in order that they might escape in the course of the confusion. Was the true 'Passover' an opting out from the obligation to make family sacrifices?

by an earthquake moments after sacrificing a youth, whose trussed-up skeleton was found on an altar in the same room, the sacrificial knife still lying on his body. Was the Biblical 'killing of the first-born' an Egyptian attempt to avert more plagues?

9. 'He turned the sea into dry land . . .'

ALTHOUGH it may seem revolutionary to ascribe the events of the Biblical Exodus to a volcanic cataclysm, the basic idea is in fact nothing new. It was suggested as long ago as 1873 by Englishman Charles Beke, who produced a pamphlet on the subject setting Exodus 13:21 and the Greek lyric poet Pindar's description of an Etna eruption side by side:

Exodus 13:21	*Pindar: Pythia 1, 22–4*
. . . by day a pillar of cloud to guide them on their journey, by night a pillar of fire to give them light . . .	By day a burning stream of smoke, but by night a ruddy eddying flame . . .

As he developed his theme, Beke had looked particularly at Exodus 19, with its dramatic description of Mount Sinai:

> . . . when morning came there were peals of thunder and flashes of lightning, dense cloud on the mountain. . . . Mount Sinai was all smoking because the Lord had come down upon it to fire; the smoke went up like the smoke of a kiln; all the people were terrified.

Not unreasonably, Beke deduced that Mount Sinai must have been a volcano, and he found the idea so stimulating that although already elderly he set out for the Sinai region in an attempt to identify the precise peak that might have been responsible. But he returned disappointed. Faced with the fact that there is nothing conceivably volcanic about south Sinai's Jebel Musa ('Mountain of Moses'), the mountain traditionally identified as the Biblical Mount Sinai, nor indeed any other mountain in the Sinai region, Beke opted instead for Arabia's Har-Nur, or 'Mount of Fire', so called because it often appears to be haloed by a fiery-looking ring. But as Beke found himself obliged to recognize, this too was non-volcanic. With a most creditable honesty, in a posthumously published account of his travels, Beke admitted: 'I am bound to confess that I was in error as regards the physical character of Mount Sinai, and that the appearances mentioned in Scripture were as little volcanic as they were tempestuous.' None the less the basic idea behind Beke's thinking refused to die. It was taken up by German scholars H. Gunkel and Eduard Meyer, and in England by Canon W.J. Phythian Adams, and also by the now somewhat discredited John Garstang, pioneer excavator at Jericho. None, however, considered Thera, because at that time hardly anyone had heard of the island or knew of its possible significance.

The man to whom any credit must go for making the first clear association between the Theran eruption and the events of Exodus was another Englishman, John G. Bennett. By sheer chance Bennett was a witness to Thera's relatively minor burst of activity in April 1925, and set on record an enthusiastic description:

> I was in Athens at the time, and as soon as it was reported that an explosion had taken place a Greek ship-owner sent out people to inform whoever might be interested that he was leaving in two hours' time for the island. . . . As we approached, we could see great clouds of dust going high up into the sky. . . . The sea was covered with pumice and sulphur; it was an extraordinary sight to see the sulphur and pumice stone as it came up from the depths. There were great thundering noises and rocks being thrown out of the centre of the crater. A new island had been formed. The sea was boiling and boiled fishes could be seen floating in the sea. Unaware of the dangers, we took a row boat and rowed out to see the new island. We bathed in the hot sea amid the pumice stone and sulphur, and then climbed on to the new part of the island. Not more than half-an-hour after we had left, the volcano blew up again. . . .

Inspired by the experience to find out everything he could about volcanic eruptions, Bennett, like Beke and the others before him, saw the logic of the idea that the Exodus plagues were volcanic in origin:

> darkness over the land, stones of hail and rocks pouring down, great winds, the Nile suddenly flooded and suddenly run dry, with frogs and flies infesting the town . . . the descriptions are strangely reminiscent of the great explosion at Krakatau, the sound of which was heard in Australia. . . .

Recognizing that only the great fifteenth-century BC eruption of Thera would have been big enough and geographically and chronologically near enough to have been responsible for such a cataclysm, Bennett realized that such a theory demanded a reappraisal of the traditional dating of Exodus, and found no difficulty in dismissing Ramesses II as the pharaoh involved in the events of the story:

> When the story of the Exodus was written, centuries after the event, Ramesses was the capital city, and the scribes used it to denote also the capitals of Egypt in earlier times. It appears for example in Genesis 47 as the city where Joseph settled his father and his brethren – at least two hundred years earlier than the Exodus. We can therefore safely disregard the references to Ramesses.

But like others who have been fascinated by Thera, Bennett became diverted by the altogether more nebulous idea that the island's collapse might have been one and the same as the famous fall of Atlantis described by Plato, and he failed to pursue the possibilities of the Exodus connection with the necessary rigour.

What Bennett let slip has quite independently been taken up by an Austrian, Dr Hans Goedicke, Chairman of the Department of Near Eastern Studies at Johns Hopkins University, Baltimore, and well known among the world's leading Egyptologists. Although at the time of writing he has yet to publish a word of his ideas, on 3 May 1981 Goedicke delivered a coolly reasoned lecture at Johns Hopkins arguing that the Thera eruption was responsible for the Exodus events. Having been booked into hospital for an operation the next day, Goedicke found himself reading from his hospital bed the world newspaper headlines his views had precipitated. It was close to the first anniversary of the Mount St Helens disaster and the *New York Times* ran the story on its front page, with other papers around the world following suit. Much to Goedicke's personal discomfiture, there was an unpleasant backlash from the fundamentalists.

Yet all Goedicke had effectively done – and that is the crux of this book also – was to show that greater credence may be attached to some of the Biblical stories than even many Biblical scholars have hitherto been prepared to believe. Goedicke held the view, outlined earlier in this book, that the people subsequently called the Israelites were simply a very heterogeneous group of settlers located in the north-eastern part of the Delta. Faced early in the fifteenth century BC with a serious reverse in their fortunes, perhaps owing to a loss of privileges or to enslavement, they sought to get away from the Delta, apparently receiving the appropriate official permission at the time that the region was riven by the calamities generated by the Thera volcano.

At this point they were faced with the dilemma of choosing a route by which to leave Egypt. There were two possible ways of getting back to their original homeland in Hebron (Genesis 50:13): the most direct was via the Wat-Hor, or Way of Horus, north-eastwards from Pi-Ramesses, which seems to have been what the Biblical writers anachronistically called the Way of the Philistines. This followed the course of the Pelusiac branch of the Nile for much of its length, and involved traversing the 'Wall of the Ruler' and its well-guarded frontier canal. According to Goedicke, provided that official permission was given, the only problem presented by this route was that in winter it could be under water if there had been Mediterranean winter storms. Alternatively, there was a route eastwards via the Wadi Tumilat, but this was a much longer way round and led out towards the exceptionally hot and arid terrain of the Sinai, where the Egyptians' copper and turquoise mines were located. It was a route to be taken only *in extremis*.

Goedicke argued that the Biblical text indicates that the Israelites began their trek by taking the more direct northerly route (every indication suggests that their departure was in spring), but then they did a strange turnabout, apparently prompted by God's instructions 'to turn back and encamp before Pi-hahiroth, between Migdol and the sea, to the east of Baal-zephon ...' (Exodus 14:2) The Exodus text is precise and detailed

Pharaoh Seti I approaching the 'Wall of the Ruler' canal, as depicted in the photograph on page 84, but incorporating now lost inscriptional and other detail recorded by nineteenth-century copyists. The (modern) letter A marks the frontier canal, and B the Sile frontier fortress. D, described in the hieroglyphs as 'The Dwelling Place of the Lion', was possibly Tell Habwe,

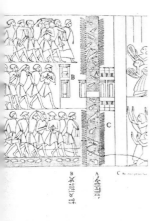

while fort E, 'The Migdol of Menm're' (fortress of Seti I) was thought by Egyptologist Sir Alan Gardiner to be the Migdol of Exodus 14: 2 and the Magdolo of Graeco-Roman times. It may have been located at present-day Tell el-Heir. The Seti relief is a particularly valuable source of information on Egypt's military outposts in the north-east during the New Kingdom period.

in its geography at this point, laying emphasis both on the proximity of the sea and on the unusual nature of the Israelite manoeuvre. It is frustrating that the locations of Pi-Hahiroth and Baal-zephon are unknown to us, although there have been a variety of attempts to identify them. Migdol, which means 'tower' or 'fortress', may refer to the Egyptian frontier post of Sile, or to another similar Egyptian military outpost in this region, Tell el-Heir, east of Sile, which was the preference of Egyptologist Sir Alan Gardiner. Such a fort, specifically called Migdol or something similar, is indicated east of Sile on the relief of Seti I (see left; also page 84), although according to a papyrus in the Cairo Museum (no. 31169) there were at least another three Migdols in the same eastern Delta area.

This brings us back to the still somewhat conjectural combination of ancient geography and Egyptian fortifications which had up to now prevented the Israelites from escaping: the 'Wall of the Ruler', the Sile fortress, the crocodile-infested canal, and in particular the 'Papyrus Swamp' (see map, page 84). Usually located by Egyptological geographers as in roughly the area of today's Lake Ballah, but rather more extensive, the 'Papyrus Swamp' sounds much like what is referred to in Exodus 13:8 as the *Yam Suph* or 'Sea of Reeds'. In the Authorized Version of the Bible, and still in the New English Bible, this has misleadingly been translated as 'Red Sea', but as most scholars are now generally agreed that the word *yam*, 'sea', includes inland bodies of water and *suph* denotes 'reed' or 'papyrus', the name signifies a sea or swamp of papyrus or reeds. Although in this particular context *Yam Suph* is unlikely to have meant the Red Sea (or Gulf of Suez) as understood today, which has no reeds along its banks, it is quite possible that in ancient times the whole region of the Bitter Lakes, Lake Timsah and Lake Ballah was virtually one continuous marshy northern extension to the present-day Red Sea. This would make sense of the fact that in 1 Kings 9:26 *Yam Suph* undeniably refers to the present-day Gulf of Suez. The reediness of the terrain in the Sile fortress area is quite evident from the relief of Seti I, in which reeds are to be seen all along the banks of the 'Wall of the Ruler' canal.

So the Israelites were faced with a considerable dilemma. Having somehow become aware that an Egyptian army was in pursuit, they would have known that, with all their accompanying families, flocks and baggage, they could never clear the frontier post (assuming they had documents granting them permission to leave) before the fast-moving chariots with their deadly archers had overtaken them. With the Mediterranean to the north of them and the 'Reed Sea' and canal to the east, the only manoeuvre to which their leaders could resort in the time available would have been to head for the nearest high ground, to give them an advantage in defence. As Goedicke noted, amid the monotonous flatness of the Delta there is in this eastern area only one elevation that might have been suitable for this purpose, a hill called Tell el-Hazzob immediately to the south of the Israelites' route. Here, Goedicke suggested, they stationed themselves for what seemed certain annihilation when there occurred the totally unexpected: the 'Miracle of the Sea' of Exodus 14, in which a massive wave swept the Egyptians away before their eyes.

Goedicke's ingenious, and to this author at least, convincing explanation of this phenomenon is that it was yet another manifestation from Thera, a *tsunami* wave of the kind which caused such devastation when Krakatau erupted in 1883, and to which Marinatos attributed some of the dislocations of masonry observed at stricken sites on Minoan Crete. The very fact that the word *tsunami* is a Japanese one (meaning 'harbour wave') underlines the unfamiliarity of such an occurrence in the west, but *tsunami* can occur in any ocean as a result of earthquake or volcanic activity. Although very fast-moving, out at sea these waves may be only two or three feet high; large ships may hardly notice them. But as they approach shallower water closer to shore, they slow down and increase in height. What may have been a two-foot bump travelling at 500 miles an hour in deep water becomes a 100-foot-high killer travelling at thirty miles per hour as it approaches a harbour. The sheer terror of the *tsunami* associated with the Krakatau eruption has been graphically described by a survivor who was near the prosperous Javanese port of Anjer, with a population about 7,500 and lying some thirty-five miles to Krakatau's east:

> I suddenly heard a cry 'A flood is coming!' and turning round I saw in the distance an enormous, black-looking mass of water, appearing at first sight mountains high, rush on with a fearful roar and lightning-like rapidity. At the next moment I was swept off my feet, and found myself struggling amidst the waters thinking that my hour was come. . . .

The survivor was saved only by getting caught up in a coconut palm. He continued:

> I looked around and a fearful sight met my eyes. Where Anjer stood I saw nothing but a foaming and furiously rushing flood above the surface of which only a couple of trees and tops of houses were visible. Presently the water fell with great rapidity and flowed back into the sea. I saw it ebb away from under my feet. I again stood on firm ground. But what a sight met my half-stupefied gaze. It was a scene of the utmost confusion. Immense quantities of broken furniture, beams, broken earthenware, amid human corpses formed heaps and masses on every side. I crept on my knees over the ruins and the dead, often entangled amid corpses, their garments and house spoil.

Was this the type of disaster that overcame the Biblical Egyptians? The more closely the Biblical text is studied, the more convincing such an explanation seems to be. For instance, one of the most individual and still least understood characteristics of a *tsunami* is a withdrawal of the sea, often for several hours, as a precursor to the subsequent massive onrush of water. One Krakatau survivor, Dutchwoman Mrs Beyerinck, told how before the coming of the destructive wave one of her servants, Jeroemoeidi, had come to her with the story that the sea had gone 'far, far away'. When

Dr Hans Goedicke, Chairman of the Department of Near Eastern Studies at Johns Hopkins University, Baltimore, and the first professional Egyptologist to identify the Thera eruption as the catalyst of the Exodus.

Mrs Beyerinck greeted this with disbelief, Jeroemoeidi responded: 'Come and see. . . . It should now be at high tide. It is a worrying sight, for all the coral reefs along the coast, which at the lowest ebb lie a fathom below the surface, and which I can sail over in my sloop, are now dried out.' Pliny the Younger, describing the Vesuvius eruption of AD 79 reported: 'The sea appeared to have shrunk, as if withdrawn by the tremors of the earth. In any event, the shore had widened, and many sea creatures were beached on the sand.' Describing the event immediately preceding an earthquake-generated *tsunami* which hit the eastern Mediterranean in AD 365, Syrian historian Ammianus Marcellinus observed:

> . . . the sea with its rolling waves was driven back and withdrew from the land, so that in the abyss of the deep thus revealed men saw many kinds of sea creatures stuck fast in the slime; and vast mountains and deep valleys which Nature, the creator, had hidden in the unplumbed depths, then, as one might well believe, first saw the beams of the sun. Hence many ships were stranded as if on dry land, and . . . many men roamed about without fear in the little that remained of the waters, to gather fish and similar things with their hands. . . .

That this sort of phenomenon could occur even at a distance of thousands of miles is quite evident from the following account from the west coast of India – 3,000 miles from Krakatau – the morning after the eruption, but undoubtedly caused by it:

> An extraordinary phenomenon of tides was witnessed at Bandora on the morning of Tuesday last [28 August 1883], by those who were at the time on the seashore. The tide came in, at its usual time and in a proper way. After some time the reflux of the tide went to the sea in an abrupt manner and with great impetus, and the fish not having sufficient time to retire with the waves, remained scattered on the seashore and dry places, and the fishermen, young and old, had a good and very easy task to perform in capturing food-sized and palatable fish, without the least trouble or difficulty, being an extraordinary event never seen or heard of before by the old men. . . .

As related in Exodus 14:21, 'the Lord . . . turned the sea bed into dry land'. The Israelites were unexpectedly able to pass dry-shod through the 'Sea of Reeds', the eastern barrier that had apparently been holding them up, but for the pursuing Egyptians there was no such happy outcome: 'The water flowed back and covered all Pharaoh's army, the chariots and the cavalry, which had pressed the pursuit into the sea. Not one man was left alive.' This is precisely as occurred in the various examples cited of the sea receding before the onslaught of a *tsunami*, with the exception of the Vesuvius eruption described by Pliny, when the water does not seem to have returned with very great force. In contrast, in Ammianus' account,

> . . . the great mass of waters, returning when it was least expected, killed many thousands of men by drowning; and by the swift recoil of the

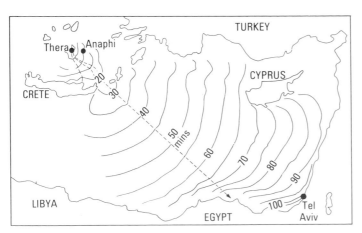

Left A refraction diagram demonstrating that a Thera *tsunami* could have reached Egypt, and been responsible for the 'Miracle of the Sea' described in Exodus 14. It is based on the researches of Japanese geophysicist I. Yokoyama, who made his calculations from quantities of sea-borne pumice found 150 feet above sea level on Thera's neighbouring island of Anaphi, and fifteen feet above sea level on the seashore north of Tel Aviv. The arrow indicates the uninterrupted line of open sea from Thera to the eastern Nile Delta. The numbers refer to the time, in minutes, estimated for a *tsunami* to have reached the points indicated.

eddying tides a number of ships . . . were found to have been destroyed. . . . Other great ships . . . landed on the tops of buildings, as happened at Alexandria. . . .

At Bandora on the west coast of India: '. . . lo! suddenly the flux came with a great current of water, more swift than horse's running. . . .'

Descriptions of the *tsunami* generated by the Krakatau and St Pierre eruptions repeatedly use the term 'wall of water' in describing the waves, precisely the words used in Exodus 14:22 – except that here, no doubt through the inaccuracy of oral transmission, the impression is given of walls of water on either side of the Israelites. As a particularly remarkable parallel to the Exodus story, there is an instance from classical sources of an army being swept away at Potidaea near Thessalonika in the year 479 BC:

> The initial ebb of the sea was so intense and lasted so long that an army seizing Potidaea had sufficient time to fall in rank and advance nearly a mile, bypassing the city from the sea side which under normal conditions was inaccessible and was protected by deep waters. Then the sea, returning with great swell, overflooded the coast and drowned the advancing army.

So the Biblical event sounds as if it was caused by a *tsunami*, especially as there are virtually no tides in any of the waters around Egypt. And it is difficult to think of anything else that could have been responsible. Three of Krakatau's four major explosions were accompanied by *tsunami*, and it seems probable that Thera in the course of its disintegration behaved in like manner. It would have been perfectly possible for a *tsunami* from Thera to have reached Egypt for, while the effects of *tsunami* vary widely from one part of a coast to another, a map reveals that a dead straight line can be drawn between Thera and the eastern Nile Delta without a single island to interrupt its path. A Japanese scientist, I. Yokoyama, has deduced that a *tsunami* from Thera could have reached Egypt in between sixty and ninety minutes (see map opposite).

But if something of this kind did happen to Egypt some time in the fifteenth century BC, surely there would have been mention of it in Egyptian literary material? In fact, even for this better-known period our documentation is scanty, particularly so with regard to the Delta, since most surviving records relate to Upper Egypt. However, according to Dr Goedicke there *is* an Egyptian reference to the Thera *tsunami*, dating from precisely the period when we might expect it, the reign of Hatshepsut, contemporary with the Late Minoan IA period at which, according to the Akrotiri excavations, occupation of Thera was abruptly terminated. At Speos Artemidos, just south of Beni Hassan in Middle Egypt, there is a rock temple of Hatshepsut with a rather enigmatic inscription carefully translated by the great Egyptologist Sir Alan Gardiner in 1946. Gardiner acknowledged it as a 'difficult text', and Goedicke has subsequently furnished his own somewhat different translation, the two versions meriting comparison side by side:

The steamer *Berouw* flung a mile and a half inland by the force of one of the Krakatau *tsunami*. It proved impossible to get it back to the sea.

Gardiner

Hearken all ye patricians, and
common folk as many as ye be, I
have done these things by the
device of my heart. I have never
slumbered as one forgetful,
but have made strong what was
decayed. I have raised up what
was dismembered, even from the
first time when the Asiatics were
in Avaris of the North Land,
[with] roving hordes in the midst
of them overthrowing what had
been made;
they ruled without Re, and he
acted not by divine command
down to my august self, I being
firmly established on the thrones
of Re.

I was foretold for a [future]
period of years as a born
conqueror. [And now] I am come
as the Sole one of Horus darting
fire against my enemies.

I have banished the abomination
of the gods, and the earth has
removed their foot[-prints].

Such has been the guiding rule of
the father of [my fathers], who
came at his [appointed] times,
even Re;

and there shall never be the
destruction of what Amun has
commanded. My command stands
firm like the mountains and the
sun's disc shines and spreads rays
over the titulary of my august
person, and my falcon rises high
above the kingly banner unto all
eternity.

Goedicke

Hear, all ye patricians and
common folk in its multitude! I
did these things by the design of
my heart, and no indolent one
could sleep because of me!
While I restored what had
decayed, I annulled the former
privileges [that existed] since [the
time] the Asiatics were in the
region of Avaris of Lower Egypt!
The immigrants [shemau] among
them disregarded the tasks which
were assigned to them,
thinking [that] Re would not
consent when the deified [i.e.
Hatshepsut's father Tuthmosis I]
assigned the rulership to my
majesty. When I was established
over on the thrones of Re
I became known through a period
of three years as a born
conqueror. And when I came as
king [i.e. became king myself], my
uraeus [the symbol of royal
power] threw fire against my
enemies!
And when I allowed the
abomination of the gods [i.e. the
immigrants] to depart, the earth
swallowed their footsteps!
This was the directive of the
Primeval Father [literally 'father of
fathers', i.e. Nun the primeval
water], who came one day
unexpectedly.
Just as it does not happen that a
command of Amun is destroyed,
my inscription will last like the
mountains! As long as the sun
shines and throws rays on the
titulary of my majesty, my name
as a ruler will be elevated – for
ever!

42 41 40

Copy of the Speos
Artemidos inscription of
which Egyptologists

8   37   36   35

As will be appreciated from the comparison, for the most part there is nothing unreasonable about Goedicke's version, which on the whole follows Gardiner quite closely, and in places makes better sense of passages whose meaning Gardiner seems to have found obscure. There is general agreement that the inscription expresses Hatshepsut's displeasure at Asiatics who had been in the familiar Avaris/Pi-Ramesses territory, and who had either been banished or allowed to depart. While these Asiatics are generally thought to have been the Hyksos, leading Egyptologists such as Oxford University's Professor John Baines have expressed surprise that they should be so much the subject of Hatshepsut's displeasure, and that she should be claiming to have restored good order after them as long as two generations after their undoubted expulsion by her great-uncle Ahmose. So could they have been the Biblical Hebrews/Israelites? We have already noted the evidence that Habiru remained in the Delta after the Hyksos departed, and the 'disregarding of the tasks assigned to them' in Goedicke's version of the Speos Artemidos inscription is strikingly evocative of the Israelites' objections to being 'made to work in gangs with officers set over them' (Exodus 1:11). Furthermore, in both the Gardiner and Goedicke translations occurs the imagery 'the earth . . . removed their foot[prints]'/'the earth swallowed their footsteps', reminiscent of the Exodus 15:12 phrase 'earth engulfed them' (New English Bible) and 'the earth swallowed them' (Jerusalem Bible), used of the 'Miracle of the Sea' incident – although in Exodus it applies it to the Egyptians whereas the inscription relates to the departed immigrants.

The part of the translation which has brought Goedicke most criticism is the one that is crucial to the inscription being interpreted as referring to the Thera *tsunami*/Biblical 'Miracle of the Sea': 'This was the directive of the Primeval Father [literally "father of fathers", i.e. Nun the primeval water], who came one day unexpectedly.' To the Egyptians, Nun meant water in all its forms, but particularly the surrounding ocean, and for this to have come 'unexpectedly', independently of the normal Nile flood, could quite plausibly denote a *tsunami*-type flood wave if Goedicke's translation is to be accepted. In 1982 one supposed expert, George Michanowsky, tried to argue that Goedicke had falsified his translation by inventing two obliterated hieroglyphs to make his text refer to Nun, but Michanowsky has been shown not to be an accredited Egyptologist; and those who are, such as Toronto's Professor Donald Redford, have pointed out that the only way the text can be reconstructed is as a reference to Nun, Goedicke's version being at least in this respect perfectly legitimate. This is not to say, however, that Goedicke's other differences from Gardiner, and his particular historical interpretation of the text, have any significant support from other established Egyptologists, and he will have an uphill task to prove his case.

But even if the Speos Artemidos inscription does provide independent evidence of a Theran *tsunami*, what of direct evidence outside Egypt? Surely any flood wave that had a major impact as far away as the Nile Delta would have been even more devastating nearer to Thera, for example on Crete, a mere sixty miles away? It is to consider this that we return to the problem

Gardiner and Goedicke
have produced different
translations.

faced by Marinatos: how the Theran evidence that the earthquake and eruption (including presumably the *tsunami*) occurred in the Late Minoan IA period is to be reconciled with the Cretan evidence that the time of dramatic, and in most cases final, destruction of the eastern sites (with the exception of Knossos), was Late Minoan IB. The problem seems to lie in the fact that everyone has been mesmerized by the supposed non-human origin of the destruction that occurred in Late Minoan IB. If an attempt is made to correlate the Egyptian and Minoan chronologies, it is evident from the tomb of Hatshepsut's vizier Senenmut that the Keftiu/Cretan tribute bearers are depicted carrying only Late Minoan IA wares, while in the tomb of Tuthmosis III's last vizier, Rekhmire, the male Keftiu represented can be seen to have had their traditional codpiece garments overpainted with kilts typical of the Mycenaean mainland, strongly indicative of the change of power on Crete that occurred at the end of Late Minoan IB (see fresco overleaf).

So could the real time when Crete was affected by the eruption of Thera have been at the end of Late Minoan IA? This view is now increasingly in favour among specialists in Minoan studies, including Professor Marinatos' successor as excavator of Thera, Professor Christos Doumas. There is in fact considerable evidence that there was a major seismic disturbance affecting Crete and surrounding Aegean islands at the end of Late Minoan IA. As has very forcefully been pointed out by Sinclair Hood, a former Director of the British School of Archaeology in Athens, and a great authority on the Minoans and Mycenaeans, Knossos and the city around it were severely damaged by a great earthquake at the end of that period (i.e. contemporary with the time of Hatshepsut, and virtually every one of the other sites mentioned in chapter 6 – Mochlos, Gournia, Pseira, Zakro, etc. – also sustained severe damage at the same time. On Kythera the site called Kastri I was destroyed; on Melos Phylakopi III:I was destroyed; on Rhodes Trianda I was destroyed, and here a very thick level of Thera ash has been identified. This widespread disaster, undeniably seismic, has attracted less attention than that which occurred in Late Minoan IB simply because the Minoans managed to clear up after it. But it may have weakened them so considerably as to explain why they were extinguished relatively easily by the later instances of destruction, which we may now attribute to human activity – with little doubt the work of the Greek-speaking Mycenaeans who took over at the palace of Knossos – of Late Minoan IB.

Apparently unnoticed by anyone previously, there is a further indication that the Thera eruption, and specifically any *tsunami* wave damage on Crete, happened at the end of Late Minoan IA. The change of pottery style denoting the Late Minoan IB period is a striking one: a sudden addition to the IA repertoire (which otherwise continued) of the liveliest representations of every form of marine life – wriggling octopus, darting fish, picturesque seashells, starfish, rocks, anything with an association with the sea. Inevitably this recalls the words of Ammianus Marcellinus' description of the event preceding the *tsunami* of AD 365: '. . . in the abyss of the deep thus

Hatshepsut, from a statue in the Metropolitan Museum, New York. Her reign, which opened with considerable flair and promise, ended in mysterious disgrace for her and her first minister Senenmut. Could the Biblical plagues have been responsible?

Tribute bearers from Crete, depicted in the tomb of Tuthmosis III's vizier, Rekhmire. Close examination has revealed that the Mycenaean Greek-style kilts worn by these men have been painted over what were formerly Minoan-style cod-pieces. Egyptologists suggest that this denotes a change of regime on Crete while Rekhmire was vizier. It is possible, therefore, that Mycenaean Greeks were responsible for the fires that destroyed Crete at the end of the Late Minoan 1B period.

Examples of the marine style of pottery typical of the Late Minoan 1B period on Crete and ancillary islands of the Aegean. Was this sudden vogue for depicting marine life a reaction to a devastating *tsunami* generated by the eruption of Thera at the end of the Late Minoan 1A period? Most identifiable traces of the damage could have been cleared up after that catastrophe, whereas the same would not have been possible after the Late Minoan 1B destruction.

revealed men saw many kinds of sea creatures stuck fast in the slime. . . .' Was it because they had suffered a battering from a *tsunami* that the Keftiu of Crete, believing themselves to have offended the deity of the sea, suddenly introduced on to their pottery depictions of every form of sea life? Although the idea cannot be proved, it strikingly supports the theory that the eruption and *tsunami* occurred in the Late Minoan IA period.

One further aspect of the matter is at least worthy of mention. In their many tangled legends the Greeks preserved the memory of a flood or floods, associated with heroes called either Deucalion or Ogyges. Because of the tidelessness of the Mediterranean, any flood on the Greek mainland is more than likely to have been generated by a *tsunami*. Curiously, according to a tradition among some of the early Church fathers, such as Eusebius, St Augustine and Julius Africanus, the Greek flood occurred at the time of the Biblical Exodus. In the words of Julius Africanus, 'We affirm that Ogyges from whom the first flood [in Attica, i.e. mainland Greece] derived its name, and who was saved when many people perished, lived at the time of the Exodus of the people from Egypt along with Moses.'

So the Biblical descriptions of the events at the 'Reed Sea' – the mysterious drying up of an impassable barrier of water, its safe crossing by the Israelites, then the sweeping away of pursuing Egyptians by a sudden and fearsome new inrush of water – all take on a new significance. Hitherto, even the most hard-headed of Jewish scholars have felt these episodes to be so central to their faith that something along these lines must have happened. In Martin Noth's words, they are the very 'bedrock of an historical occurrence'. But it is only now, in the light of Dr Goedicke's hypothesis, that it is possible to glimpse, albeit dimly, the when and why of that occurrence. However, if Goedicke's theories, and the re-dating, are to be accepted, what happened afterwards? Was there such a person as Moses? Were there really forty years of wandering in the wilderness? Might there have been more historical truth to the Biblical fall of Jericho than archaeologists such as the late Dame Kathleen Kenyon would have had us believe?

10. *Forty years in the wilderness*

WHILE it might seem remiss, if not downright negligent, to have come three-quarters of the way through a book on the Biblical Exodus with hardly a mention of the great leader Moses, this omission has been quite intentional. As remarked earlier, aside from the Biblical narratives, all written at a relatively late date, there is no reliable independent attestation of a historical character identifiable as Moses, and only by first setting the Exodus events within a credible historical context can some form of understanding of who Moses *may* have been begin to emerge.

First, however, even if we provisionally accept Dr Goedicke's theory identifying the Biblical plagues and 'Miracle of the Sea' with Thera's eruption and *tsunami*, there are powerful objections to be faced in connection with his placing of the Biblical story in the reign of Hatshepsut. For instance, the Bible contains not the slightest suggestion that the pharaoh with whom Moses dealt was a woman, i.e. Hatshepsut. Also it seems to indicate that whoever the pharaoh was at the time of the Exodus events he or she had their palace or headquarters somewhere close to the Israelite settlements in the Pi-Ramesses/Goshen area. Otherwise Moses would have been unable to have his apparently frequent audiences with the pharaoh. Since Hatshepsut, and all the other Eighteenth Dynasty rulers (with one exception, the heretic Akhenaten), had their capital at Thebes, 400 miles to the south, it scarcely seems plausible that an Israelite leader could readily have dealt with any Eighteenth Dynasty pharaoh; even Akhenaten was based 200 miles upriver at what is now called el-'Amarna. Only in Ramesses II's Nineteenth Dynasty did the pharaohs move their base to Avaris/Pi-Ramesses, in the Delta. This fact remains one of the best reasons for continuing to date the Exodus to the thirteenth rather than the fifteenth century BC.

However, there is one simple answer to these objections – one which, in all the century and a half of the Eighteenth Dynasty, is peculiar to the closing years of the reign of Hatshepsut. We have already learned how she unconstitutionally seized power from the rightful pharaoh, Tuthmosis III, at a time when he was too young to be able to rule on his own. Although little is known about this early period of Tuthmosis III's life, he was undoubtedly sent off for military training, and continued to be a pharaoh in name throughout that period, dating his reign from before Hatshepsut's usurpation. Where Tuthmosis III went for training is unrecorded, but it is possible to make a very good guess. Later in his life, long after he had

Pharaoh Tuthmosis III (1479–25 BC, inclusive of Hatshepsut period), from a sculpture in the British Museum. Known to have been sent away from Thebes for military training during Hatshepsut's usurpation, Tuthmosis may have been the pharaoh resident in the Delta at the time of Moses and the Biblical plagues.

succeeded Hatshepsut, he added a wing to Karnak's Temple of Amon. On its north wall he had carved a detailed account of the military campaigns that he conducted almost annually after he came to power at the age of about thirty, and from this it is clear that the first of these was an invasion of Canaan at the head of a highly trained, highly organized army within as little as two or three months of Hatshepsut's death.

Tuthmosis' departure point from Egypt is specifically described as the frontier fortress of Sile – part of the barrier that would have prevented the Israelites' escape. The land to the west of this, Goshen and the environs of whatever remained of Avaris/Pi-Ramesses, would have been the most logical station for any army defending against eastern attack, and it is more than likely that Tuthmosis III received his military training, and when old enough set about the training of others, in this very region. The likelihood that this is so is quite evident from the already quoted description of Pi-Ramesses from Merneptah's reign: 'the marshalling place of your chariotry, the mustering place of your army, the mooring place of your ships' troops'. No doubt before Tuthmosis III, when it was Avaris, the Hyksos favoured it for the same reason.

So if the young Tuthmosis III was the ruler with whom the Israelite leader dealt, he would have had his headquarters, and no doubt his own subsidiary court, in the very same region as that of the Biblical Goshen. Furthermore, there are circumstances towards the end of Hatshepsut's reign which suggest that some unspecified misfortune had occurred, which conceivably could have been the disasters in the Delta. Although previously Senenmut had guided Hatshepsut's every triumph, and was whispered to have been her lover, six years before her death he suddenly fell from grace, and his portraits in his tomb were mutilated even within Hatshepsut's own lifetime. Was he blamed for the chaos in the Delta? Similarly, although there is no evidence that Tuthmosis III staged any coup (if he had he would hardly have dared campaign abroad so soon after Hatshepsut's death), nor are there other signs of vindictiveness in his character, about half-way through his reign he ordered a systematic campaign for the erasure of Hatshepsut's memory. Her statues were destroyed, her obelisks walled up, her portraits and titles obliterated; and later monarchs in their turn deliberately omitted Hatshepsut's name from lists of their predecessors. Was all this because something in Hatshepsut's reign was thought to have brought a curse upon her country? Assuming that some of Tuthmosis III's troops were swept away by a *tsunami* or some such disaster, and that this calamity had occurred a few years before Hatshepsut's death, he would have spent the intervening time getting his army up to full strength again and would have been able to begin campaigning immediately after her death.

So was Tuthmosis III the pharaoh who confronted Moses? If he was, Moses would have found himself dealing with a considerably more forceful personality than the overrated Ramesses II. A mummy purported to be that of Tuthmosis III was one of those found in the cache discovered by Emil Brugsch (see page 23), and because of its short, stocky build and the

In Egyptian lists of their pharaohs, Hatshepsut's name was ignored after her death, as if she had never existed. Was this because as a woman her seizure of power broke with convention? Or because she and Senenmut were blamed for the series of disasters that occurred during her reign?

pharaoh's militaristic reputation, Tuthmosis III has been labelled 'Egypt's Napoleon'; which is unfair to Tuthmosis because his empire was far more long-lasting than the Frenchman's. If Moses' Exodus was in his time, then more than likely it would have been Tuthmosis' building of garrisons along the Via Maris (the direct route through northern Sinai into Canaan), and his relentless campaigning in Canaan itself, that would have kept the Israelites wandering in the wilderness, unable to make a direct approach to their promised land.

But who was Moses? Interestingly, his name is an Egyptian one meaning 'is born', the same as 'mosis' in Tuthmosis' own name. And although in the Introduction we noted reasons for doubting the truth of certain aspects of the Biblical story of his birth (see page 12), there are clues in that account which suggest that he had a relatively well-to-do Egyptian upbringing. During the Eighteenth Dynasty it was not uncommon for the children of subject foreign princes to be brought up in the Egyptian court – the apparent reason being to gain their loyalty in adult life – and perhaps Moses was one of these, though in his case the intention clearly failed. As the Biblical scholar George Mendenhall has argued, the possibility that Moses spent some time at a royal court is indicated by the similarity between the covenant which he is described as having set up between God and the Israelite people and the sort of covenant between lord and vassal that was common around the middle of the second millennium BC among such people as the Hittites. The form is in each case almost identical: the lord's identification of himself and his titles, 'I am the Lord your God'; a statement of his past munificence, '. . . who brought you out of Egypt'; a requirement of loyalty and obedience, 'You shall have no other god to set against me; you shall not make a carved image . . .' – and so on. There are also some hints that Moses is likely to have had military training. The use of trumpets as a system of military signalling (Numbers 10:4); the deployment of spies for intelligence gathering (Numbers 13:17-20); implementation of conscription, and arranging troops into fighting divisions with battle standards (Numbers 1 and 2); all are comparatively sophisticated forms of military organization which Moses may have learned from the Egyptians. Intriguingly, the idea of an 'ark' as a portable god-house is also typically Egyptian. On his military campaigns Tuthmosis III travelled with a portable shrine, the cabin of a ceremonial boat housing an image of the god Amon – 'he who is hidden' – and Egyptian armies paraded before it, regarding it as their divine protection, in a manner reminiscent of the Israelites' subsequent use of their ark as described in 1 Samuel 4:4-6. Like the Israelite ark, the Egyptian one could be opened only by specially privileged persons, in this case the pharaoh and his most senior priests.

As described in Exodus 2:11-15, Moses, on killing an Egyptian, became a renegade against pharaonic authority, fleeing for his life east across the Sinai. This is very reminiscent of a tale that had been popular among the Egyptians since the Middle Kingdom, that of Sinuhe, the Egyptians' Marco Polo. Sinuhe, on the point of dying of thirst, found rescue in the traditional hospitality of desert nomads: 'I was parched . . . I said: "This is the taste of death!" [But then] I lifted up my heart . . . for I had heard the sound of the lowing of cattle, and I spied Asiatics. The sheikh among them . . . gave me water while he boiled milk for me. I went with him to his tribe. . . .' Similarly, Moses appears to have received sanctuary with a Midianite tribe in the territory beyond the Sinai, east of the Gulf of Aqaba, actually marrying Zipporah, a young woman from that tribe.

Although the Bible provides only the briefest information about this episode of Moses' career, it is perhaps not stretching credulity to view it as the most formative in his life. After the ease and languor of an Egyptian court it must have been a revelation to live among a tent-dwelling people whose very survival would have been dependent on their ability to read a landscape – to know in a dry gully the likeliest spot to dig for water, to know in a world without signposts or maps the likeliest direction of the next pasturage, to know sources of food in the driest-looking desert. Moses would have observed with wonder the confidence and good order with which such tribes could be led and moved from one place to another, a wonder echoed by European traveller De Lascaris' description of the migration of a Bedouin tribe in the early nineteenth century:

> Mehanna having ordered the departure of the tribe, the next morning by sunrise not a single tent was standing; all was folded up and loaded, and the departure began in the greatest order. Twenty chosen horsemen formed the advance guard; then came the camels with their loads, and the flocks; then the armed men, mounted; after these the women. . . . It was truly wonderful to witness the order and celerity with which the departure of eight or nine thousand persons was effected. . . . When they halted, the Bedouins sprang to the ground, fixed their lances and fastened their horses to them; the women ran on all sides, and pitched their tents near their husbands' horses; and thus, as if by enchantment, they found themselves in the midst of a large city.

That Moses, whoever he was, must early in his life personally have crossed the Sinai desert and experienced at first hand the nomadic way of life in both its disciplines and its rigours seems incontestable from all that followed – not least his identification with, and qualification for leadership of, the oppressed Habiru back in the eastern Nile Delta.

In considering again who these Habiru or Israelites were, we must continue to avoid the old stereotyped Sunday School images. Historical references to Habiru in Canaan around the end of the fifteenth century and the first half of the fourteenth century BC, suggest they were a mixed, classless assortment rather than any distinctive ethnic group, and there is no reason to think those who left Egypt in the Biblical Exodus were any different. Exodus 12:38 specifically describes them as 'a large company of every kind' or, in the words of the old Authorized Version, 'a mixed multitude'. In fact to this day, despite widespread public ideas to the contrary, there is nothing that can be classified as a Jewish type. In the words of the anthropologists

Huxley and Haddon, 'The Jews can rank neither as nation nor even as ethnic unit, but rather as a socio-religious group carrying large Mediterranean, Armenoid and many other elements, and varying greatly in physical characters.' For instance, several of the Levites described in the Bible as involved in the Exodus have Egyptian names – Phinehas, Merari, Hophni, Moses himself and possibly his brother Aaron and sister Miriam, the latter referred to as a 'prophetess' (Exodus 15:20). That does not mean that these people were 'Egyptian' – this term, too, lacks any specific racial connotation – but they certainly appear to have been so long Egyptianized that they had no Semitic names to fall back on.

There were almost certainly many lower-class remnants from the Hyksos/Canaanite period of occupation who stayed in the Delta after their fellow countrymen left – no doubt caught up in the subsequent oppression and as eager as their fellow slaves for some opportunity to escape. The presence of a Canaanite element among the Israelites is indicated by the repeated instances in which groups of Moses' followers lapsed into Canaanite forms of paganism. Examples are the idolatry before the golden calf of Exodus 32 (a 'beautiful little bull of wrought bronze', a Near Eastern weather god, was found in the excavations of Canaanite Hazor), and the ease with which some adopted the sexual licentiousness of the Moabite religion (which, from the Biblical descriptions, was closely related in this respect to the Canaanite religion) in Numbers 25:1-2.

Uneasily rubbing shoulders with these assorted groups would have been the people with whom Moses now most closely identified himself: the tribal, nomadic, tent-dwelling descendants of Abraham and Isaac and Joseph, keepers of the innumerable flocks and herds that grazed in the Delta. Repeatedly the Bible refers to their 'flocks . . . and herds in immense droves' (Exodus 12:38), mobile food stocks that would inevitably dwindle during the privations of the years that lay ahead. The base camp for these nomads was perhaps what the Bible calls 'Succoth' – the term means 'tabernacles', or portable dwellings, suggesting that it was not a permanent city. After the evacuees left Pi-Ramesses, this was their first port of call en route to freedom. Inevitably the menfolk, presumably previously confined to some work camp at Pi-Ramesses, would have needed first to collect their wives and children, tents and animals before they began their journey proper.

According to Exodus 12:37 the men alone in the refugee band numbered 600,000, which would have meant some two million persons in all – yet another figure that is impossible to believe since, based on available land, the entire population of Egypt at the time is unlikely to have been more than this. Although some scholars have scaled the figure down to as few as 600, a more reasonable estimate (and no one can do more than guess) has been made by Oxford Biblical scholar John Wenham. Using a variety of Biblical clues he has suggested a fighting force of about 18,000 men and a total for the whole migration of about 72,000. This may still be somewhat high, it being necessary to allow sufficient numbers for the capture of a moderate-sized city, but not so many as to make survival in desert conditions impossible.

The nature of the terrain that the group faced when they had made good their escape now concerns us. To the European the word 'desert' usually evokes an image of endless miles of rolling sands, as in the Sahara; but the Sinai is not like that. Nor does it have the interminable stony slopes that typify much of the Rub al-Khali desert of Saudi Arabia. Basically the Sinai is an arid, gravelly plateau, with hillier territory principally in the south. It does rain in the Sinai, but a mere inch a year, and the Bible and climatologists are agreed that it is unlikely to have been significantly better watered in the time of Moses. For peoples used to the plenty of the Delta it could only have seemed a fearful place; hence the heartfelt cry of Numbers 11:5: 'Think of it! In Egypt we had fish for the asking, cucumbers and water-melons, leeks and onions and garlic. Now our throats are parched. . . .'

But, as is attested by the several thousand Bedouin, along with their sheep, goats and camels, for whom the Sinai provides a home to this day, it does support life. For herds there is a fair supply of camelthorn bushes. In places there are green *wadis* and even springs of water. Nevertheless, survival, particularly for a group as large as even our own conservative estimate, would have depended in large measure on the leadership's know-how, and Moses would have been under considerable pressure to call upon everything he had learned during his earlier crossing of the same terrain.

It is not difficult to appreciate the sense of wonder he would have provoked in his followers when he used the ancient Bedouin technique of digging down into the apparently long-dried-out bed of a *wadi* in order to reach the sub-surface water left from winter rains. Just how miraculous the results of this technique can seem to be, especially when they yield copious supplies of water, has been vividly conveyed by Major C.S. Jarvis, British Governor of the Sinai during the 1930s:

> Several men of the Sinai Camel Corps had halted in a dry wadi and were in the process of digging about in the rough sand that had accumulated at the foot of a rock-face. They were trying to get at the water that was trickling slowly out of the limestone rock. The men were taking their time about it and Besh Shawish, the colour sergeant, said: 'Here, give it to me!' He took the spade of one of the men and began digging furiously in the manner of NCOs the world over who want to show their men how to do things but have no intention of keeping it up for more than a couple of minutes. One of his violent blows hit the rock by mistake. The smooth hard crust which always forms on weathered limestone split open and fell away. The soft stone underneath was thereby exposed and out of its apertures shot a powerful stream of water. The Sudanese, who are well up in the activities of the prophets but do not treat them with a vast amount of respect, overwhelmed their sergeant with cries of: 'Look at him! The prophet Moses!'

As numerous writers have remarked, the other apparent 'miracles' in the Sinai are all not only explicable by the terrain but are such characteristic results of it that they effectively enhance the case for many Bible stories being the genuine product of folk memory. The annual migration of quails from Africa to Europe each year takes some of them directly across the Sinai, and the birds quite commonly settle there for short periods to regain strength after their long flight across the sea. Accordingly, when we read in Exodus 16:13, 'That evening a flock of quails flew in and settled all over the camp', we may infer not only that this actually happened but that the hungry Israelites, well-versed in the use of throwsticks from bird hunting in the Delta, killed the birds with considerable efficiency. Similarly, as has frequently been noted, there really is a 'manna' to be found in the Sinai. As German traveller Bernard de Breitenbach described more than five hundred years ago,

> In every *wadi* throughout the whole region of Mount Sinai there can still be found 'bread of heaven' which the monks and the Arabs gather, preserve and sell to pilgrims and strangers who pass that way. This same bread of heaven falls about daybreak like dew or hoarfrost and hangs in beads on grass, stones and twigs. It is sweet like honey, and sticks to the teeth. We bought a lot of it.

Both the Biblical and the Breitenbach stories have been positively confirmed in recent years by two Hebrew University scholars, Friedrich Bodenheimer and Oskar Theodor. 'Mann es-Samâ' or 'bread of heaven', as the Bedouin call it to this day, consists simply of honey-like deposits produced by one of the Sinai's commonest shrubs, the tamarisk. In Bodenheimer's words it is 'peculiarly sweet . . . most of all like honey when it has been left for a long time to solidify', and although its supply is unpredictable, an adult can gather some four pounds of it in a single morning.

But if these elements of the Biblical story carry almost complete credibility, an altogether more difficult problem is that of trying to trace the route the Israelites may have taken in their travels across the Sinai. Bedouin place names which carry Mosaic associations are absolutely no help. Since the Sinai Bedouin hold Moses' memory in just as high regard as do Jews and Christians, they have liberally sprinkled his name around their landscape with scant regard for whether the original Moses ever set foot anywhere near. South of Suez there are the 'Uyun Musa, or 'Moses' Springs', purportedly where Moses watered his flocks every evening on the way to his home at Mount Sinai after having grazed them in the Delta – a round trip of some 500 miles! Just under fifty miles further south Hammam Far'un, 'Pharaoh's Bath', is a hot spring from which the Egyptian pharaoh's breath is said to issue after the Red Sea closed over him. Sixty miles further south again Moses supposedly had his bath, Hammam Musa, at springs near the port of aṭ-Ṭur. The Jebel Musa, or Mountain of Moses, where Moses is reputed to have received the Ten Commandments, carries more credibility, because at least as far back as the fourth century AD the redoubtable traveller Egeria knew of its Mosaic associations. This and its slightly higher companion, the Jebel Katrina, are the tallest peaks in the whole of the Sinai peninsula. At their feet lies the famous St Catherine's Monastery built by

Below '. . . they have made themselves a calf of molten metal, and have worshipped it . . .' (Exodus 32:38). Some of the 'mixed multitude' who joined Moses on the flight from Egypt may well have been devotees of the old Canaanite religion, for whom the bull was a weather god. Was this the origin of the famous Biblical story of the 'golden calf'? Certainly Canaanite influence has been detected in several of the Biblical Psalms. This bronze figurine was found at Hazor.

Above The Sinai wilderness. Although parts such as this could scarcely support any life, others have sufficient vegetation to sustain several thousand Bedouin and their flocks, even to this day.

The throwstick in use for fowling in the Delta, as depicted in the tomb of Nakht at Thebes. This implement was so closely identified with Asiatics that a throwstick symbol was often a determinative for Canaanite names in Egyptian hieroglyphs. Curiously, it seems to have been an Eighteenth-Dynasty fashion for throwsticks to be carved in the shape of a snake, reminiscent, perhaps, of Moses' rod turning into a snake in Exodus 7?

the Byzantine Emperor Justinian in the sixth century AD to mark the spot where Moses saw the 'burning bush', while not far away the er-Raha plain is said to have been the only one in all Sinai big enough for Moses to address the entire assembly of Israelites.

But theories concerning the routes and the stopping places used by the Israelites in their wanderings in the Sinai are as diverse as the scholars who put them forward. For Dr Goedicke, one particularly plausible site as an Israelite halt is the ancient Egyptian turquoise-mining centre known today as Serabit al-Khadim, a little to the north-west of the Jebel Musa in a beautiful setting, with a large, pastel-coloured plain to the north and strange black hills to west and east. The Egyptians sent numerous expeditions here from the Old Kingdom onwards, to find and dig out the highly prized turquoise from fissures in the purplish-grey sandstone. Because the work was unpleasant, Asiatic labour was often used, a fact which has led some scholars to assume that the Israelites would have sought out Serabit al-Khadim as a place they would find allies, while others have thought it would have been avoided because it would bring them once more into confrontation with Egyptian troops. Irrefutably the site has strong associations with Hatshepsut and Tuthmosis III, both of whom, according to inscriptions, did much to beautify the now largely ruined temple to the cow goddess Hathor, known to the Canaanites as 'Ba'alat' or 'The Lady'.

It is in this latter connection that Serabit al-Khadim has perhaps its greatest interest. Dotted around the site have been found curious inscriptions in signs reminiscent of, but distinctively different from, the familiar hieroglyphs of ancient Egyptian writing. It was Petrie who rightly recognized that these must have been scrawlings by Serabit al-Khadim's Asiatic mining community, but it took patient detective work by Sir Alan Gardiner to make the first halting steps towards deciphering them. Taking a set of four signs,

$$\sqsubset \!\!\! \urcorner \, O \,) \, \times$$

Gardiner recognized the first as reminiscent of the Egyptian 'house' hieroglyph, in north-west Semitic/Hebrew *bayit*, or 'b'; the second as the Egyptian 'eye' hieroglyph, in Semitic *ayin*, a breathing symbol represented by the mark ', and the last as the crossed sticks mark, in Semitic *tau*, ancestor of our own 't'. Guessing that the third sign was an ox-goad, Semitic *lamed*, 'l', Gardiner read b'lt, 'Ba'alat', 'The Lady', the Canaanites' title for Hathor. Called 'Proto-Sinaitic', the signs are of very considerable interest in their own right because, as a simplification of the cumbersome Egyptian hieroglyphic (for inscriptions) and hieratic (on papyrus) systems of writing, they are a stage in the development of both the later Hebrew and our own alphabet. And since they can be dated to around the fifteenth-century BC Hatshepsut/Tuthmosis period, their other intriguing feature is that they indicate that at this time there must have been at Serabit al-Khadim Semites speaking a language close to that of the Biblical Israelites.

Were these Canaanites attracted this far south into the Sinai by high Egyptian wages? Could they have been Asiatic slaves brought over to work the mines under guard? Is it possible even that they were the Biblical Israelites themselves, those still attached to Canaanite deities recording their allegiance as they passed through? With Hathor as a cow goddess it might even be tempting to attribute the 'golden calf' incident of Exodus 32:1–6 to a spontaneous act of Hathor worship by this faction. Goedicke believes emphatically, although he has yet to make his reasons clear, that the Proto-Sinaitic inscriptions were made by the Biblical Israelites.

But to be realistic, it is best to acknowledge that there is nothing in all the Sinai that can be regarded as a definite trace of the Israelites having passed through that region, and that as they were a nomadic people there is no reason why after three and a half thousand years there should be. Of all Biblical sites in the Sinai that might conceivably be expected to carry traces of any settlement by the Biblical Israelites, the likeliest would be Kadesh Barnea, which is where they are described as having stayed the longest (Deuteronomy 1:46), perhaps for as much as thirty-eight years (2:4). It was from Kadesh Barnea that Moses sent out twelve spies to reconnoitre Canaan (Numbers 13:3–21), and it was also here that Moses' sister Miriam died and was buried (Numbers 20:1).

As with all other Biblical locations in the Sinai, there is no universal agreement on where Kadesh Barnea might have been, the main Biblical information being that it was between the wilderness of Paran (Numbers 13:3), and the Wilderness of Zin (Numbers 13:21), on the frontier of Edom (Numbers 20:17), and obviously a convenient point from which to plan further progress. Despite a complaint about water associated with Kadesh (Numbers 20:1–13) it would need to have had a good water supply in order to sustain a community of even a few thousand over a period of years. Accordingly, a site favoured from the very earliest years of this century by, among others, Sir Leonard Woolley (discoverer of Ur) and T.E. Lawrence has been Ain el-Qudeirat, set in the deep, narrow Wadi el-Ain, or 'Valley of the Spring', probably the best source of water in the whole north of Sinai, and to this day providing good irrigation for many acres of fruit and nut trees. But excavations carried out at Ain el-Qudeirat within the last ten years by Israeli archaeologist Rudolph Cohen have found nothing definitely earlier than a fortress of the tenth century BC. There was some crude, hand-made 'Negev ware' pottery which, because it has no fashion or style to it, could date from up to five hundred years either side of 1000 BC. Cohen has suggested this might have been pottery of the nomadic tribe into which Moses married, but could it have been that of the Israelites themselves? Or could Ain el-Qudeirat be the wrong location? It is simply impossible to tell.

If we accept that the Exodus occurred in the time of Hatshepsut and Tuthmosis III, and thus assume that the Israelites would have been wandering in the Sinai some time towards the end of the fifteenth century BC, one major anomaly still exists. According to Numbers 20:14–18,

From Kadesh Moses sent envoys to the king of Edom. . . . 'Grant us passage through your country. We will not trespass on field or vineyard,

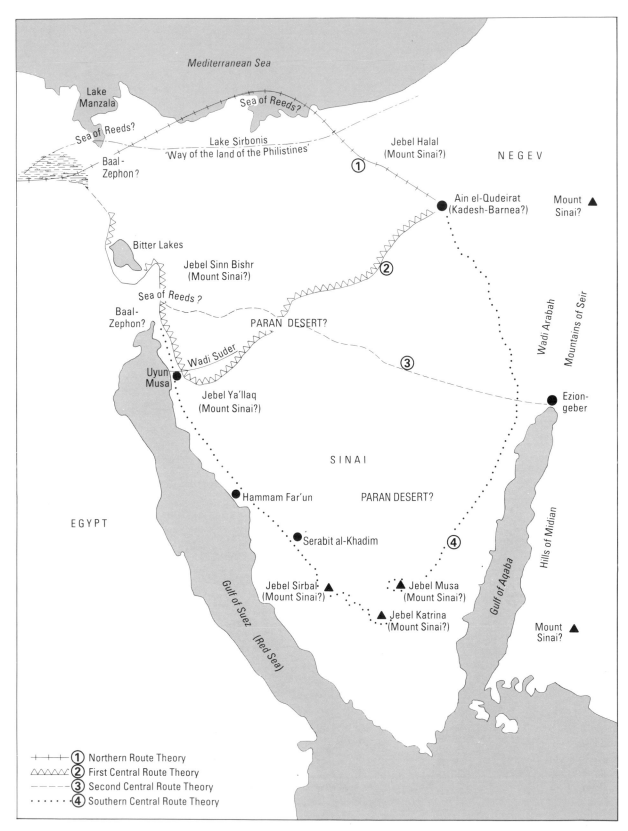

Left Some of the alternative theoretical routes taken by the Israelites to cross the Sinai:

1 *The Northern Route*
This suggests that the Israelites first turned north towards the Mediterranean coast, Biblical Baal-Zephon being identified as the temple of Zeus Casius on the tongue of land just west of Lake Sirbonis (Sinai governor Major Jarvis favoured this as the site of the 'Miracle of the Sea'). The Israelites would then have turned south-east towards Ain el-Qudeirat, Moses receiving the Ten Commandments on the Jebel Halal to the west of Ain el-Qudeirat.

2 *The first Central Route Theory*
This identifies the present-day Bitter Lakes with the Sea of Reeds, and suggests that after travelling south for a short distance along the coast east of the Gulf of Suez, the Israelites turned north-east towards Ain el-Qudeirat. Mount Sinai would have been Jebel Sinn Bishr which, though not very high, is a landmark, and near enough to Egypt to correspond with the Biblical order of events. The nearby Wadi Suder could have provided necessary water and pasturage.

3 *The Second Central Route Theory*
This follows the same route as 2 as far as the Sea of Reeds but suggests that after that the Israelites went directly east via the way of al-Hajj 'Way of the Pilgrims' towards Ezion-geber (present-day Eilat), Mount Sinai being located either in the hills of Midian to the east of the Gulf of Aqaba or in the mountains of Seir to the east of the Wadi Arabah. Such arguments are based on texts which locate Mount Horeb/Sinai and the Paran desert in the land of Midian (Exodus 3: 1; 4: 27; 1 Kings 11: 17-18) and others which locate it at Mount Seir (Genesis 14: 6; Numbers 3: 37; Deuteronomy 33: 2; Judges 5: 4-5; 1 Kings 9: 26). For those who hold this theory, Kadesh-Barnea would have been somewhere near the border of Edom (Deuteronomy 1: 2, 19; Judges 11: 16).

4 *The Southern Route*
This suggests that Baal-Zephon was just north of the topmost point of the Gulf of Suez, the latter being identified as the place of the 'Miracle of the Sea' because the difference between high and low tides there can be as much as six feet. The Israelites are then thought to have journeyed southwards, Mount Sinai being either the traditional Jebel Musa or its neighbour Jebel Katrina. But it is difficult to envisage a substantial number of Israelites surviving in that southern terrain for as long as the year referred to in Numbers 10: 11-12.

Ain el-Qudeirat in the Sinai. Although topographically the most likely site of the Biblical Kadesh-Barnea, where the Israelites are said to have stayed for thirty-eight years (Deuteronomy 2:14), no remains identifiable as Israelite have yet been found here. This may have been because as nomads they chose to use perishable utensils or the so-called 'Negev' ware, plentiful at Ain el-Qudeirat and elsewhere, but undatable (and therefore archaeologically largely useless) because of its crude, handmade character.

or drink from your wells. We will keep to the king's highway; we will not turn off to right or left until we have crossed your territory.' But the Edomites answered, 'You shall not cross our land. If you do, we will march out and attack you in force.'

The ancient route known as the 'king's highway' ran northwards from the Gulf of Aqabah along a line east of the Dead Sea and the Jordan (see map opposite). This same route was followed for thousands of years; in places its path can still be traced by aerial photography. According to the Bible, at the time when the Israelites were about to make their entry into their promised land it was controlled by no fewer than three kingdoms, those of the Edomites (Numbers 20:14-21), the Moabites (Numbers 21:13), and the Amorites under a king called Sihon (Numbers 21:21-6).

However, in the early 1930s American archaeologist Nelson Glueck conducted a survey of the surface pottery to be found in these areas – a standard archaeological technique to determine the phases of occupation of any area – from which he concluded that from the Middle Bronze Age I, that is, about the nineteenth century BC, until the thirteenth century BC there was virtually no settlement in these regions. At most they were occupied by a few nomads who could have put up no resistance to any large numbers of incoming Israelites. Modern scholars' almost unquestioning acceptance of these findings has been one of the main reasons why a fifteenth-century BC date for the Exodus has failed in recent years to be more seriously considered.

Furthermore, Glueck's deductions have seemed to be supported by the archaeological findings of others. A commanding site called Buseirah, thought to have been the Edomite capital Bosrah (Amos 1:12) has been excavated in recent years by Crystal Bennett of the British School of Archaeology in Jerusalem. She found it to date from no earlier than the eighth century BC, with absolutely no previous trace of occupation. Similarly, the impressive Tell Hesban, thought to have been the Moabite capital Heshbon (Numbers 21:25-8), received five seasons of intensive excavation by Dr Siegfried Horn of Andrews University, Michigan. Again the earliest remains were found to be of the eighth century BC.

But as it happens – although textbooks and encyclopaedias have yet to make the appropriate adjustments – in recent years there has been a radical about-face in attitudes to at least this aspect of Glueck's work. In 1971 the Biblical scholars H.J. Franken and W.J.A. Power published a review in the scholarly journal *Vetus Testamentum* demonstrating the flaws in both Glueck's methodology and his conclusions. Pottery shapes which Glueck did not personally recognize he omitted from publication, and more recent surveys, such as one conducted by Emory University, have called Glueck's whole chronology into question. As remarked by the eminent Egyptologist W.A. Ward as early as 1975, 'It is now evident from recent finds that [Glueck's] view will have to be modified in that some areas east of the Jordan river seem to have maintained a settled population throughout the

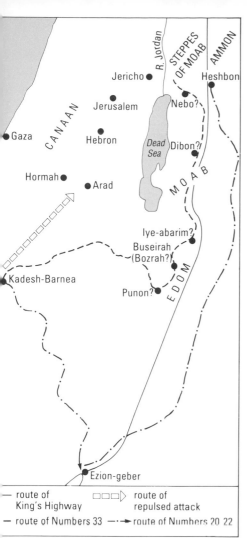

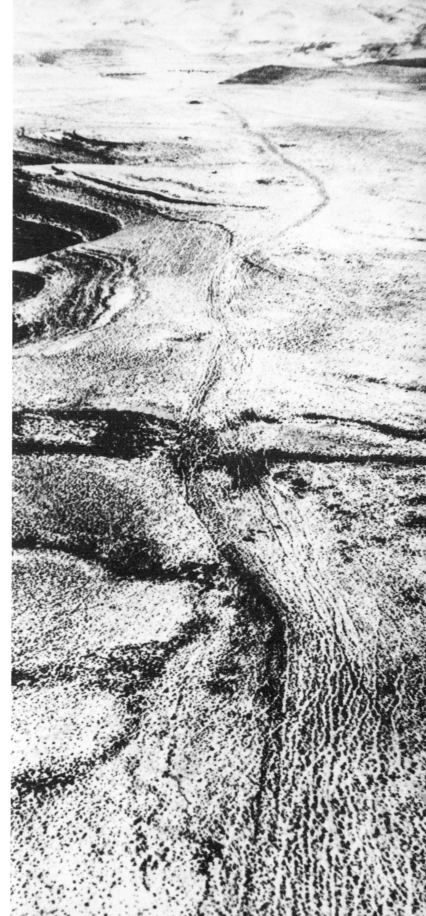

above The route of the 'King's Highway', and
the two different routes from Kadesh-Barnea
which strands of the Biblical narrative suggest
the Israelites may have taken. According to
Numbers 33, which lists in detail the Israelites'
movements, they turned eastward to Punon,
then northward to Iye-abarim in Moabite
territory, passing Dibon and Nebo, and finally
reaching 'the plains of Moab, near the Jordan
opposite Jericho'. But according to Numbers 20–
the Edomite king was hostile and they were
forced to make a detour of his territory, which
meant an awkward journey, probably via Ezion-
geber and the eastern desert, to fight Sihon,
King of Heshbon, and Og, King of Bashan,
before ending up again encamped across the
Jordan from Jericho. Biblical scholars suggest
the different traditions may indicate two
independent sets of wanderings, one by the
'Leah Tribes', the other by the 'Rachel Tribes'.

right The King's Highway.

Middle and Late Bronze Age period.' Aware of the mounting tide of criticism, Glueck himself retracted many of his arguments on this aspect of the matter before he died.

Similarly, despite the undoubted competence of Mrs Bennett's and Dr Siegfried Horn's excavations at Buseirah and Tell Hesban, from literary evidence alone it is quite evident that there was occupation of Edom at least as far back as the thirteenth century BC, and by implication earlier still. The report quoted earlier (page 30) from an Egyptian frontier official of the time of Merneptah is worth repeating: 'Another communication to my [lord], to [wit: We] have finished letting *the "Shosu" tribes of Edom* pass the fortress [of] Merneptah . . . to keep them alive and to keep their cattle alive.' Even those now refuting Glueck's findings acknowledge that pottery of the Middle and Late Bronze Ages is 'relatively sparse' on the east bank of the Jordan, but we would expect little else if the tribes of this region had the same transitory and nomadic tendencies that we have ascribed to the Biblical Israelites.

Almost certainly the reason why the Israelites asked the Edomites and others for permission to pass through their territory, and at least in the case of the Edomites behaved with due caution when permission was refused, was because the Edomites were too much like themselves, living in tents and, despite cultivating fields and vineyards, having few encumbrances to prevent them from moving to other pastures should circumstances require. Glueck's objection to a fifteenth-century date for Exodus need be considered an obstacle no longer.

11. *The Canaan conquest controversy*

ATTRACTIVE though the Thera eruption may be as a means of explaining the Biblical Exodus and setting it in a historical context, there is one essential criterion that needs to be satisfied: that the Biblical conquest of Canaan can be seen to fit into this revised chronology. As already established, the Thera eruption may be placed approximately in the first half of the fifteenth century BC, the reign of Hatshepsut having been, in our chronology, between 1473 and 1458 BC. In the Bible we are told that the wanderings in the wilderness lasted for forty years (Numbers 32:13). While the need to treat Biblical numbers with caution has already been stressed, it is unlikely that the Israelites would have preserved in their traditions the memory of such a painful and shameful episode – full of grumblings and backslidings – unless something like it had happened. Numbers 32:13 stresses that 'the whole generation was dead which had done what was wrong' at the time when the first serious incursions into Canaan began, so we should be looking to the period between the end of the fifteenth century and the middle of the fourteenth for a new date for the conquest. How does this square with what is known of Canaan at that period from history and archaeology? Yet again we approach a hornet's nest of scholarly controversy.

As already shown, the reign of Tuthmosis III (c1458–1425), following Hatshepsut's death, provides an eminently satisfactory explanation for why the Israelites would not have been able to make an immediate invasion of Canaan, and why they would have been unable to take the shortest and easiest route into the country – the 'Way of the Sea', or 'road towards the Philistines' as it is referred to in Exodus 13:17. During his reign Tuthmosis III trundled Egypt's most efficient army ever, bristling with horse-drawn chariots and highly trained archers, at least seventeen times up and down this road, which provided flat terrain ideal for his pitched battle type of warfare. It seems that Tuthmosis' male predecessors had already set up command posts controlling watering places along this route, and had the Israelites travelled along it, slow-moving and no doubt inadequately armed as they were, they could have been cut down with ease. The purpose of Tuthmosis III's repeated marches to and fro was to remove any possibility of a Hyksos/Canaanite resurgence, and thus so firmly establish Egyptian power and influence beyond its boundaries that Canaan could effectively act as a buffer against any threats from further afield, such as those from the up-and-coming Hittites and Mitanni to the north and north-east. He

Above The northern Canaanite fortress of Hazor. Along with several other sites, Hazor's defences were reinforced before the end of the Middle Bronze Age with steeply sloping ramparts. A sudden large population increase, perhaps from an influx of refugee Hyksos from Egypt, seems to have been responsible for the creation of a Lower City.

A typical Canaanite dignitary, from a bronze plaque found at Hazor. Despite frequent attacks from Egypt during the century or so after the Hyksos defeat, Canaan appears to have been allowed to retain a reasonable measure of strength and prosperity.

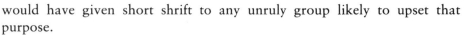

would have given short shrift to any unruly group likely to upset that purpose.

But what precisely was the nature of Tuthmosis III's power over Canaan at this time? Did he leave behind a trail of slaughter and burnt-out cities? If that was the case it is surely odd that he should have needed to return to the region seventeen times, particularly as his famous victory at Megiddo early in his campaigning took Egyptian power as far north as he would ever succeed in doing.

It is evident that at the height of their power the Canaanites had developed remarkably strong defences. In a manner reminiscent of the castle building of the European Middle Ages, they created huge artificial mounds round their cities, built up of alternating layers of stones and beaten earth to prevent undermining, and made so steep and sloping that it was difficult for any enemy even to reach the walls, let alone to scale them. Archaeologically these defences, found at widespread Canaanite sites such as Lachish, Shechem, Megiddo, Jericho and Hazor, are one of the most characteristic features of the last phase of the Middle Bronze Age, referred to as Middle Bronze Age IIB and IIC by most archaeologists. The culture associated with this period is Canaan's most prosperous. Several of the cities show strong signs of having received sudden influxes of their fellow countrymen in the wake of the Hyksos/Canaanite expulsion from Egypt. Dr Kathleen Kenyon noted that Jericho had been 'considerably enlarged' shortly before the end of the Middle Bronze Age, and Dr Yigael Yadin identified at Hazor in Galilee the sudden building of a complete Lower City in the same period. But the difficulty that now arises is that every Canaanite city of the time is mute. To discover what happened and when, too often our only resource is a series of often contradictory interpretations of precisely when any one archaeological phase may be fitted into the context of Egyptian history. The problem is particularly acute in relation to the undoubtedly savage destruction of most of Canaan's major fortified cities at the end of the Middle Bronze Age, *whenever that was*. Because Egypt is known to have taken over a substantial area of Canaan as a part of its empire, it has been widely assumed that the Middle Bronze Age destructions must have been the work of the early Eighteenth Dynasty pharaohs in the immediate wake of the expulsion of the Hyksos – that is, Ahmose and his successors, with the exception of the unwarlike Hatshepsut. Undoubtedly these rulers were responsible for some destruction. Ahmose, for instance, is described in the tomb of his sea-captain namesake as having spent three years besieging 'Sharuhen', according to recent interpretations thought to have been the site today called Tell el-Ajjul, which would have been at the very entrance to ancient Canaan. Tuthmosis I is thought to have pushed on farther up the coastal strip and, as already remarked, Tuthmosis III took Megiddo, a campaign which we know much about because he recorded his annals in great detail on the walls enclosing the sanctuary of Amon at Karnak.

But as is clear from these very annals, Tuthmosis III, having brilliantly outflanked the army that the various Canaanite city states had assembled for their defence, and having caused the survivors to take refuge within Megiddo's walls, behaved with nothing but magnanimity when the city's occupants surrendered some months later. He took no lives, and did not even depose or imprison the captured Canaanite princes. Instead he simply required of each of them an oath of loyalty – one no doubt of the very same pattern as the Ten Commandments – then allowed them to return to their former territories. And Megiddo itself shows no sign of any destruction at the period to which its capture by Tuthmosis is attributable. Tuthmosis, though by no means a boastful man, claimed the victory, which was over a coalition of most of the leading Canaanite princes, to be equivalent to 'the capture of a thousand towns', and he was most likely right. He was able to return to Egypt with more than 2,000 captured horses. He had also secured supply lines for one of Egypt's most badly needed commodities, timber: 'Every year real cedars of Lebanon are felled for me and brought to my court. . . . When my army returns, they bring as tribute the cedars of my victory.'

Although he brought back sons and daughters of Canaanite princes to the Egyptian court, this was probably not in order to hold them hostage but to give them a suitable education and upbringing so that, on the death of any royal father in Canaan, they could be sent back to take over the administration with reinforced loyalty. On these terms Canaanite princes were allowed not only to retain their own corps of men-at-arms but also to supplement them with contingents of Egyptian troops. Similarly, nothing is known to suggest that the Egyptians in any way tried to suppress the Canaanite religion: they were tolerant of the religions of others, even to the point of incorporating foreign gods into their pantheon. In the last phase at Jericho there are strong indications of Egyptian influence in the styling of furniture and ornaments. When, a generation after the time of Tuthmosis III, Pharaoh Amenophis III ordered forty 'unblemished' concubines from the vassal prince at Gezer (an important Canaanite city dominating the route leading off the 'Way of the Sea' towards Jerusalem), he very properly included a substantial down payment in silver. Overall, while it seems to have been Egyptian policy to keep Canaan regularly 'milked' (hence Tuthmosis III's repeated expeditions), it was also in the long-term interests of Egypt to keep Canaan prosperous and in good order, in the words of one authority, 'a chain of strong, fortified urban settlements'.

Gratifyingly, from the point of view of fitting this into Thera's chronology, these events appear to be in accord with the Biblical picture of post-Exodus Canaan as brought back to Moses by the twelve spies he had sent out from Kadesh Barnea:

> . . . the land to which you sent us . . . is flowing with milk and honey . . . its inhabitants are sturdy, and the cities are very strongly fortified. . . . Amalekites . . . live in the Negev, Hittites, Jebusites and Amorites . . . live in the hill country, and the Canaanites . . . live by the sea and along the Jordan. (Numbers 13:27–9)

'Palestinian bichrome ware'. Until recently this pottery had been widely interpreted as Palestinian, and indicative of the beginning of Canaan's Late Bronze Age. But new scientific techniques have conclusively shown it to be an import from Cyprus, overturning many previous assumptions.

Although it might be objected that there is no mention of Egypt or Egyptians in this list, there is no reason why there should have been, since the outward appearance to any spies would have been that Canaanites, and the other closely related peoples mentioned, remained in charge. Their reports of having seen strong fortifications are corroborated by the Bible reference to the strong walls and obviously well-organized opposition that the Israelites encountered at Jericho and elsewhere. Archaeology suggests that these fortifications date from the Middle Bronze Age: Late Bronze Age Canaan, as a later chapter reveals, was typified by weak, unwalled settlements.

But while this picture accords with the view of Canaan in the early New Kingdom period as it is understood by Egyptologists today, the specialization in archaeological circles is such that some investigators, for example Dr Kathleen Kenyon, have seen it differently, perhaps because they have focused their minds rather too exclusively on what they have turned up with the spade in Palestine itself. As already noted in chapter 2, Kenyon interpreted the destruction of the prosperous Middle Bronze Age city of Jericho as having been the work of the Egyptians shortly after they had expelled the Hyksos, leaving throughout the Late Bronze Age little more than a ghost town for Joshua to walk into at the end of that period.

It is almost inevitable in a situation fraught with so many inconsistencies that some scholar should take it upon himself to rationalize the discrepancies; this task has fallen to Dr John Bimson, lecturer in Old Testament Studies at Trinity Theological College, Bristol, who made it the subject of his PhD thesis, *Re-dating the Exodus and the Conquest*, published in 1978. As Bimson argues, the mistake of contemporary archaeology has been to set the end of the Middle Bronze Age too early, on the basis of the (in most cases) unwarranted assumption that it was the Egyptians who were responsible for these particular destructions. The exact date at which the Middle Bronze Age ended has always been a subject of disagreement among scholars, and Bimson's solution is a radical one of moving it about a century and a half to around the end of the fifteenth century, cutting into part of what had previously been ascribed to the Late Bronze Age. Even more radical is his attribution of the destruction at the end of this period to Joshua and his fellow Israelites.

Dr Bimson's reasons for reaching such conclusions are unavoidably technical. To Biblical scholars one of the most characteristic features of the Late Bronze Age in Canaan has been a type of pottery called 'Palestinian bichrome ware'. However, Bimson has revealed certain fallacies in the thinking associated with it: in particular that the recent discovery that it was an import from Cyprus overturns many assumptions concerning both its date and the date of archaeological levels at which it is found.

The most gratifying feature of Bimson's research is that he has reached conclusions about the dating of the conquest which are essentially compatible with an Exodus at the time of the Thera eruption, yet in doing so he has at no stage taken the Thera eruption into his thinking. His concern has been to find a new compatibility between the Bible and the archaeolog-

Dr John Bimson (*left*), lecturer in Old Testament studies at Bristol's Trinity Theological College. By bringing forward the conventional dating of the end of the Middle Bronze Age, Bimson attributes the destruction of Canaan's Middle Bronze Age cities to Joshua and the Biblical Israelites. His theory has not as yet won a consensus in the world of Biblical scholarship, although most scholars admit to a certain confusion in the current state of knowledge. With him at the excavation site at Khirbet Nisya is Dr David Livingstone (see page 173).

BC	Conventional dating	Bimson redating	
1900	MIDDLE	MIDDLE	Hebrews enter Egypt
	Senwosret III		
1800	BRONZE	BRONZE	
1700	AGE	AGE	
1600	HYKSOS DOMINATION	HYKSOS DOMINATION	Bondage?
1500	END OF MIDDLE BRONZE AGE	END OF MIDDLE BRONZE AGE	Bondage Exodus
	Hatshepsut		
	Tuthmosis III LATE		
1400	Amenophis III	LATE	Conquest of Canaan
	Akhenaten BRONZE	BRONZE	
1300		AGE	Judges
	Ramesses II AGE		
	Merneptah		
1200			
	IRON AGE		Philistines

Dr John Bimson's controversial redating of the end of the Middle Bronze Age, shown in comparison with conventional dating set out in the left-hand column

ical record, and this, he finds, *only* exists if the Exodus and Conquest events are set in the fifteenth century BC rather than the thirteenth. The circumstances of the fall of Jericho demonstrate the soundness of his reasoning.

The Israeli president General Chaim Herzog, an expert on military matters old as well as new, has pointed out one reason why the Biblical story of the fall of Jericho ought to be regarded as historically based: that it accords so well with what would, for reasons of geography, necessarily have been a first military objective for anyone invading Canaan from the east as, according to the Bible, the Israelites did. For anyone making a direct approach into Canaan from Egypt, Jericho would have been a relatively minor backwater, difficult to get to and therefore unlikely to have been of any great military interest to the Egyptians. But for the Biblical Israelites, coming from the inhospitable desert country to the south-east, its position would have been crucial. Not only did it command the fordable stretch of the Jordan that the Israelites needed to cross in order to press westwards, it also controlled the most practicable, stream-cut route they could take to reach the highlands that would have been their next objective. Furthermore, for a people parched after too long in the desert it offered a first taste of fertile land and an abundant water supply.

If, as Bimson argues, late Middle Bronze Age Jericho was the town contemporary with Joshua, there can be no doubt, as Kathleen Kenyon's excavations have shown, that it would have represented a serious obstacle for anyone as poorly equipped to carry out a siege as the Israelites must then have been. Despite considerable subsequent erosion of the site, Dr Kenyon found its fortifications, as at other sites of the period, to have consisted of 'a great rampart, consisting of an enormous fill of imported material, faced by a thick layer of plaster', together with a revetting wall whose remains she described as 'the most impressive fragment of the defences of Jericho at any period'. Patchily preserved behind these walls, she found evidence of closely packed, small-roomed houses, and single-booth shops at street level, some with jars still full of grain left unconsumed when the inhabitants were overtaken by the disaster that marked Middle Bronze Age Jericho's fall.

What was that disaster? Could it have been something like that described in the Book of Joshua? As Bimson has noted, both in the Bible and as revealed at Middle Bronze Age Jericho, the prelude to the drama that followed appears to have been some form of epidemic. According to Joshua 2:1, immediately before crossing the Jordan and attacking Jericho the Israelites were settled at a place – apparently near by – called Shittim (in Hebrew 'the acacias' – present-day location unknown) where, judging by their debauchery with Moabite women as described in Numbers 25:1, they dallied for some while. During this same period, according to Numbers 25:9, although we are told frustratingly little about it, no fewer than 24,000 Israelites are said to have died of a plague. While we should adopt the usual conservatism with regard to the number, we can at least assume that the epidemic was serious.

Kathleen Kenyon noted in the course of her excavations that 'some catastrophe caused high mortality on an occasion very late in the history of Middle Bronze Age Jericho'. She had observed a sudden incidence of multiple burials in tombs of the late Middle Bronze Age, whole families, adults, adolescents and children all being laid together, as if they had died at much the same time. In considering the cause of death Dr Kenyon ruled out famine because the bodies had been supplied with substantial haunches of meat as their food for the afterlife. She also ruled out that these were victims of the actual sack of Jericho: '. . . it is unlikely that casualties would have been buried with such rich equipment, and . . . unlikely that the survivors would have carried out elaborate burial ceremonies at all. . . .' Accordingly, her conclusion was that these people must have died from some 'virulent disease', such as a plague.

There was something else that was odd about these burials: they were unusually well preserved. Unlike in Egypt, when corpses buried in the hot dry sand remain intact without the need for mummification, in Israel bodies usually decay, and all that remains is the bones, with pots and other durable grave goods. But in these particular 'plague' tombs at Jericho, far more was preserved in recognizable form: furniture, matting, basketry, wig materials, scraps of clothing, the joints of meat for the afterlife, and the bodies themselves, sometimes with skin, flesh and hair still intact, and even with the shrivelled remains of their brains inside their skulls.

Intrigued, Kathleen Kenyon sought advice from two separate specialists, F.E. Zeuner and S. Dorell, both of whom arrived at essentially the same conclusion. Quite soon after the 'plague' burials there must have been some form of local seismic activity, such as an earthquake, which released poisonous gases into the tombs and killed the bacteria and insects which would normally have brought about rapid decay of the organic materials. Zeuner pointed out that two of the three tombs he had specially studied had suffered heavy internal rock falls, and Dr Kenyon herself noted that the walls of these and other tombs appeared to have been strangely 'twisted and fractured'.

A plague followed by an earthquake? Bimson has been by no means the first to suggest that the other strange Biblical events immediately preceding Jericho's fall – the damming of the Jordan, and the collapse of the town walls – may have been due to earthquake activity. The region is regularly subject to such events, lying as it does in a huge and still active rift valley extending through the Dead Sea, along the Red Sea to the Ethiopian highlands, and finally to the great lakes of East Africa. Of the many Palestinian earthquakes that have been recorded this century, one of the most serious occurred shortly after three o'clock in the afternoon of 11 July 1927. At least 500 were killed and a further 700 injured, many hundreds of buildings collapsed, and there were four serious rock falls or landslides along the Jerusalem to Jericho road. Great clefts in the ground appeared in the Jordan valley. But from a Biblical point of view the most interesting feature of this event is that one of the landslides stopped the flow of the Jordan for twenty-one and a half hours at Jisr ed-Damiye, a little to the north of Jericho. It appears that something very similar also happened during the Crusades. Inevitably these events recall that which Joshua 3 describes, and specifically notes as happening at a time when the river was in full flood:

> Joshua rose early in the morning, and he and all the Israelites set out from Shittim and came to the Jordan . . . the water coming down from upstream was brought to a standstill; it piled up like a bank for a long way back, as far as Adam [Jisr ed-Damiye?], a town near Zarethan. The waters coming down to the Sea of the Arabah, the Dead Sea, were completely cut off, and the people crossed over opposite Jericho.

If an earthquake stopped the flow of the Jordan at the time when Joshua and his fellow Israelites were in the vicinity, could not the same event or a closely following shock wave have caused a fatal breach in Jericho's defences – the famous tumbling down of its walls? And is it beyond the bounds of probability that this was the very same quake which preserved the bodies of Jericho's recent plague victims?

The Bible makes it clear that Joshua and his Israelites showed no leniency towards those they conquered – unlike Tuthmosis III and his Egyptian army. Moses' instructions are explicit in Deuteronomy 7:5 and are repeated in 12:2-3: 'This is what you must do to them: pull down their altars, break their sacred pillars, hack down their sacred poles and destroy their idols by fire. . . .' The inhabitants of Jericho would already have been badly weakened from the combined effects of plague and earthquake. Joshua and the Israelites 'destroyed everything in the city; they put everyone to the sword, men and women, young and old, and also cattle, sheep and asses. . . . They then set fire to the city and everything in it.' Only objects of metal were saved. Dr Kenyon, in her book, *Archaeology in the Holy Land*, has described her archaeological findings from the Middle Bronze Age levels at Jericho in readily comparable terms:

> The evidence for the destruction is . . . dramatic. All the Middle Bronze Age buildings were violently destroyed by fire. . . . This destruction covers the whole area, about 52 metres by 22 metres, in which the buildings of this period surviving the subsequent denudation have been excavated. That the destruction extended right up the slopes of the mound is shown by the fact that the tops of the wall-stumps are covered by a layer about a metre thick of washed debris, coloured brown, black and red by the burnt material it contains; this material is clearly derived from burnt buildings farther up the mound.

The same theme is repeated in her references to Jericho in her contribution to the *Cambridge Ancient History*: 'Walls and floors are hardened and blackened, burnt debris and beams from the upper storeys fill the rooms, and the whole is covered with a wash from burnt walls.'

So the archaeological picture for Middle Bronze Age Jericho is one of plague followed by earthquake, followed by fiery destruction by opportunist

Right Houses from Middle Bronze Age Jericho, with a street and drain on the left. At top right layers of burning can clearly be seen, together with foundations of the same Late Bronze Age wall shown on page 49.

Interior of one of the multiple graves from Jericho, showing comparatively well-preserved organic remains, on the right a Middle Bronze Age bed, and to the left a table with a wooden platter. The unusual state of preservation is thought to be owing to bacterial activity having been abruptly checked by poisonous gases leaking into the tombs as a result of an earthquake shortly after the burials took place.

Opposite '[the tribe] Judah did not take Gaza with its territory, or Ashkelon with its territory ...' (Judges 1:18). Continuing Egyptian influence at Canaanite towns which the Israelites failed to take is exemplified by this magnificent anthropoid coffin, from the reign of Ramesses II, unearthed at Deir el-Balah just south of Gaza. Inside, archaeologists found two skeletons almost touching each other, together with a quantity of jewellery and utensils of bronze and alabaster. Cruder versions of the same type of anthropoid sarcophagus were adopted by the Philistines after their infiltration of Canaan in the reign of Ramesses III.

Site	Biblical account	Archaeological evidence	Agree-ment
Jericho (Tell-es Sultan)	Major, strongly fortified city captured and burnt by Joshua (Joshua 6:1–24)	At Middle Bronze Age level evidence of a major fortified city suffering decisive destruction by earthquake and fire	Yes
Ai (et-Tell?)	Major, strongly fortified city captured, burnt and made a permanent ruin (Joshua 8:19–28)	No evidence of occupation of et-Tell site during Middle Bronze Age period	No
Bethel (Beitin?)	Captured by the tribe of Joseph. Inhabitants slaughtered (Judges 1:22–5)	At Beitin evidence of destruction of Middle Bronze Age IIC city, followed by scanty subsequent occupation	Yes
Hazor (Tell-el Qedah)	A royal city captured and burnt by Joshua, then subsequently reoccupied by the enemy (Joshua 11:10–12)	Evidence of destruction of Middle Bronze Age IIC city by fire, then subsequent reoccupation	Yes
Debir (Tell Beit Mirsim)	A royal city captured and its inhabitants slaughtered (Joshua 10:39; Judges 1:11)	Stratum D, the Middle Bronze Age IIC city, 'completely destroyed, then abandoned for a comparatively long time'	Yes
Lachish (Tell ed-Duweir)	Captured and the inhabitants slaughtered (Joshua 10:31–3)	Last phase of Middle Bronze Age level destroyed in violent conflagration	Yes
Hebron	An Anakim city captured and its inhabitants slaughtered (Joshua 10:36–7)	A populous town with rampart fortifications up to the end of the Middle Bronze Age, whereupon occupation ceased throughout Late Bronze Age	Yes
Hormah (Tel Masos or Khirbet el Meshâsh)	A Canaanite city (Zephath) captured and renamed by the tribe of Judah (Judges 1:17; Number 14:21)	Fortified with ramparts at end of Middle Bronze Age, then occupation ceased throughout Late Bronze Age period	Yes
Dan (Tell Dan)	Formerly known as Laish, captured and burnt by Danite tribe, inhabitants killed, then town rebuilt for Danite occupation (Judges 18:27)	The Middle Bronze Age IIC city 'destroyed by a massive conflagration', evidence of some form of reoccupation	Yes
Gibeon	Population enslaved, but city apparently preserved (Joshua 9:10)	Extensive occupation in Middle Bronze Age period, but no walls, indicating that invaders would have had no need to make conventional attack	Yes
Arad (Tel Malhata)	Arad's king defeated in battle shortly before main Israelite invasion (Numbers 21:2–3)	A strongly fortified Canaanite city destroyed by firee towards the end, but not at the end, of the Middle Bronze Age period	Yes

raiders who clearly saw so little value in even the site of the city that they subsequently abandoned it for generations. The Biblical story of Jericho's fall is broadly compatible with every aspect of the archaeological findings; yet this fact has been discounted by those who believe the story to be a late piece of fiction, and Joshua to have lived at the time of Ramesses II, when Jericho lay a ruin.

It is this apparent absurdity that Dr John Bimson's re-dating hypothesis has sought to rectify. The acid test for his theory is to look at which other sites besides Jericho show a close correspondence between the Biblical conquest account and the archaeological findings for the end of the Middle Bronze Age. The best way of doing this is in precisely the chart form adopted in Chapter 2 to show the lack of correspondence between the Biblical conquest story and archaeological findings for the Late Bronze Age. Now the degree of compatibility is remarkable (see opposite and compare with the chart on page 40).The single anomaly is Ai, a special case which we will consider shortly. The contrast between this list and the earlier one is itself justification for the broad sense of Bimson's arguments. And the list of corresponding points can be amplified by including those towns which, as we are told with convincing candour in Judges 1:27-33, the Israelites did not manage to take:

> [The tribe] Manasseh did not drive out the inhabitants of Beth-Shan with its villages, nor of Ta'anach . . . and Megiddo with the villages of each of them; the Canaanites held their ground in the region. . . . [The tribe] Ephraim did not drive out the Canaanites who lived in Gezer, but the Canaanites lived among them there. . . .

It is precisely in these sites that continuity of occupation has been found between the end of the Middle Bronze Age and the Late Bronze Age, and where there has been archaeological evidence of destruction, independent information shows that it was the Egyptians who were responsible for it, and the Egyptians who kept up the continuity. Thus at Megiddo, which Tuthmosis III took after a siege but preserved intact, archaeology shows no destruction level and interrupted occupation. At Beth-Shan no destruction level at the end of the Middle Bronze Age has been found, and there is evidence of continuous Egyptian influence right up to the reign of Ramesses III. At Ta'anach some signs have come to light of a limited destruction at the end of the Middle Bronze Age; here the proximity of the town to Megiddo, and its subsequent speedy return to prosperity, suggest that Tuthmosis III applied minimum force while he bided his time besieging Megiddo. As for Gezer, although excavations there were botched in the early years of this century, the correspondence that was exchanged between Egypt and Gezer in the reign of Amenophis III, a generation after Tuthmosis III, clearly indicates that it had not been razed up to that time. And this continuity of occupation has been confirmed by more recent archaeology.

As mentioned, there is one apparent anomaly – Ai – which, as described in Chapter 2, does not fit a Late Bronze Age dating either. But, as might be

If the Israelite conquest of Canaan is dated to the end of the Middle Bronze Age, the Bible and archaeology agree.

171

Above Ruins thought to have been part of Biblical Bethel, at modern Beitin. The photograph looks towards Et-Tell, long thought to have been the Biblical town of Ai.

Locations of the traditional sites of Biblical Ai and Bethel (Beitin and Et-Tell), and the alternatives (Bireh and Khirbet Nisya) proposed by David Livingston and Dr John Bimson. Supporting the Livingston/Bimson view, between Bireh and Khirbet Nisya is the area's tallest mountain, the Jebel et-Tawil, corresponding to Genesis 12: 8; Khirbet Nisya is smaller than Gibeon and Jericho, corresponding to Joshua 10: 2 and 7: 2–3 (whereas Et-Tell is larger than both); and Khirbet Nisya has a ravine to the north and north-west, corresponding to Joshua 8: 11. The western side of the Jebel et-Tawil would have provided an ideal site for the ambush described in Joshua 8: 12. In addition, Bireh fits better than Beitin with the Biblical information that Bethel lay on a major north-south route from Jerusalem to Shechem (Judges 21: 19), and lay on the natural border between Judah and Israel (Joshua 16: 1–2 and 18: 13).

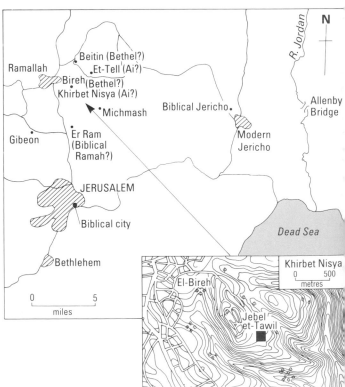

A Middle Bronze Age
dagger of a similar type to
that found at Khirbet Nisya
by U.S. Bible scholar David
Livingston. Livingston
believes Khirbet Nisya to
have been the true site of
Biblical Ai, and his most
recent excavations have
revealed a considerable
amount of Middle Bronze
Age pottery at the site,
although no building
remains of the period.
Livingston attributes this to
later Byzantine settlers
having cannibalized the
Middle Bronze Age
buildings.

expected, Dr Bimson has an answer to this one: et-Tell, for all its impressive fortress-like appearance, has simply been misidentified as the Biblical Ai. This argument, acceptable enough at face value, does in fact become more complex when it is realized that et-Tell has been long identified with Ai principally because it is the one obvious site east of Beitin, almost universally thought to have been the Biblical Bethel, and Joshua 7:2 specifically tells us that Ai was 'east of Bethel'. So Bimson's argument demands not only that Ai has been misidentified, but that Bethel has as well; an unpalatable argument for most scholars because etymologically the Beitin-Bethel association makes a lot of sense.

Here, however, Bimson has one ally, American Biblical scholar David Livingston, who has shown not only how poorly Beitin and et-Tell tally geographically with Biblical and other early information relating to Bethel and Ai, but also that there are two nearby sites that satisfy the early descriptions much better: el-Bireh, which he believes to have been the true Bethel, and a small tell called Khirbet Nisya, which he believes to have been the true Ai. Between these two is a mountain, the Jebel et-Tawil, or 'tall one' – which corresponds much better to the mountain described in Genesis 12:8 as having been between Bethel and Ai than do the mere valley and small hill that lie between Beitin and et-Tell. Unfortunately el-Bireh has too much present-day habitation on it to make practical any excavations to determine if it could have been the Biblical Bethel, but Khirbet Nisya is much more accessible. After four seasons Livingston has now found sufficient evidence there to establish that whether or not it was Ai, it was at least occupied at the end of the Middle Bronze Age, and then left abandoned in the Late Bronze Age. This precisely corresponds with the Bimson chronology in which Joshua took Ai at the end of the Middle Bronze Age, the site thereafter being left a ruin in accordance with Joshua 8:38 – 'So Joshua burnt Ai to the ground, and left it the desolate mound it remains to this day.'

It should be stressed that the Bimson thesis, appealing as it is, has yet to be accepted by any consensus of scholars; but it dovetails so neatly with the arguments advanced earlier for re-dating events that the crucial question now seems to be this: when, in relation to Egyptian chronology, was Joshua's 'conquest', and what was its extent? For while Egypt had the military power that Tuthmosis III gave it, and was making repeated expeditions into Canaan, it would have been most unwise for the Israelites to venture anywhere near an Egyptian army. How easily they could have been taken is evident from accounts of the campaigns of Tuthmosis III's equally warlike son Amenophis II on two surviving stelae, one from Memphis, the other from Karnak. After making clear Amenophis' continuance of Tuthmosis' policy of raids into Canaan, the stelae list the human booty Amenophis brought back with him: '. . . princes of Retenu: 127; brothers of princes: 179; Habiru: 3,600; living Shosu: 15,200; Kharu: 36,300; living Neges: 15,070; the adherents thereof: 30,652: total 89,800 men, similarly their goods without limit.'

The numbers, which do not tally too well, are vastly larger than anything claimed by Amenophis II's father, and seem to indicate that the main purpose of the expedition had been to collect slaves to support the luxurious way of life to which New Kingdom Egypt was becoming increasingly accustomed. The 'Kharu', probably synonymous with the Hurrians, are thought to have been the Biblical Horites of Genesis 36:30, who according to Deuteronomy 2:12 were displaced by the Edomites whose opposition to the Israelites was noted in the previous chapter. Since we find the term 'Shosu' used in the time of Merneptah to describe tribes from Edom, it may be assumed that these were Edomites. The presence of these two groups suggests that Amenophis simply rounded up like stray cattle any non-urban, semi-nomadic peoples who happened to come within his reach. Of considerable interest is the reference to 'Habiru', the first mention of them since the wall painting showing them working Delta winepresses in the time of Hatshepsut. Were they members of one of the Israelite tribes who had come from Egypt, and had perhaps by this stage strayed a little too far into Canaan? Or were they a branch of the Habiru who had nothing to do with the Biblical Israelites? Whichever was the case, their numbers are noticeably smaller than those of the other groups – in spite of which the Egyptians did not lump them with one of the other peoples, but distinguished them from the rest.

Despite his apparent aggressiveness, Amenophis II in fact conducted only two campaigns, retiring for his last seventeen years to enjoy the fruits of his slaving expeditions. His successor Tuthmosos IV (c1401-1391) negotiated peace with the Mitanni to Canaan's north-east, so that the need for a firm grip on Canaan began to lessen. This slackening process continued during the long succeeding reign of Amenophis III (c1391-1353), notable for major innovations in art and architecture, and for a new fashion for transparent gowns for both men and women. Amenophis III broke with tradition in his choice of a principal wife by marrying a commoner, Teye. With all these distractions he was disinclined to keep a grip on foreign affairs.

Assuming that our re-dating of Exodus is valid, if there was any opportune time for the Israelites/Habiru to infiltrate where they could into Canaan, it would have been now, and, sure enough, havoc attributed to *some* form of Habiru (whether or not they were anything to do with the Biblical Israelites) is well attested from Amenophis III's reign and that of his successor, the notorious heretic Akhenaten. In 1887 a peasant woman happened to be digging at Tell el-Amarna, site of the short-lived capital Akhenaten built for himself half-way between present-day Cairo and Luxor, when she came across several clay tablets with cuneiform writing which she promptly took to a local dealer. When they eventually reached European scholars through the usual trading channels their significance was realized and a major excavation was begun at the original location, which the peasant woman was able to point out. Eventually a total of 377 of these tablets was retrieved. They turned out to be part of Amenophis III and Akhenaten's one-time Canaan correspondence files, written mostly in Akkadian (though

he heretic pharaoh khenaten (c 1353-35 BC), hose strange appearance as been attributed to andular disorders. If Dr imson's redating of the raelite entry into Canaan valid, the Israelites would ready have gained a bstantial foothold in anaan by Akhenaten's ign, pottery of the second hase of the Late Bronze ge having been found at khenaten's short-lived pital, Tell el 'Amarna. riking parallels have been oted between Akhenaten's lymn to the Aten' and the 4th psalm, but Atenism is nown to have been tablished at the Egyptian urt for some while before khenaten's reign.

sometimes strongly tinged with Canaanite dialect), because this was the international language of the day.

It was immediately evident that these so-called 'Amarna tablets' are largely a one-way correspondence from Canaanite vassal monarchs to their overlord pharaoh, indicating a continuance up to this point of the benign relationship instituted by Tuthmosis III. But now there was trouble which, apart from a few petty squabbles between one Canaanite king and another, can broadly be summed up in one word: 'Habiru'. Shuwardata, responsible for the Hebron hill country region in the reign of Akhenaten, complains:

> Let the king, my lord [i.e. Akhenaten], learn that the chief of the Habiru has risen [in arms] against the lands which the god of the king, my lord, gave me; but I have smitten him. And let the king, my lord, know that all my brethren have abandoned me, and it is I and 'Abdu-Heba [who] fight against the chief of the Habiru.

Since 'Abdu-Heba, responsible for Jerusalem, seems from previous correspondence to have been an arch enemy of Shuwardata's, clearly the unnamed chief of the Habiru must have been a formidable foe. In a separate letter 'Abdu-Heba, confirming Shuwardata's story, pleads for Egyptian archers, obviously considered the best defence against the raiders:

> Let the king turn his attention to the archers and let the king, my lord, send out troops of archers [for] the king has no lands [left]. The Habiru plunder all the lands of the king. If there are archers [here] in this year the lands of the king, my lord, will remain [intact]; but if there are no archers [here] the lands of the king, my lord, will be lost.

That Akhenaten, his religious reforms apparently occupying all his attention, shut his ears to Canaanite problems, is evident from a later letter from the same 'Abdu-Heba informing him that the problem had now reached even the Egyptian border post of Sile:

> ... now the Habiru capture the cities of the king ... Behold, Turbazu has been slain in the [very] gate of Sile ... Behold Simreda, the townsmen of Lachish have smitten him, slaves who had become Habiru. Yapti has been slain [in] the [very] gate of Sile, [yet] the king holds his peace.

Convenient though it would be to believe that these Habiru were one and the same as Joshua and his fellow Israelites, in fact this cannot be so, and Dr Bimson has prudently avoided claiming this. For instance, Joshua 10:3 actually names some of the petty kings responsible for different cities at the time of the Biblical invasion: Adonizek of Jerusalem, Hoham of Hebron, Piram of Jarmuth, Japhia of Lachish and Debir of Eglon. Not only do the Amarna tablets name the kings of Jerusalem and Hebron as 'Abdu-Heba and Shuwardata, but others also fail to match. Nor do the events of the Biblical invasion correspond to those that can be understood from the Amarna letters.

But that is not to say that the Israelites may not have been part of this

One of the famous Tell el 'Amarna tablets, part of the foreign correspondence files of pharaoh Amenophis III (c 1391–53 BC) and his son Akhenaten. The tablets, written mostly in Akkadian the international diplomatic language of the time, include many reports of disturbances to Canaanite urban life by seemingly rootless bands of 'Habiru'. While it is tempting to identify these intruders as the Biblical Hebrews, scholars rightly point out that the names of Canaanite kings quoted in the tablets are quite different from those mentioned in the Biblical record.

same broad Habiru movement at roughly this time. For instance, the Amarna correspondence notably omits any mention of Jericho. Was this because it had already fallen to Joshua, perhaps just before the Amarna files began? Furthermore, according to the Amarna tablets one location that was particularly receptive to the Habiru was the hill town of Shechem, a little to the north of Ai. As 'Abdu-Heba bitterly remarks, '. . . shall we do like Lab'ayu [the vassal prince responsible for Shechem], who gave the land of Shechem to the Habiru?' It is in just this area that the Israelites' ancestors are described in the Bible as having bought land in the time of Jacob (Genesis 33:19). When Joshua arrives here he not only meets no resistance, he makes a covenant alliance with the inhabitants, who appear to have been members of his people who did not go down to Egypt. He also buries the bones of Joseph, brought all the way from Egypt, and he makes his own deathbed speech here.

The Biblical scholar G.E. Mendenhall has made the somewhat controversial deduction that whatever and whenever Joshua's invasion may have been, in real terms it was probably neither very large nor very important. The real force of change within Canaan, he claims, was some form of 'peasants' revolt', an uprising of the non-urban population against the leaders of the various city states still paying lip service to Egyptian rule. In fact there is no reason why this should not have been the way the so-called 'conquest' of Canaan actually happened, the influx of Habiru from Egypt (i.e. the Biblical Israelites) combining with the relaxing of Egyptian control to trigger an overthrow of the old regime by those Habiru who had stayed behind.

There is one final intriguing clue that Joshua's invasion may have been around the time of, or shortly before, the reigns of Amenophis III and Akhenaten. As will be recalled, Jericho fell at a time when plague was ravaging Canaan. And the Amarna tablets too record a plague, albeit in the form of denials by a vassal anxious that such news might further deter Akhenaten from sending any aid: '. . . they are trying to commit a felony when they report in the presence of the king, "There is plague in the lands!" Let not the king, my lord, listen to the words of these men! There is no plague in the country! Things are as healthy as ever!' In fact this plague appears to have been so serious and so widespread that it even reached Akhenaten's court at el-Amarna, and was most likely responsible for the deaths in quick succession of Akhenaten's beloved daughters and the queen mother, Teye. Twenty years later it had reached the Hittites. It seems reasonable that this was the very same disease that smote both the Biblical Israelites and the inhabitants of Jericho.

12. *The Exodus and future research*

In a book of this kind there can be no firm conclusions. However vigorously the case for a reconsideration of the dating of the Biblical Exodus is argued, it has to be acknowledged that because Biblical sources are based on oral traditions, nothing in the Bible story of the Exodus conquest can be regarded as strictly historical, and for this reason all archaeological parallels, however convincing, must be treated with caution. Dr Bimson's hypotheses, as outlined in the previous chapter, have as yet no consensus of scholastic support, many scholars for the present preferring to believe the Exodus and conquest stories to be largely myth, rather than that there may have been something wrong in the traditional way of matching Palestinian pottery periods and Egyptian chronology.

While such attitudes are understandable, it should be stressed again that although those who assembled the Exodus and conquest traditions did so with more consideration for theology than for history, recording events as signs of divine intervention, yet for that very reason they had a serious concern for truth. Which people other than the Jews have been so blazingly honest about their faults that they chose to chronicle their every grumble over food and water in the wilderness (Exodus 15:22-6; 16:2-3; 17:2-7; Numbers 11:4-6); their murmuring against their own God-inspired leaders (Numbers 12:1-2; 14:2-3; 16:12-14); their turning away from the God who led them out of Egypt (Exodus 32:1-6 and in most of the prophetic books in the latter part of the Old Testament)? So why should they have lied about the plagues or the flood wave that saved them from their Egyptian pursuers? And why should they have invented a story such as that of the capture of Jericho?

Dr Manfred Bietak's identification and excavation of Avaris/Pi-Ramesses, Professor Marinatos' finds on Thera, Dr Hans Goedicke's controversial linking of the Thera eruption with the Biblical Exodus, and Dr Bimson's equally controversial re-dating of the Biblical Conquest have all occurred only in very recent years, and their full validity and relation to each other – if they are indeed valid and related – will undoubtedly take many more years to be fully realized. None the less, recent researches in these fields have revealed surprising new findings lending much support to some of the new theories.

For instance, the Late Bronze Age archaeological period that followed the destruction of the Canaanite cities had, curiously, not been the subject of

Egypt	BC	Canaan	Biblical events
MIDDLE Senwosret III KINGDOM	— 2000 — — 1900 — — 1800 — — 1700 —	MIDDLE BRONZE AGE	Time of Joseph
HYKSOS DOMINATION	— 1600 —		
THERA ERUPTION Hatshepsut Tuthmosis III NEW Amenophis III Akhenaten Ramesses II Merneptah KINGDOM Ramesses III	— 1500 — — 1400 — — 1300 — — 1200 — — 1100 — — 1000 —	Egyptian incursions Tuthmosis' Victories _ _ _ 'Habiru' invasions/uprisings - - - - - - - - - - - LATE BRONZE AGE - - - - - - - - - - - Coming of Philistines IRON AGE	Bondage Exodus from Egypt Wanderings Infiltration of Canaan Judges Philistines

A tentative redating of the Biblical events, based on the revised chronology demanded by linking the Exodus to the Thera eruption, and to Dr John Bimson's redating of the Israelite 'conquest'. Compare the conventional view shown in the chart on page 16.

Left Lump of pumice, scientifically identified as having come from the Thera eruption of the Minoan period. It was found at the Eighteenth-Dynasty Egyptian settlement of Gurrob in the Faiyum region of Egypt, south-west of present-day Cairo. It is worn from apparent domestic use as an abrasive, and was probably brought to Gurrob by traders.

specialist study in its own right until Israeli-born Hebrew University archaeologist Dr Rivka Gonen devoted her PhD thesis to it in 1979. Her findings so surprised her tutor, distinguished Israeli archaeologist Dr Benjamin Mazar, that he insisted she check them no fewer than three times.

For as Dr Gonen had assembled what was to be the first comprehensive master list of all known Late Bronze Age sites in Canaan, it had become apparent that they had been dramatically reduced, both in size and number, from those that had existed in the Middle Bronze Age. Even when, by the thirteenth century BC, the number of settlements had returned to something approaching that of the Middle Bronze Age, often they covered only about 45 per cent of the area occupied previously, an indication, as Dr Gonen reasoned, that 'the Late Bronze Age was a time of dramatic weakening of the urban fabric'. It was almost equally surprising that, of the seventy-seven sites on her list, all but two, or at most three, were unwalled, as was the case when some small semblance of urban life returned to post-Middle Bronze Age Jericho.

Although the full implications of Dr Gonen's findings (like those of many others), have yet to be properly assessed, it is difficult to avoid the conclusion that the non-urban character of Late Bronze Age Canaan must date from around and after the time of the Habiru disruptions described in the Amarna letters, rather than before, when the impression created is one of still ordered city-states. This in itself strongly corroborates Dr Bimson's changing of the date of the end of the Middle Bronze Age. The lack of city walls in these Late Bronze Age sites was presumably unimportant to the incoming population, suggesting that they were nomadic. Dr Gonen, conscious of the fact that nomads do not necessarily leave lasting traces of their presence, particularly in towns, turned her attention to Late Bronze Age burials, suspecting that this might be the one feature by which occupation of a site by Biblical Israelites might be detected. She found that in the Canaanite low country and foothills, the areas most closely connected with the Canaanites and the Egyptians, pit burials seemed to be the norm. But in the hill country – the territory most often associated in the Bible with Israelite infiltration – the fashion over many centuries was for cave burials, generation after generation of families being buried in this way, in the manner of the cave tomb purchased by the patriarch Abraham (Genesis 23:19–20). Significantly, Dr Gonen found that some of these cave burials had no signs of settlement near by, lending credence to the theory that there were nomads in the vicinity but that the burial plots were the only remaining indications of their presence.

It is beyond the scope of this book to explore the ways in which archaeology may corroborate the Biblical book of Judges, except to point out that by dating the conquest of Canaan to around the reigns of Amenophis III and Akhenaten, i.e. the mid-fourteenth century BC, some 150 years are allowed for the Judges period prior to the coming of the Philistines: less than the 350 years prescribed in the Bible (see chart opposite and compare with that on page 16), but rather more convincing than the thirty or so years (without counting any time for wanderings in Sinai) that would be allowed by a dating to the time of Merneptah. During this period it may be guessed that the Israelites remained non-urban, ranging with their herds around the hill country and open spaces of Canaan and Transjordan, raiding and in turn being raided in the time-honoured manner (e.g. 1 Chronicles 7:21 and 8:13), and only gradually changing their habits to a more settled way of life. This would have allowed normal Egyptian life to continue at those towns too strong or too near the coast for them to take, such as Megiddo and Beth-Shan inland and Gaza and Ashkelon on the coast. This would conform precisely to the information of Judges 1 and to indications of Egyptian presence found at these sites. Accordingly, by the time Merneptah ordered his patently hollow inscription 'Israel is laid waste; his seed is not', the Israelites would have been settled in their land for something over a century, quite long enough to have achieved official recognition, and to have set down roots that have survived more than three millennia of further attempts to eradicate them.

With the first post-Egyptian attempt to wipe them out, the invasion of the Philistines, we arrive at last at what can be accepted as firm history. In typical Ramessid fashion Pharaoh Ramesses III (*c*1194–1163) emblazoned the story of his famous victory against the 'Sea Peoples' all around the walls of his funerary temple at Medinet Habu on the west bank of the Nile at Thebes. Included among the supposedly conquered peoples are the *P–l–s–t* who, Egyptologists and others usually agree, must have been the Biblical Philistines. But this was no more than typical Ramessid boasting, and these peoples were not as conquered as the Medinet Habu inscriptions would have us believe. A separate document, the British Museum's forty-five-foot-long Harris papyrus, discovered under a heap of mummies in 1855, lets slip that the *P–l–s–t*, despite having been 'made ashes', were in fact assigned special places to settle. As the Israelites soon found out to their cost, one of those places was south-west Canaan, where the Philistines demonstrated the one tactical advantage they had over all other comers: weapons of iron, hardened by new forging techniques, which made all bronze weapons obsolete. It was the beginning of a new era, the Iron Age; but that is another story.

If the Biblical Exodus and conquest are wrongly dated, they are doomed to remain outside the canon of history, as indeed they have been up to the present time. But if this book even begins to set them in their correct historical context, then a fascinating new era of opportunities for deeper understanding is about to open up: many of the major research programmes touched on here – of Dr Manfred Bietak, Dr Hans Goedicke, Dr John Bimson and Dr Rivka Gonen among others – have been by no means exhausted, and some have hardly yet begun.

After more than a century during which Egyptologists have devoted most of their attentions to the easy pickings of Middle and Upper Egypt, now the importance of the flat and uninteresting-looking Delta in Egypt's pharaonic past is being recognized. As Dr Bietak's pioneering excavations have

The fierce naval battle between Pharaoh Ramesses III and the 'Sea Peoples' (known to have included the Biblical Philistines), as depicted on a wall relief from Ramesses III's mortuary temple at Medinet Habu near Thebes. The battle seems to have been fought in the waters of the eastern Nile Delta. The Sea Peoples can be identified by their round shields, the Egyptians by rectangular ones, and the Peleset, or Philistines, by their feather headdresses. In the Egyptian boats (with lion-headed prows) the oars are in use, whereas in the Sea Peoples' they are not, suggesting that the latter were caught by surprise.

shown, the artefacts discovered may not be spectacular, but they can clear up many decades of misunderstandings about where the Biblical Israelites spent their years of oppression. At Tell el-Dab'a, alias Pi-Ramesses, alias Avaris, Dr Bietak still has much work to do, and many finds still to publish; but this is merely one of many sites, even if it is the most important. With the amount of attention now being devoted to the Delta, inevitably there will be further surprises in store.

Dr Goedicke, for instance, has yet to publish anything of his finds at Tell Hazzob; instead he has cloaked them in mystery, to the chagrin of his Egyptological colleagues. And he has yet to provide the world with a full scholarly explanation for why he now so confidently attributes the Exodus events to the Thera eruption. In April 1985, at the time this book was in its final stages, he gave a new lecture at Johns Hopkins University not only reaffirming his previous views, but also outlining fresh material which he believes reinforces them. He now interprets further elements in Hatshepsut's enigmatic Speos Artemidos inscription as attesting to the Thera eruption and *tsunami*, among them his reading of Hatshepsut's stated reason for dedicating the shrine to the lioness goddess Pakhet: '. . . as [she opened] the roads for the water-torrent without drenching me, in order to catch the water'. He comments: 'I cannot think of any other explanation for the "water-torrent" than to see in it the flood-wave or *tsunamis* . . . generated by the Thera explosion.'

But all Dr Goedicke's theorizing, as he rightly recognizes, can be dismissed as mere empty words unless he can back these up with positive evidence that effects from the Thera eruption really did have a substantial impact on the Nile Delta in the fifteenth century BC. For instance, are there still traces of ash from Thera below the several feet of silt that the Nile has added to the Delta since the Biblical Israelites walked there? Preliminary surveys have shown that the water table lies a mere foot below the surface in most places, so special techniques of core drilling are required to reach the levels at which Theran ash might be found. But Dr Goedicke, as he reported in his second Exodus lecture, has succeeded in attracting the most highly respected technical assistance:

> To enthuse someone to join in the project was not an easy task, because it meant not only a lot of work, but also generating the necessary funds. After more than two years Dr Daniel Stanley from the Smithsonian Institution became convinced. Although we suffered undesired delays, considerable progress has been made. An initial drilling program is in place and scheduled to begin in September [1985]. In the meantime cores from unrelated drillings are being studied and first results indicate a specific level containing traces of natural glass, i.e. volcanic ash.

What of findings on Thera itself? After the prodigious pace of excavation set by the ebullient Professor Marinatos, his successor Dr Christos Doumas has proceeded very much more slowly, but arguably with much greater thoroughness and concern that no tiny detail should be missed. On his own

Professor Christos Doumas at the Akrotiri excavation site on Thera. Successor to the ebullient Professor Marinatos, he has proceeded with the excavations at a slower, if more thorough, pace. Vital further clues to the date and circumstances of the Thera eruption may still lie beneath the pumice.

estimates there is at least another hundred years' work at Akrotiri alone if excavation continues at its present pace; and that does have its frustrations. Could the pumice still conceal the remains of a palace, perhaps with still intact, readable archives such as those found at Tell el-Amarna? If, as is likely, these were written in Cretan linear A, the language itself would have to be deciphered first, so any discovery that might reveal the date of the Thera eruption by that method lies a long way into the future.

The technique normally used to establish precise dates in such circumstances is radiocarbon dating, but this has proved worse than useless in the case of Thera. Readings obtained from foodstuffs stored and trees killed at the time of the eruption have varied so wildly, between 2590 BC, plus or minus 80 years, to 1100 BC, plus or minus 190 years, that it is generally thought that the eruption itself must have affected the materials' normal radioactive decay (which radiocarbon dating measures).

Accordingly, hopes are now pinned on two other scientific methods, neither as yet totally satisfactory, but offering important future possibilities. The first of these, dendrochronology, is based on the ways in which trees' growth rings show significant variations each year, according to fluctuations of climate. The world's oldest known living trees are the bristlecone pines of California, and as two University of Arizona geoscientists, Valmore La-Marche and Katherine Hirschboeck, have observed, some of the rings exhibit frost damage which can be directly related to years when the world's climate has suffered from the after-effects of a volcanic eruption. LaMarche and Hirschboeck have been able unequivocally to point out frost damage rings for 1902 and 1884 which clearly mark the aftermath of the Mount Pelée and Krakatau eruptions. On bristlecone samples known to have rings representative of the second millennium BC, LaMarche and Hirschboeck have therefore looked for frost rings that might denote the Thera eruption. They have found one for the year 1626 BC, but this seems too early, at least according to current understanding of second-millennium chronology, and it is generally thought that their method is insufficiently specific, there being years of very cold summers without volcanic activity, and vice versa.

Altogether more promising is the second method, based on the layer of ice deposited each year on the Greenland icecap. However remote this may seem from the Biblical Exodus, every year a layer of fresh ice nearly eight inches thick is deposited on Greenland (compressing to around an inch in the course of millennia), each layer containing and preserving a sample of the pollutants which happen to be in the earth's atmosphere in the year. As in the case of tree rings, the layers can be read off year by year.

Three Danish geophysicists, Drs Hammer, Clausen and Dansgard, have observed that layers from years in which there have been major eruptions show a markedly greater acidity than the rest, to such a degree that high peaks of acidity can be considered to be entirely due to volcanic activity. The problem with this dating method is the difficulty of obtaining icecap cores in sufficiently good condition for reliable readings to be obtained back

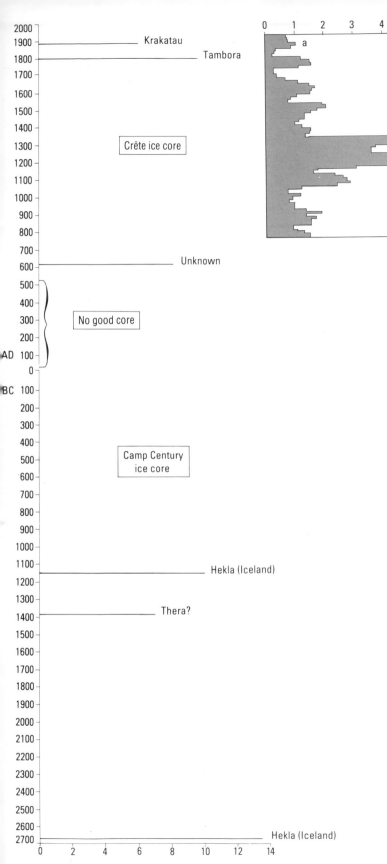

As determined from core samples from the Greenland ice-cap, high acidity levels are linked to years of known volcanic eruptions (see *left*); *inset* details of the acidity peak of 1816, the 'year without a summer', after the Tambora eruption of 1815. This diagram is greatly simplified and minor fluctuations in acidity levels (as in the inset) are not shown.

to the second millennium BC. A twelve-hundred-foot core from a central Greenland site called Crête provided very significant acidity peaks back to AD 553, but was broken beyond that point. Another, four-thousand-foot long one from Camp Century, to the north-west, provided layers back to 100,000 BC, but with the last two thousand years missing. The Camp Century core therefore incorporated the period that would have included the Thera eruption, but its layers are not so precisely datable, making all the more intriguing its only notable peak between what can be roughly computed as the twenty-sixth and eleventh centuries BC (see chart opposite). The date, as estimated by Hammer, Clausen and Dansgard, seems to be 1390 BC, plus or minus fifty years; that is a few decades later than might be expected, but they concede: 'The dating can be further improved to plus or minus ten years if and when a deep central Greenland ice core becomes available.' It is conceivable that, as ice core technology improves, they may eventually be able to date the Thera eruption with such precision that all the rest of the shaky chronology of the second millennium BC could be hung on this event. It is a fascinating prospect.

Before concluding our survey of possible future developments we should not ignore the Biblical archaeology still being vigorously pursued within Israel itself. Will Dr David Livingston find conclusive evidence that Khirbet Nisya really is the site of Biblical Ai? Will some conclusive proof become available that Dr John Bimson's re-dating of the end of the Middle Bronze Age is the correct one? Even within the last decade great strides have been taken towards a better understanding of the Old Testament period, and there is no reason why this progress should not continue, even to the extent of decisively overturning the new ideas advanced in this book.

But if there is still so much uncertainty, and still so much yet to be discovered, is there anything that this survey of the Exodus enigma can claim to have achieved? I hope this: that while the Biblical Exodus and conquest stories, based as they are on oral traditions, may not in the form in which they have come down to us be quite as accurate as fundamentalists would have us believe, none the less real events can be glimpsed behind them which, if the Goedicke and Bimson re-datings are valid, can be set much more firmly into the context of history than before. Because the concern of this book has been to get the setting right, inevitably much detail relating to the Moses and Joshua of Biblical tradition has been neglected, though not with the intention of depriving them of credibility. Why should we not believe that a leader with the Egyptian name of Moses had the daring and initiative to seize a moment of confusion and whisk his people to a precarious safety from under the very rods of their captors? Would not this same temerity become a very hallmark of Jewishness, from the shepherd boy's slingstone that felled the armoured Goliath, to the coolheadedness that rescued civilian Israelis from a twentieth-century Goliath at Entebbe?

And although to some it may seem an affront even to suggest that a volcano, rather than the Old Testament Yahweh, could have been responsible for such happenings as the Biblical plagues and the 'miracle of the

Unconventional but intriguing new techniques may one day help to provide a precise date for the Thera eruption. Examination of the rings of the world's oldest trees, California's bristlecone pines (*left*), has revealed clear signs of frost damage for years in which the world's weather has been severely disrupted by volcanic eruptions. And the layers of ice deposited annually on the Greenland ice-cap (*below*) are known to have significantly higher levels of acidity in years in which the world's atmosphere has been polluted by major volcanic eruptions. Although neither method can yet provide the means of pin-pointing the date of the Thera eruption, future research may well provide greater accuracy.

sea', is such thinking really so unacceptable in our age of rationalism? Should we instead believe that three and a half thousand years ago God behaved like a tyrant, taking sides and hurling thunderbolts, *tsunamis* and goodness-knows-what-else at his people's enemies? Is that not closer to what we expect of the gods of the pagans? Or is the message of the Exodus story the rather more subtle one of God being at his most active in times of apparent disaster and hopelessness, of having his own way of reducing the mighty, and allowing the meek to throw off the shackles of oppression? Is it any less possible that God can work through a volcano than through a human being?

We are confronted with two choices. We can believe, with some hard-headed scholars to back us up, that there is virtually no historical base for the Biblical Exodus: that the tales of plagues and parting waters have no connection with whatever happened at the time of the Thera eruption, and that the whole story is a piece of pious Jewish fiction. Or we can believe that when Thera erupted three and a half thousand years ago there happened to be a people in captivity in Egypt who viewed its accompanying havoc as their literally heaven-sent opportunity for escape; that they seized that opportunity, and were so astounded by their success and accompanying adventures that they enshrined it all – hazy though the details may be – in a folk memory and celebration which they have preserved to this very day.

Chronology of Egypt's pharaohs

MIDDLE KINGDOM

Twelfth Dynasty (c1991–1783)
DATE OF ACCESSION
1991 Amenemhet I
1971 Senwosret I (Sesostris)
1929 Amenemhet II
1897 Senwosret II
1878 Senwosret III
1844 Amenemhet III
1799 Amenemhet IV
1787 Nefrusobk

*Thirteenth Dynasty (c1787–
after 1640)*
approx. 70 kings, mostly short-lived
and obscure

Fourteenth Dynasty
various minor kings contemporary
with Thirteenth Dynasty

SECOND
INTERMEDIATE PERIOD
(c1640–1532)

Fifteenth Dynasty (Hyksos)
? Salitis
? Khian
1585 Apophis
1542 Khamudi

Seventeenth Dynasty (Theban)
1640 Inyotef v & others
? Djehuti
? Seqenenre Ta'o II
1555 Kamose

NEW KINGDOM

Eighteenth Dynasty (c1550–1307)
1550 Ahmose
1525 Amenophis I (Amenhotep)
1504 Tuthmosis I (Thutmose)
1492 Tuthmosis II
1479–1425 Tuthmosis III
1473–1458 Hatshepsut
1427 Amenophis II
1401 Tuthmosis IV
1391 Amenophis III
(Amarna period)
1353 Amenophis IV/Akhenaten
1335 Smenkhare'
1333 Tut'ankhamun
1323 Aya
1319 Haremhab (Horemheb)

*Nineteenth Dynasty
(The Ramessides)
(c1307–1196)*
1307 Ramesses I
1306 Seti I (Sethos)
1290 Ramesses II

1224 Merneptah (Merenptah)
1214 Seti II
1204 Sitpah
1198 Twosre

Twentieth Dynasty (c1196–1070)
1196 Sethnakhte
1194 Ramesses III
1163 Ramesses IV
1156 Ramesses V
1151 Ramesses VI
1143 Ramesses VII
1136 Ramesses VIII
1131 Ramesses IX
1112 Ramesses X
1100 Ramesses XI

THIRD
INTERMEDIATE PERIOD
(c1070–712)

Twenty-first Dynasty	c1070–945
Twenty-second Dynasty	945–712
Twenty-third Dynasty	c828–712
Twenty-fourth Dynasty	724–712
(Sais)	

Dates and most pharaohs' names are
based on the chronology adopted in
John Baines and Jaromir Málek's
Atlas of Ancient Egypt (Phaidon,
Oxford 1980).

The following notes, references and bibliography are intended for readers wishing to explore further the issues raised in *The Exodus Enigma*. In the interests of simplicity, sources appear in the notes only in an abbreviated form, except in the case of very specialized publications. Full publishing details in bibliography.

Notes and references

Introduction

p9   The Jewish seder: for an excellent account of the ceremony and its history, see Chaim Raphael's *A Feast of History*.

p10   The earliest Exodus manuscript: see F.M. Cross *The Ancient Library of Qumran*, p184.

p12   Sargon birth story: see J.B. Pritchard *Ancient Near Eastern Texts*, p119.

p14   'J', 'E', 'P' and 'D': for an introduction and further bibliography, see Bernhard W. Anderson *The Living World of the Old Testament*, also the entry under 'Exodus' in the *Encyclopaedia Judaica*.

p15   Domestication of the camel: see, among other sources, Peter J. Ucko (ed.) *The domestication and exploitation of plants and animals*, Duckworth, London, 1969. There are some objections to this view, with claims of a depiction of a load-carrying camel from Egypt *c*3000 BC and archaeological evidence from Mari *c*25,000 BC, but the general absence of references to the camel in pictorial and literary material seems to indicate late domestication.

p15   Philistine invasion: for the most up-to-date and authoritative work, see Trude Dothan *The Philistines and their Material Culture*.

p18   'Lo, the wretched Asiatic . . .': quotation from the Instructions to Merikare, translated John A. Wilson, in Pritchard *Ancient Near Eastern Texts* (1969 edition), pp414-18.

p18   Quotation from B.K. Waltke, from p36 of his article 'Palestinian Artefactual Evidence . . .' quoted in bibliography.

p18   'Hapiru', 'Habiru' and 'Hebrews': for a detailed discussion with references to most of the relevant literature, see H.H. Rowley *From Joseph to Joshua*, pp38-56.

p18   Quotation from J.W. Jack: from p10 of his *The Date of the Exodus* in *The Light of External Evidence*.

1. *The Exodus pharaoh mystery*

p19   Gemini IV view of Nile Delta: see Paul D. Lowman, Jr, 'New Knowledge of Earth from Astronauts' Photographs', *National Geographic*, November 1966, pp644, 645.

p20   Biblical numbers: for a discussion of the relevant thinking, see Yehuda T. Radday 'A Bible Scholar Looks at BAR's Coverage of the Exodus', *Biblical Archaeology Review*, November–December 1982, pp69, 70.

p23   Brugsch's discovery of the 1881 mummy cache: this is vividly described in more detail in C.W. Ceram's popular classic *Gods, Graves & Scholars*, pp167-9.

p23   Quotation from Maspero: from Maspero's official report as translated in Ange-Pierre Leca's *The Cult of the Immortal*, pp26-8.

p24   X-radiography of Ramesses II's mummy: for a most authoritative account of medical examinations of this and other pharaonic mummies, see James Harris and Edward Wente *An X-Ray Atlas of the Royal Mummies*.

p24   Merneptah's mummy: see Harris and Wente, as above, also S.G. Shattock 'A report upon the pathological condition of the aorta of King Mernephtah, traditionally regarded as the Pharaoh of the Exodus', *Royal Society of Medicine of London, Proceedings of the Pathology Section 2*, 122-7, 1909.

p25   Merneptah stele: translation by J.H. Breasted *Ancient Records of Egypt* III §617. For John A. Wilson's comments, see his *Burden of Egypt*, p255.

p28   Location of Pithom and Ramesses: for an author-

p28 itative discussion of this matter, see the articles 'Pithom and Raamses . . .' by E.P. Uphill.

p28 Excavations by Montet at Tanis: see Montet *Les Nouvelles Fouilles de Tanis* (1929-32).

p28 'Ramesses' inscription: see Uphill, *op cit* p306.

p28 Quotation from G.E. Wright, from his *Biblical Archaeology*, p60.

p28 Quotation from K.A. Kitchen *Ancient Orient and Old Testament*, p59, note. I owe both this and the preceding quotation to Dr John Bimson's *Redating the Exodus and Conquest*, p33.

p30 Tanis and its lack of stratification before Twenty-first Dynasty: see J. van Seters *The Hyksos*, pp132-7, 140-2, 147-51.

p30 Merneptah text: from Papyrus Anastasi VI (British Museum 10245). Translation as quoted in Pritchard *Ancient Near Eastern Texts*, p259.

p30 Excavations by Naville at Tell el-Maskhutah: see E. Naville *The Store City of Pithom and the Route of the Exodus*.

p31 Excavations by John S. Holladay: see his excavation report listed in the bibliography.

2. *When did the walls tumble down?*

p35 Excavations by Garstang: see his *Palestine Exploration Fund Quarterly Statement* articles 1930, 1931, 1935 and 1936, also the popular book *The Story of Jericho*, written in association with his son, J.B.E. Garstang.

p35 Excavations by Dr Kathleen Kenyon: see bibliography.

p35 Quotation from Dr Kenyon: from her *Archaeology in the Holy Land*, pp181, 182.

p37 Quotation from Dr Kenyon: from her *Digging Up Jericho*, p263.

p37 Dr Kenyon's arguments against Late Bronze Age remains of Jericho having been removed by erosion: from her booklet *The Bible and Recent Archaeology*, p42.

p37 Martin Noth's aetiological interpretation of Jericho story: see his *History of Israel*, p149, n2.

p38 Dr Kenyon's argument that the Israelites would not have recognized the Jericho mound as a ruin: see her *The Bible and Recent Archaeology*, p42.

p39 Dr Joseph Callaway's excavations at et Tell: see his articles in the *Bulletin of the American Schools of Oriental Research*, nos 178 (1965), pp13-40; 196 (1969), pp2-16; and 198 (1970), pp7-31.

p41 Excavations at Tel Malhata (Arad): see Y. Aharoni and R. Amiran 'Excavations at Arad: Preliminary Report on the First Season, 1962', *Israel Exploration Journal* 14, pp131-47.

p41 Excavations at Tel Masos (Hormah): see Y. Ahar-oni, V. Fritz and A. Kempinski 'Tel Masos (Khirbet el-Meshash)', *Israel Exploration Journal* 22, p243.

p41 Excavations at Hebron: see P.C. Hammond's reports in *Revue Biblique*, nos 72 (1965), pp267-70; 73 (1966), pp566-9; and 75 (1968), pp253-8.

p41 Quotation from Pritchard: from p318 of his article 'Culture and History' in J.P. Hyatt (ed.) *The Bible in Modern Scholarship*, Nashville, 1965, pp313-24.

p41 Yigael Yadin's excavations at Hazor: see his *Hazor* listed in bibliography. His discussion of the Sisera problem appears in chapter 16.

3. *The real Biblical 'Ramesses'*

p44 Quotation from Herodotus: from Book 2 of his *Histories*, translation by Aubrey de Selincourt, Penguin Classics, 1954, p108.

p44 Tracing of original Pelusiac branch of the Nile: see article by Sneh and Weissbrod listed in bibliography.

p45 Changes to the topography of the Nile Delta since ancient times: for the most comprehensive and authoritative study, see Karl Butzer *Early hydraulic civilization in Egypt*.

p45 Quotation '. . . the forefront of every foreign land . . .': from Anastasi Papyrus III, 9.

p45 Papyrus with reference to 'Great of Victories': from Anastasi Papyrus II, 1.

p45 Essay of schoolboy Pai-Bes: from Anastasi Papyrus III, 2, as translated in E.P. Uphill 'Pithom and Raamses . . .', *op cit*.

p47 Egeria: an excellent translation of her account of her pilgrimages is Rev. John Wilkinson's *Egeria's Travels*, SPCK, London, 1972.

p47 Excavations by Mahmoud Hamza: see his report listed in bibliography.

p47 Glazed tiles from Qantir: see report by W.C. Hayes listed in bibliography.

p47 Base of Ramesses II statue from Tell-el-Shafei: see article by Shehata Adam in *Annales du Service des Antiquités de l'Égypte* 55 (1958), pp306, 318-24 and pls 27, 28.

p47 Unearthing of remains from houses of important Ramessid officials: see article 'Khata'na-Qantir' by Dr Labib Habachi, pp479-544. The Paser lintel is depicted in plate XX.

p48 Excavations by Dr Bietak: see reports listed under his name in bibliography, especially his Mortimer Wheeler Archaeological Lecture 'Avaris and Piramesse . . .' Some important information on his excavations since 1979 is to be found in his recent article 'Problems of Middle Bronze Age Chronology . . .'.

p51 Extract from Manetho's *History of Egypt*, quoted from Josephus *Against Apion* 1, 75–90, translated H.St J. Thackeray (Loeb Classical Library, 1926), pp193–9.

4. *The coming of the Hebrews*

p56 'Khnum-Khufu . . . Smiting the nomads': see Gardiner and Peet *The Inscriptions of Sinai*, vol 1, pl 11, nos 5, 7.

p56 Pepi 1 and reference to 'Sand Dwellers': see Pritchard *Ancient Near Eastern Texts*, p228.

p56 Date of Ipuwer Papyrus. I have followed Barbara Bell 'The Dark Ages in Ancient History', p11, in assigning the Ipuwer Papyrus to the First Intermediate Period. According to Bell 'most Egyptologists consider it more probably belongs to the First. The most compelling argument is given by Erman (*The Ancient Egyptians*, 1927), who points out that the work is undoubtedly older than the "Instruction of Amenemhet", since the latter quotes a passage, interpolated in corrupt form where it makes no sense, from the "Admonitions", where, on external grounds, the passage certainly belongs.' But van Seters, in *Journal of Egyptian Archaeology* 50 (1964), assigns the document to the Second Intermediate Period. Immanuel Velikovsky in his famous *Ages in Chaos* (Doubleday, 1952), argued that the document was an Egyptian account of the Biblical plagues, but the language is far too early for this.

p57 Dr Barbara Bell: see her 'Climate and the History of Egypt' listed in the bibliography.

p57 Text referring to 'Wall of the Ruler . . . to oppose the Asiatics and to crush the Sand Crossers': from the 'Prophecy of Neferty' from the First Intermediate Period, as translated by J.A.Wilson in Pritchard's *Ancient Near Eastern Texts*, see pp444–6.

p57 Quotation from chancellor Nefer-yu: translation by W.C. Hayes quoted in Bell 'The Dark Ages in Ancient History', p11.

p57 Tomb of Khnumhotep: many authorities discuss this famous painting from the tomb, and differ on the type of eye paint being brought by the entourage. According to W.F. Albright in his *Archaeology of Palestine*, p208, 'As a whole this group perfectly illustrates the very ancient story in Genesis 4:19–22 where the family of Lamech is described as including specialists in pastoral life, in playing the lyre, and in copper and iron [*sic*]

working. Since it is unlikely that the dress of the Palestinian semi-nomad changed appreciably in the following century or two, we can scarcely go wrong if we picture Jacob and his family as clad in much the same way.'

p59 Shosu: for by far the most authoritative work on this variety of Asiatic, see Raphael Giveon *Les Bédouins Shosou des Documents Égyptiens*.

p59 Habiru in Mari and Nuzi tablets: see chapter one of Robert Davidson and A.R.C. Leaney's *Biblical Criticism*, especially pp41–4.

p61 Orbiney Papyrus: for full text see translation in Pritchard's *Ancient Near Eastern Texts*, pp23–5.

p61 Professor Redford's views on the Joseph story: as a balance to these, see Kenneth A. Kitchen's review of Redford in *Oriens Antiquus* 12, 3 (1973), pp233–42.

p62 The Brooklyn Papyrus: the list of household slaves appears on the verso of Papyrus Brooklyn 35. See W.C. Hayes *A Papyrus of the Late Middle Kingdom in the Brooklyn Museum*, 1955, pp89–92; also, for Professor William Albright's appraisal, his article 'Northwest-Semitic Names in a list of Egyptian Slaves from the Eighteenth Century BC', *Journal of the American Oriental Society* 74 (1954), p232.

p64 Tutu: for scenes of Tutu's investiture, see Norman de Garis Davies *The Rock Tombs of El Amarna*, VI, pls 17–20.

p64 Quotation 'The finest of their fields are ploughed for us . . .' derives from the Carnarvon Tablet 1, found in western Thebes, and appears to be a schoolboy's copy from a contemporary inscription. For the full text see Pritchard *Ancient Near Eastern Texts*, p232.

p65 Grave of Asiatic woman at Tell el-Maskhuta: for a more detailed account of the finds, see John S. Holladay *Tell el Maskhuta*, pp44, 45.

p65 Dr John Bimson: his arguments for dating the Israelite arrival in Egypt to the time of Senwosret III appear in his article 'A Chronology for the Middle Kingdom and Israel's Bondage', *S.I.S. Review (Journal of the Society for Interdisciplinary Studies)* vol III (1979), pp64–9.

p67 Quotation from Dr Barbara Bell: from her article 'Climate and the History of Egypt', p258.

p67 Quotation from W.C. Hayes: from his 'The Middle Kingdom in Egypt', revised *Cambridge Ancient History*, fascicle 3 (1961), pp44–5.

p70 Viziers of Senwosret III: for what is known, see W.K. Simpson 'Sobkemhet, a Vizier of Sesostris III', *Journal of Egyptian Archaeology* 43 (1957), pp26–9, '*Slaves in every kind of hard labour*'.

5. 'Slaves in every kind of hard labour'

p71 Seqenenre's mummy: for a somewhat lurid account of this see Ange-Pierre Leca's *The Cult of the Immortal*, p64. Further information is to be found in G.E. Smith's *The Royal Mummies*, and Harris & Wente's *X-ray Atlas*.

p71 Papyrus Sallier: this is Papyrus Sallier I (British Museum 10185), and dates from the late Nineteenth Dynasty, somewhat later than the events described. The full text appears in Pritchard's *Ancient Near Eastern Texts*, pp231, 232.

p73 Ugarit text on making of composite bow: quotation derives from Yadin's *The Art of Warfare in Biblical Lands*.

p73 The Kamose Stela: see Labib Habachi *The Second Stela of Kamose* (Verlag J. J. Augustin, Gluckstadt, 1972).

p73 Inscriptions from tomb of Ahmose: the tomb is at el-Kab in Upper Egypt, and a full translation is to be found in Pritchard *Ancient Near Eastern Texts*, pp233, 234. See also Gunn & Gardiner 'The Expulsion of the Hyksos'.

p74 Inscription '300 *baw* ships of cedar . . .': this is quoted in van Seters *The Hyksos*, p170.

p75 Scene from tomb of Puyemre: the tomb is no 39 at Thebes, and is described in detail in Norman de Garis Davies *The Tomb of Puyemre at Thebes* (Metropolitan Museum of Art. Tytus Mem. Series 2–3), New York, 1922–3. The winepress scene is described on pp64ff. For a discussion of the winepress workers as Habiru, see T. Save-Soderbergh 'The *'prw* as Vintagers in Egypt', *Orientalia Suecana* I (1952), pp6–14.

p75 Tomb of the great herald Antef: no 155 at Thebes. Although in this example the winepress scene is now rather badly damaged, fortunately a good copy was made last century by the early Egyptologist Sir Richard Burton. This is preserved in the British Library as Brit. Mus. Add. Mss. 25644, 120.

p75 Egyptian empire-building campaigns in Canaan; for the most recent and authoritative assessment of these, see James M. Weinstein 'The Egyptian Empire in Palestine' listed in bibliography.

p77 Hatshepsut and Tuthmosis III: for entertaining background reading on this historical episode, see Newby *Warrior Pharaohs*, chapter 3 and Romer *Romer's Egypt*, chapter 9.

p80 Tomb of Senenmut: see the drawings of Mrs N. de Garis Davies in *Bulletin of the Metropolitan Museum of Art, New York*, The Egyptian Expedition 1924–5, p42, fig. 1 and p43, fig. 2.

p81 Tomb of Rekhmire: see the report by Norman de Garis Davies listed in the bibliography.

p81 Left arm fractures. This observation derives from Ange-Pierre Leca's *Cult of the Immortal*, and is not backed up by specific examples, so must be treated with reserve. Even if the observation is correct, it would need to be established whether the fractures occurred in life, or resulted from subsequent handling of the mummies, which can be very brittle.

p83 Artificial waterway north of Lake Timsah: see William Shea 'A date for the Recently Discovered Eastern Canal . . .'

p83 Recommendations to Merikare: see J.A. Wilson's translation as quoted in Pritchard's *Ancient Near Eastern Texts*, pp414–18.

p83 Sinuhe: Sinuhe's story was a popular one in ancient Egypt, and manuscripts relating it have survived from the late Twelfth to the Twenty-first Dynasties. The translation quoted is from Pritchard's *Ancient Near Eastern Texts*, p19.

p83 Relief of Seti I: from the Hippostyle Hall of Amon's Temple at Karnak. It is discussed in detail in Shea, *op cit*, and in Giveon *Les Bédouins Shosou*, pp39ff.

p85 Quotation from W.A. Ward: from his *Egypt and the East Mediterranean World*, p34.

6. Crete: a strange swath of destruction

p86 Harriet Boyd Hawes: her archaeological report on Gournia is listed in the bibliography, but for background concerning her life, see her posthumous 'Memoirs of a Pioneer Excavator in Crete' as published in *Archaeology*, Summer and Winter 1965, also the entry under her name in *Notable American Women: A biographical dictionary*.

p86 Quotations from Harriet Boyd's 'Memoirs' are from *Archaeology*, loc. cit., p269.

p88 Quotation 'The conflagration . . .': see Harriet Boyd *Gournia*, p21.

p89 Seager's excavations on Pseira and Mochlos: see bibliography. The quotation regarding human bones derives from p301 of his 'Excavations on the island of Mochlos'. No analysis or proper record appears to have been made of these bones, which are of the only known human victims of the Late Minoan IB destructions. There is no record of their having been preserved.

p89 Nirou Khani: S. Xanthudides' report appeared in the Greek archaeological journal *Archaiologike Ephemeris* in 1922, pp1–25. But for a summary and the findings on related sites, see the opening chapter of Professor Denys Page's *The Santorini Volcano and the Desolation of Minoan Crete*.

p89 Kato Zakro: for a non-technical account of the excavations, see Nicholas Platon's *Zakros* listed in the bibliography. The quotation on the fire is from pp288, 289, that on the valuable objects from p00.

p90 Quotation '. . . huge stones' is from Platon, *op cit*, pp286, 287.

p91 Professor Marinatos' excavations at Amnisos: most relevant information is to be found in his *Antiquity* article, p434.

p92 Plate tectonics: for an introduction to the most up-to-date understanding of these processes, see D.C. Heather *Plate Tectonics*.

p92 For a detailed account of the 1925–6 eruption and earthquake activity associated with Thera, see a series of articles by Professor N. Kretikos, Professor of Seismology at the University of Athens, cited by Marinatos: 'Sur la sismicité des Cyclades et de la Crète', *Annales de l'Observatoire d'Athènes*, 1925, IX, 36; 'Sur les phénomènes sismiques produits avant et depuis l'éruption du volcan de Santorin', *loc. cit*, 1926, VIII, 2ff, also the same publication 1928, X, pp47ff. It is also worth noting that a similar eastern Mediterranean earthquake of 12 October 1856 destroyed or damaged all but 18 of 3,620 houses in Heraklion, passed along the north coast of Crete to the extreme east, then by way of the distant islands of Kasos and Karpathos to Rhodes, where great damage was done to the castle, towers, mosques and houses, finally causing some minarets and houses to fall in Cairo and Alexandria. This latter information was noted by Sir Arthur Evans in his *Palace of Minos* vol II, pp315ff. A particularly violent eruption of Thera, clearly visible from Crete by night and by day (see J.E.H. Skinner *Roughing it in Crete in 1867*, Richard Bentley, London, 1868) pp146ff, followed ten years later.

p93 Marinatos' article in *Antiquity*: see bibliography. The editors' cautionary footnote appears on p439.

p93 Ninkovich and Heezen: see bibliography.

p96 Monkey's head from Thera: see article by Aris N. Poulianos 'The Discovery of the First Known Victim of Thera's Bronze Age Eruption', *Archaeology*, 1970, pp229–30.

7. Pillar of fire

p97 Height of ash cloud: for discussion see p112.

p97 Historical geography of Thera: for the most recent and authoritative introduction to the subject, see Christos Doumas *Thera, Pompeii of the ancient Aegean* listed in bibliography.

p103 Recollections of Emily Vermeule: from her little-known article 'The Promise of Thera, A Bronze Age Pompeii', *Atlantic Monthly*, December 1967, pp83–94.

p103 Excavations at Akrotiri: during his lifetime Marinatos managed to keep up a lively output of archaeological reports on his progress. These are listed under his name in the bibliography. Since his death the flow of information has slowed, and his successor, Doumas, acknowledges that much awaits publication.

p105 Tell el-Yahudiyeh juglets found on Thera: see paper by Professor Paul Aström 'Three Tell el Yahudiyeh Juglets in the Thera Museum', *Acta of the First International Scientific Congress on the Volcano of Thera*, Athens, 1971, pp415–19.

p106 Professor Peter Warren on Ship Procession fresco: see his article 'The Miniature Fresco from the West House at Akrotiri, Thera, and its Aegean Setting'.

p106 Similarity of Ship Procession landscape to topography west of Akrotiri: see Doumas *Thera*, pp55, 56.

p108 Sequence of Thera eruption: see Doumas *Thera* pp134–8, also his 1974 article 'The Minoan eruption of the Santorini volcano'.

p112 Royal Society of London report on Pelée eruption: see Anderson & Flett listed in bibliography. For a more recent, popular account of this eruption, see Gordon Thomas & Max Morgan-Witts' *The Day Their World Ended*.

p112 Disintegration of Thera volcanic cone: see H. Pichler & W.L. Friedrich 'Mechanism of the Minoan Eruption of Santorini' in *Thera and the Aegean World* (see bibliography) vol II, pp15–30.

p112 For information on the Bezymianny eruption of 1956 (which was preceded by a massive earthquake in November 1952), see H. Tazieff *When the earth trembles* (Hart-Davis, London, 1964), p115. For estimates of the height of the Krakatau eruption plume, see Simkin & Fiske (listed in bibliography), p54, n17.

p113 Professor Luce: his *The End of Atlantis* (Thames & Hudson, London, 1969) is well presented, but even if the demise of Thera was responsible for the Atlantis legend, Plato's account of it is third-hand and so garbled that it is historically valueless.

p113 Sir Denys Page and identification of the Thera eruption with the demise of Late Minoan IB Crete: see his *The Santorini Volcano and the Desolation of Minoan Crete* in bibliography, also his later paper 'On the Relation between the Thera eruption and the Desolation of Eastern Crete c1450 BC' in *Thera and the Aegean World*.

p113 James Money's observations: see his article 'The destruction of Akrotiri' in *Antiquity* 47, 50–3.

Doumas' article 'The Minoan eruption of the Santorini volcano' is a reply to it.

p114 Geological arguments on likely interval between earthquake and eruption: see P. Hedervari 'An attempt to correlate some archaeological and volcanological data regarding the Minoan eruption of Santorin' in *Acta of the First International Scientific Congress op cit*, pp257-76, also C. Blot 'Volcanism and Seismicity in Mediterranean Island Arcs' in *Thera and the Aegean World*, pp33-44.

8. *Were these the plagues?*

p115 Mount St Helens eruption: the descriptions of events and the destruction caused are taken from a graphically illustrated souvenir booklet *Mount St Helens Holocaust, a diary of destruction* produced by *The Columbian* newspaper of Vancouver, Washington.

p116 Krakatau eruption: by far the most authoritative account is Tom Simkin and Richard S. Fiske's *Krakatau 1883* listed in bibliography. This includes scientific appraisal and numerous eyewitness accounts.

p119 Sounds of the Krakatau eruption: see Simkin & Fiske, p174.

p119 Quotation 'Thousands of tongues of fire . . .': from Simkin & Fiske, p84.

p119 Verbeek report on Krakatau: the first translation from the Dutch is published in Simkin & Fiske, pp169-279.

p119 Sir Stamford Raffles' account of the Tambora eruption: see his *The History of Java* vol 1 (London, 1820), pp25-8.

p120 The 'year without a summer': see Stommel & Stommel 'The Year without a Summer' listed in bibliography.

p120 Pliny the Younger's account of Vesuvius: the translation is from J.J. Deiss's recently republished *Herculaneum*, pp11-15.

p122 Description of ashfall by captain of *Berbice*: for his full account, see Simkin & Fiske, p102.

p123 Killing of marine life: for information concerning historical instances of this, and coloration of the sea-water, see the monumental work by the Abbé Pègues, *Histoire de Santorin ou Thera* (Paris, 1842). Besides the underwater effects, gaseous vapours from Thera have caused fainting, headaches, vomiting and sometimes suffocation, and have been blamed for more long-term ailments such as angina and bronchitis. The brilliant white walls of Thera's houses have sometimes been turned green or rust-red by these gases.

p123 Gordon Thomas and Max Morgan-Witts: see their book on the Pelée disaster listed in the bibliography. The plague of ants and centipedes is described on pp137-40, that of the snakes on pp147-9.

p127 Infant burial in jars: see Yadin *Hazor*, pp38-9.

p127 Unearthing of evidence of human sacrifice at Arkhanes: see 'Drama of Death in a Minoan Temple' by Yannis Sakellarakis and Efi Sapouna-Sakellaraki, *National Geographic* vol 159, 2 (1981), pp205-22, also S. Elliott 'Archanes, Human Sacrifice in Minoan Crete', *The Athenian* vol 6 no 77, March 1980, pp22-30.

9. *'He turned the sea into dry land . . .'*

p128 Beke pamphlet of 1873: this was entitled *Mount Sinai a Volcano*.

p128 Beke's posthumously published book: this was entitled *Discoveries of Sinai in Arabia and of Midian*, and was published in London in 1878. Beke's 'confession' appears on p436.

p128 Gunkel and Meyer: see H. Gunkel *Deutsche Literaturzeitung* 24 (1903), col 3058f, and E. Meyer *Die Israeliten und ihre Nachbarstämme* (Halle, 1906), pp69ff.

p128 Canon Phythian Adams: see his *The Call of Israel* listed in bibliography.

p129 John G. Bennett: see his *Systematics* article 'Geophysics and Human History' listed in bibliography. His eyewitness account of the 1925 eruption of Thera appears on pp142, 143. (*Systematics* was a quarterly publication by the Coombe Springs Press, Kingston upon Thames, but has long ceased publication.)

p129 Bennett's dismissal of Ramesses II as pharaoh of the Exodus: this appears in his article, p151.

p130 Doctor Hans Goedicke: although he has published nothing himself, his views have essentially been set out in an article by Hershel Shanks 'The Exodus and the Crossing of the Red Sea, According to Hans Goedicke', *Biblical Archaeology Review* vol 7, 5 (September–October 1981), pp42-52. *Biblical Archaeology Review* subsequently published a lively literature both attacking and defending Dr Goedicke. See articles by Oren and Krahmalkov listed in bibliography.

p132 Mechanisms of *tsunami* waves: these are still comparatively little understood, but for an interesting modern assessment, see an anonymous article 'Tsunami and Other Waves' published in *The New Pacific*, July-August 1978, pp17-20 (excerpted from 100AI, the magazine of Lloyd's Register of Shipping; and from NOAA, the magazine of the National Oceanic and Atmospheric Administration, and other material provided by the International Tsunami Information Center in Honolulu).

p132 Account of *tsunami* devastation at Anjer: for the full account, and that of other eyewitnesses, see Simkin & Fiske, p79.

p133 Account of withdrawal of the sea by Jeroemoeidi: see Simkin & Fiske, p83.

p133 Description of recession of the sea, from Ammianus Marcellinus. This is from the translation of his works in the Loeb Classical Library, 26, 10, 15-19.

p133 Account of withdrawal of the sea at Bandora, India: a report from the *Bombay Catholic Examiner* reprinted in the *Times of Ceylon*, 18 September 1883, quoted with other examples in Simkin & Fiske, p147.

p135 I. Yokoyama: see his paper 'The tsunami caused by the prehistoric eruption of Thera' in *Thera and the Aegean World* vol I, pp277-83.

p136 Gardiner's translation of the Speos Artemidos inscription: see his article 'Davies's Copy of the Great Speos Artemidos Inscription' listed in the bibliography.

p136 Goedicke's alternative translation of the Speos Artemidos inscription: this was included in Hershel Shanks' *Biblical Archaeology Review* article, p49.

p137 Professor John Baines: see his *Atlas of Ancient Egypt*, p43.

p137 Claims by George Michanowsky: see Hershel Shanks 'In Defense of Hans Goedicke' in *Biblical Archaeology Review*, May–June 1982, pp48-52.

p139 Overpainting of Keftiu cod-pieces: see N. de Garis Davies *The Tomb of Rekh-mi-Re*.

p139 Sinclair Hood: for his arguments against the Thera eruption having been responsible for the Late Minoan IB destructions on Crete, see his paper 'Traces of the Eruption Outside Thera' in *Thera and the Aegean World* vol I, pp681-90.

p139 Thera ash on Rhodes: see C. Doumas & L. Papazoglou 'Santorini tephra from Rhodes', *Nature* vol 287, 25 September 1980, pp322-4.

p141 Quote from Julius Africanus: from the extracts from his works as translated in A. Roberts and J. Donaldson's *The Ante-Nicene Fathers* vol VI, Michigan, 1951, p132.

10. *Forty years in the wilderness*

p145 Tuthmosis III's Annals: see the translation of these in Pritchard *Ancient Near Eastern Texts*, pp234ff.

p146 George Mendenhall on the parallels between Is-

raelite covenant tradition and Hittite treaties: see G.E. Mendenhall *Law and Covenant in the Ancient Near East*, Pittsburgh, Biblical Colloquium 1955; and *Biblical Archaeologist* XVII, 2 (May 1954), pp26-46 and 3 (September 1954), pp49-76.

p146 Quotation from 'The Story of Sinuhe': see Pritchard *Ancient Near Eastern Texts*, p19.

p147 De Lascaris' description of departure of a Bedouin tribe: from his 'Secret Mission among the Bedouin' published in Bayard Taylor's *Cyclopaedia of Modern Travel: A Record of Adventure, Exploration and Discovery for the past Fifty Years* (Cincinatti, 1846), p443.

p148 Quotation from Huxley and Haddon: from Anthony Barnett's *The Human Species* (Penguin, revised edition, 1961), pl 63. Barnett does not give the original source.

p148 John Wenham's estimate of the number of those taking part in the Exodus: see J.W. Wenham 'Large Numbers in the Old Testament' listed in the bibliography.

p149 C.S. Jarvis: see his *Yesterday and Today in Sinai* (London, 1936).

p150 Bernard de Breitenbach: he was Dean of Mainz, and wrote an account of his pilgrimage to Sinai in 1483. I owe the quotation and translation to Werner Keller *The Bible as History*, pp129, 130.

p150 Bodenheimer on 'Manna': see F.S. Bodenheimer 'The Manna of Sinai', *Biblical Archaeologist* 10, 1949, pp2-6.

p150 Routes of the Exodus: for an excellent, balanced discussion of the different theories, with sources, see the entry under 'Exodus' in *Encyclopaedia Judaica*, Jerusalem, 1971, also an interesting study made by Dr Menashe Harel in an article in *The Jerusalem Post*, 20 April 1970.

p152 Serabit el Khadim: see Raphael Giveon's *The Stones of Sinai Speak*, listed in bibliography. Giveon devotes several chapters to this remote site.

p152 Gardiner's decipherment of the 'Proto-Sinaitic' script: see Gardiner & Peet listed in bibliography.

p153 Rudolph Cohen's excavations at Ain el-Qudeirat: see his article 'Did I excavate Kadesh-Barnea?' listed in bibliography.

p156 Nelson Glueck: for his arguments that the Edomite and Moabite territories were virtually uninhabited between the nineteenth century BC and the thirteenth century BC, see his 'Explorations in Eastern Palestine' II and III, pp138 and 268 respectively, listed in bibliography; also the 1940 edition of his *The Other Side of the Jordan*, pp114 and 125-47.

p156 Crystal Bennet's excavations at Buseira: see her reports listed in bibliography.

p156 Doctor Siegfried Horn at Tell Hesban: for a summary of his findings, see Magnus Magnusson's *BC*, pp75-6.

p156 Franken and Power in *Vetus Testamentum*: see bibliography.

p156 Emory University survey in Transjordan: see report by J.M. Miller in Adrian Hadidi's *Studies in the History and Archaeology of Jordan I*.

p158 Glueck's modification of his views: see the 1970 edition of his *The Other Side of the Jordan*, and note the changes he made to key passages in the 1940 edition.

p158 Quotation from W.A. Ward: from his article 'A possible new link between Egypt and Jordan during the reign of Amenhotep III', *Annual of the Department of Antiquities of Jordan and Amman* 18 (1973), pp45-6.

11. *The Canaan conquest controversy*

p161 New-style Canaanite defences: for an excellent description, see Kathleen Kenyon *Archaeology in the Holy Land*, pp161-5.

p161 Egyptian incursions into Canaan: see Weinstein 'The Egyptian Empire in Palestine' listed in bibliography.

p162 Excavations at Megiddo: see archaeological report by G. Loud listed in bibliography.

p163 Palestinian Bichrome Ware: see chapter 5 of Bimson's *Redating the Exodus and Conquest* for Bimson's demonstration of the circular reasoning used by scholars to identify the beginning of the Late Bronze Age. Important background reading is Claire Epstein's now outdated *Palestinian Bichrome Ware*. For an explanation of the scientific methods by which 'Palestinian Bichrome Ware' has been identified as an import from Cyprus, see article by Artzy, Asaro and Perlman listed in bibliography.

p165 Herzog on the fall of Jericho: see Herzog & Gichon *Battles of the Bible* listed in bibliography.

p166 Kathleen Kenyon on multiple burials at Jericho: see her *Digging up Jericho*, pp254, 255.

p166 Zeuner on preservation of organic remains at Jericho: see his *Palestine Exploration Quarterly* article listed in bibliography.

p166 Earthquake activity in Palestine: for a comprehensive catalogue of all recorded incidents since 64 BC, see D.H. Kallner-Amiran's article listed in bibliography, which provided information on quake of 11 July 1927. See also next day's issue of *The Times* of London.

p167 Quotation 'Walls and floors are hardened . . .': from p17 of Dr Kenyon's 'Palestine in the Middle Bronze Age' in the *Cambridge Ancient History*.

p171 Continuous occupation from Middle to Late Bronze Age at Megiddo: see Epstein, *op cit*, p172.

p171 Continuous occupation from Middle to Late Bronze Age at Beth-Shan: see Kenyon's 'Palestine in the Time of the Eighteenth Dynasty', pp15-17.

p171 Limited destruction at Ta'anach: see article by P.W. Lapp 'Taanach by the Waters of Megiddo', p8. He notes that the city quickly recovered and went on to 'one of its most flourishing eras'.

p173 Doctor John Bimson on mis-identification of Ai and Bethel: see his *Re-dating the Exodus and Conquest*, pp201-14.

p173 Arguments of David Livingston: see his 'Location of Biblical Bethel and Ai Reconsidered', *Westminster Theological Journal* 33/1 November 1970, pp20-40; the objections to this by A.F. Rainey 'Bethel is still Beitin' in the May 1971 issue of the same journal, pp175-88, and Livingston's reply to Rainey 'Traditional Site of Bethel Questioned' in the November 1971 issue, pp39-50.

p173 Livingston's excavations at Khirbet Nisya: so far these have only been reported in a minor journal, the ABR *Encounter* published by the Associates for Biblical Research of Philadelphia.

p173 Stelae of Amenophis II: the less damaged of these is no 6301. For a full translation, including the extract quoted, see Pritchard *Ancient Near Eastern Texts*, pp245-7.

p175 Egyptian power in Canaan in the reigns of Amenophis II and Tuthmosis IV: see Raphael Giveon's article 'Thutmosis IV and Asia', pp54-5: 'in reality the interval of seventeen years between the last Asiatic campaign of Amenophis II [year 9] and his death [year 26] was certainly a period of deterioration of Egyptian power in Asia'.

p175 The Amarna letters: see the texts of a selection of these letters translated by W.F. Albright and George E. Mendenhall, in Pritchard *Ancient Near Eastern Texts*, pp483ff.

p176 Letter of Shuwardata: this is letter RA, xix, p106, on p487 of Pritchard, *op cit*.

p176 Letter of 'Abdu-Heba: EA, no 286, on pp487, 488 of Pritchard, *op cit*.

p176 Second letter of 'Abdu-Heba: EA, no 288, on pp488, 489 of Pritchard, *op cit*.

p178 Letter of 'Abdu-Heba: '. . . shall we do like Lab'ayu': EA, no 289, on p489 of Pritchard, *op cit*.

p178 G.E. Mendenhall's 'peasants' revolt' theory: see his 'The Hebrew Conquest of Palestine', p75: 'There was no statistically important invasion of Palestine at the beginning of the twelve tribe system of Israel. There was no radical displacement of population . . . In summary there was no real conquest of Palestine at all; what happened instead may be termed . . . a peasants' revolt against the network of interlocking Canaanite city states'.

12. *The Exodus and future research*

p181 Dr Rivka Gonen: her doctoral dissertation had not been published at the time of this book going to press, but see her article 'Urban Canaan in the Late Bronze Period', also a report of a lecture by her (given to those excavating at Khirbet Nisya) in ABR *Encounter* 12, 1982, p2.

p182 The Philistines: see Trude Dothan's *The Philistines and their Material Culture*, also her summary article 'What we know about the Philistines' in *Biblical Archaeology Review*, July–August 1982, pp20–44.

p184 Dr Goedicke's April 1985 lecture: I am greatly indebted to Dr Goedicke for making available to me a copy of the unpublished text.

p185 Radiocarbon-dating of organic remains from Thera: see G.A. Weinstein and P.P. Betancourt 'Problems of Interpretation of the Akrotiri Radiocarbon Dates', *Thera and the Aegean World* vol I, pp805–14, also H. Pichler & W. Friedrich 'Radiocarbon dates of Santorini volcanics', *Nature* 262, 29 July 1976, pp373, 374.

p185 Frost-rings as a means of dating the Thera eruption: see article by LaMarche and Hirschboeck listed in bibliography.

p185 Greenland ice sheet evidence as a means of dating the Thera eruption: see Hammer, Clausen and Dansgaard article listed in bibliography.

Bibliography

ACTA of the First International Scientific Congress on the Volcano of Thera (Athens, 1971)

ALBRIGHT, W.F., *The Archaeology of Palestine* (Penguin Books, Harmondsworth, revised edn, 1956)

ANDERSON, B.W. *The Living World of the Old Testament* (Longman, London, 1958)

ANDERSON, T. & FLETT, J.S., 'Report on the Eruptions of the Soufrière in St Vincent and on a Visit to Montagne Pelée in Martinique' (Part I *Royal Society of London Philosophical Transactions* Series A. v.200, 1903, pp353-553)

ARTZY, M., ASARO, F. & PERLMAN, I., 'The Origin of the "Palestinian" Bichrome Ware' (*Journal of the American Oriental Society* 93, 1973, pp446-61)

AVI-YONAH, M. (ed.), *Encyclopaedia of Archaeological Excavations in the Holy Land* (4 vols, Oxford University Press, 1976)

BAINES, J. & MÁLEK, J., *Atlas of Ancient Egypt* Phaidon, Oxford, 1980)

BELL, B., 'The Dark Ages in Ancient History: I, The First Dark Age in Egypt' (*American Journal of Archaeology* 75, 1971, pp1-16)

'Climate and the History of Egypt' (*American Journal of Archaeology* 79, 1975, pp223-69)

BENNET, C.M., 'Excavations at Buseira, Southern Jordan, Preliminary Reports' (*Levant*, V, VI, VII, IX)

BENNETT, J.G., 'Geophysics and Human History' (*Systematics, the Journal of the Institute for the Comparative Study of History, Philosophy and the Sciences* vol I no 2 September 1963, pp127-56)

BIETAK, M., *Tell el-Daba* II (Österreichische Akademie der Wissenschaften, Vienna, 1975)

'Avaris and Piramesse: Archaeological Exploration in the Eastern Nile Delta', Mortimer Wheeler Archaeological Lecture, 1979 (*Proceedings of the British Academy* 65, 1979, pp225-90)

'Problems of Middle Bronze Age Chronology: New Evidence from Egypt' (*American Journal of Archaeology* 88, 1984, pp471-85)

BIMSON, J.J., *Re-dating the Exodus and Conquest* (Journal for the Study of the Old Testament Press, Department of Biblical Studies, University of Sheffield, 1978;

republished 1981, Almond Press, Sheffield – page numbers quoted in this book refer to the Almond Press edition).

BREASTED, J.H., *Ancient Records of Egypt* (Chicago, 1906)

BUTZER, K., *Early hydraulic civilization in Egypt* (Chicago, 1976)

CALLAWAY, J.A., 'The 1964 Ai (et-Tell) Excavations' (*Bulletin of the American Schools of Oriental Research* 178, 1965, pp13-40)

'The 1968-69 Ai (et-Tell) Excavations' (*Bulletin of the American Schools of Oriental Research* 198, 1970, pp7-31)

CHRISTOPOULOS, G.A. (ed.), *History of the Hellenic World: Prehistory & Protohistory* (Ekdotike Athenon, Athens, 1982)

COHEN, R., 'Did I excavate Kadesh-Barnea? Difficulty of site identification and absence of Exodus remains poses problem' (*Biblical Archaeology Review*, May/June 1981, pp20-33)

CROSS, F.M. Jr, *The Ancient Library of Qumran* (Duckworth, London, 1961)

DAICHES, D., *Moses, Man in the Wilderness* (Wiedenfeld, London, 1975)

DAVIDSON, R. & LEANEY, A.R.C., *Biblical Criticism, The Penguin Guide to Modern Theology* vol 3 (Penguin, Harmondsworth, 1970)

DAVIES, N. de G., *The Tomb of Rekh-mi-Re at Thebes*, 2 vols (New York, 1943, 44)

DEISS, J.J., *Herculaneum, Italy's buried treasure* (New York, 1985)

DORRELL, S., 'The Preservation of Organic Remains in the Tombs of Jericho' (Appendix L of Kenyon's *Excavations at Jericho* vol I, pp704-17)

DOTHAN, T., *The Philistines and their Material Culture* (Yale University Press, New Haven & London, 1982)

DOUMAS, C.G., 'The Minoan eruption of the Santorini volcano' (*Antiquity* XLVIII, 1974, pp110-15)

Thera, Pompeii of the ancient Aegean (Thames & Hudson, London, 1983)

EDGERTON, W.F., *The Tuthmosid Succession* (Chicago, 1933)

EDWARDS, I.E.S., GADD, C.J., HAMMOND, N.G.L. & SOLLBERGER, E., *Cambridge Ancient History* vol II, parts 1 & 2 (Cambridge University Press, 1973 and 1975)

ENCYCLOPAEDIA JUDAICA (Jerusalem, 1971)

EPSTEIN, C., *Palestinian Bichrome Ware* (E.J. Brill, Leiden, 1966)

EVANS, A.J., *The Palace of Minos*, 5 vols (London, 1921–35)

FISHER, R.V., SMITH, A.A. & ROOBOL, M.J., 'Destruction of St Pierre, Martinique by Ash Cloud Surges May 8 & 20, 1902' (*Geology* 8, 1981, pp472–6)

FRANKEN, H.J. & POWER, W.J.A., 'Glueck's "Explorations in Eastern Palestine" in the light of recent evidence' (*Vetus Testamentum* 21, pp118–23)

GARDINER, A.H., 'Davies's Copy of the Great Speos Artemidos Inscription' (*Journal of Egyptian Archaeology* 32, 1946, pp43–56)

GARDINER, A.H. & PEET, T.E., edited & completed by ČERNÝ, J. *The Inscriptions of Sinai*, 2 vols (London, 1952, 1955)
'The Ancient Military Road between Egypt and Palestine' (*Journal of Egyptian Archaeology* 6, 1920, pp99–116)

GARSTANG, J., 'Jericho' (*Palestine Exploration Fund Quarterly Statement*, 1930, pp123–32)

GARSTANG, J., & GARSTANG, J.B.E., *The Story of Jericho* (London, 1948)

GIVEON, R., 'Thutmosis IV and Asia' (*Journal of Near Eastern Studies* 28, 1969, pp54–9)
Les Bédouins Shosou des Documents Égyptiens (E.J. Brill, Leiden, 1971)
The Stones of Sinai Speak (Gaukuseisha, Tokyo, 1978)
The Impact of Egypt on Canaan (Orbis Biblicus et Orientalis, Fribourg, 1978)

GLUECK, N., 'Explorations in Eastern Palestine II' (*Annual of the American Schools of Oriental Research* 15, 1935)
'Explorations in Eastern Palestine III' (*Annual of the American Schools of Oriental Research* 18 & 19, 1939)
The Other Side of the Jordan (American School of Oriental Research, New Haven, 1940; see also revised edition, Cambridge, Mass., 1970)

GONEN, R., 'Urban Canaan in the Late Bronze Period' (*Bulletin of the American Schools of Oriental Research* 253, Winter 1984, pp61–73)

GRAY, J., *The Canaanites* (Thames & Hudson, London, 1964)

GREENBERG, M., *The Hab/piru* (American Oriental Society, New Haven, 1955)

GUNN, N., & GARDINER, A.H., 'The Expulsion of the Hyksos' (*Journal of Egyptian Archaeology* V, 1918, pp48–54)

HABACHI, L., 'Khata'na Qantir' (*Annales du Service des Antiquités de l'Egypte* 52, 1954, pp443–559)

HADIDI, A. (ed.), *Studies in the History and Archaeology of Jordan* I (Dept of Antiquities, Amman, 1982)

HAMMER, C.U., CLAUSEN, H.B., & DANSGAARD, W., 'Greenland ice sheet evidence of post-glacial volcanism and its climatic impact' (*Nature* vol 288, 20 November 1980, pp230–5)

HAMZA, M., 'Excavations of the Department of Antiquities at Qantir (Faqûs District)' (*Annales du Service des Antiquites de l'Egypte* 30, 1930, pp31–68)

HARRIS, J.E., & WENTE, E.F. (ed.), *An X-Ray Atlas of the Royal Mummies* (Chicago University Press, 1980)

HAWES, H.B., with WILLIAMS, B.E., SEAGER, R.E. & HALL, E.H., *Gournia, Vasiliki and other Prehistoric Sites on the Isthmus of Hierapetra, Crete*, Excavations of the Wells-Houston Cramp Expeditions 1901, 1903, 1904 (American Exploration Society, Philadelphia, 1908)

HAYES, W.C., *Glazed Tiles from a Palace of Ramesses II at Kantir* (New York, 1937)

HEATHER, D.C., *Plate Tectonics* (Edward Arnold, London, 1979)

HERZOG, C., & GICHON, M., *Battles of the Bible* (Weidenfeld, London, 1978)

HOLLADAY, J.S., *Cities of the Delta, Part III, Tell el Maskhuta, Preliminary Report on the Wadi Tumilat Project 1978, 79* (Undena Publications, Malibu, 1982)

HOYT-HOBBS, A. & ADZIGIAN, J., *Fielding's Egypt & the Archaeological Sites* (Fielding, New York, 1984)

HUTCHINSON, R.W., *Prehistoric Crete* (Penguin, Harmondsworth, 1962)

KALLNER-AMIRAN, D.H., 'A revised Earthquake Catalogue of Palestine' (*Israel Exploration Journal* 1, 4, 1950, pp223–46)

KELLER, W., *The Bible as History* (Hodder & Stoughton, London, 1956)

KENYON, K.M., *Digging Up Jericho* (Ernest Benn, London, 1957)
Excavations at Jericho vols I and II (London, 1960 and 1965)
'Amorites & Canaanites', *Schweich Lecture to the British Academy* (London, 1966)
Archaeology in the Holy Land (Ernest Benn, London, 4th edn, 1970)
'Palestine in the Middle Bronze Age' (in revised *Cambridge Ancient History* – see under Edwards, I.E.S.)
'Palestine in the Time of the Eighteenth Dynasty' (in revised *Cambridge Ancient History, loc. cit.*)
The Bible and Recent Archaeology (Colonnade, London, 1978)

KITCHEN, K.A., *Ancient Orient and Old Testament* (London, 1966)

KRAHMALKOV, C., 'A critique of Prof Goedicke's Exodus Theories' (*Biblical Archaeology Review*, September/October 1981, pp51–4)

LaMarche, V. & Hirschboeck, K.K., 'Frost-rings in trees as records of major volcanic eruptions' (*Nature* 307, 12 January 1984, pp121–6)

Lange, K., & Hirmer, M., *Egypt, Architecture, Sculpture, Painting in Three Thousand Years* (Phaidon, London, 3rd edn, 1961)

Lapp, P.W., 'Taanach by the Waters of Megiddo' (*Biblical Archaeologist* 30, 1967, pp2–27)
'The 1968 Excavations at Tell Ta'annek' (*Bulletin of the American Schools of Oriental Research* 195, 1969, pp2–49)

Leca, Ange-Pierre, *The Cult of the Immortal, Mummies and the Ancient Way of Death* (Souvenir, London, 1980)

Livingston, D., 'Location of Biblical Bethel and Ai Reconsidered' (*Westminster Theological Journal* 33/1, November 1970, pp20–40)

Loud, G., *Megiddo II, Seasons 1935–39* (Oriental Institute Publications, University of Chicago, vol 62, 1948)

Magnusson, M., *B.C., The Archaeology of the Bible Lands* (Bodley Head, London, 1977)

Marinatos, S., 'The Volcanic Destruction of Minoan Crete' (*Antiquity* 13, 1939, pp425–39)
Excavations at Thera, 7 vols (Athens, 1967–73)

Mazar, B., 'The Middle Bronze Age in Palestine' (*Israel Exploration Journal* 18, 2, 1968, pp65–97)
'The Early Israelite Settlement in the Hill Country' (*Bulletin of the American Schools of Oriental Research* 241, 1981, pp75–85)

Mendenhall, G.E., 'The Hebrew Conquest of Palestine' (*Biblical Archaeologist* 25, 1962, pp66–87)

Montet, P., *Les Nouvelles Fouilles de Tanis, 1929–32* (Paris, 1933)

Muhly, J.A., 'How Iron Age Technology Changed the Ancient World' (*Biblical Archaeology Review*, November/December 1982, pp46–55)

Naville, E., *The Store-City of Pithom and the Route of the Exodus* (1st edn, 1884, 2nd edn rev. 1903)

Newby, P.H., *Warrior Pharaohs, The Rise and Fall of the Egyptian Empire* (Guild, London, 1980)

Ninkovich, D., & Heezen, B.C., 'Santorini tephra' (*Submarine geology and geophysics, Colston papers* vol 17, Bristol, 1965, pp413–52)

Noth, M., *The History of Israel* (2nd edn, A. & C. Black, London, 1960)

Oren, E., 'How Not To Create a History of the Exodus – A Critique of Professor Goedicke's Theories' (*Biblical Archaeology Review*, November/December 1981, pp46–53)
'Migdol: A New Fortress on the Edge of the Eastern Nile Delta' (*Bulletin of the American Schools of Oriental Research* 256, 1984, pp7ff)

Page, D.L., *The Santorini Volcano and the Desolation of Minoan Crete* (Society for the Promotion of Hellenic Studies, Supp. Paper 12, London, 1970)

Pegues, Abbé, *Histoire de Santorin ou Thera* (Paris, 1842)

Phythian-Adams, W.J., *The Call of Israel* (Oxford University Press, 1934)

Pichler, H., & Schiering, W., 'The Thera eruption and Late Minoan IB Destruction on Crete' (*Nature* 267, 30 June 1977, pp819–22)

Platon, N., *Zakros, The Discovery of a Lost Palace of Ancient Crete* (Charles Scribner, New York, 1971)

Pritchard, J.B., *Ancient Near Eastern Texts Relating to the Old Testament* (Princeton University Press, 1955; revised edition, 1969)

Raphael, C., *A Feast of History* (Weidenfeld, London, 1972)

Redford, D.B., *A Study of the Biblical Story of Joseph, Genesis 37–50* (E. J. Brill, Leiden, 1970)
Akhenaton, The Heretic King (Princeton University Press, 1984)

Romer, J., *Romer's Egypt* (Michael Joseph/Rainbird, London, 1982)

Rossiter, S., *The Blue Guide: Greece* (Ernest Benn, London, 1977)

Seager, R.B., 'Excavations on the Island of Mochlos, Crete, in 1908' (*American Journal of Archaeology* 13, 1909, pp273–303)
Excavations on the Island of Pseira, Crete (Philadelphia, 1910)

Shanks, H., 'The Exodus and the Crossing of the Red Sea According to Hans Goedicke' (*Biblical Archaeology Review*, September/October 1981, pp42–52)

Shea, W., 'A Date for the Recently Discovered Eastern Canal of Egypt' (*Bulletin of the American Schools of Oriental Research* 226, 1977, pp31–8)

Simkin, T., & Fiske, R.S., *Krakatau 1883, The Volcanic Eruption and its Effects* (Smithsonian, Washington DC, 1983)

Smith, G.E., *The Royal Mummies: General Catalogue of Egyptian Antiquities in Cairo Museum* (Cairo?, 1912)

Sneh, A., & Weissbrod, T., 'Nile Delta: The Defunct Pelusiac Branch Identified' (*Science* 180, 1973, pp59–61)

Stommel, H., & Stommel, E., 'The Year without a Summer' (*Scientific American* 240, 6, 1979, pp134–40)
Thera and the Aegean World, Papers and Proceedings of the Second International Scientific Congress, Santorini, Greece, August 1978 (2 vols, London, 1980 – by far the most comprehensive and up-to-date collection of scholarly papers relating to the Bronze Age eruption of Thera)

Thomas, G., & Morgan-Witts, M., *The Day Their World Ended* (Souvenir, London, 1969)

Uphill, E.P., 'Pithom and Raamses: Their Location and

Significance' (*Journal of Near Eastern Studies* 27, 1968, pp291-316, and part 2, 28, 1969, pp15-39)

VAN SETERS, J., *The Hyksos: A New Investigation* (New Haven, 1966)

WALTKE, B.K., 'Palestinian Artifactual Evidence Supporting the Early Date for the Exodus' (*Bibliotheca Sacra* 129, pp33-47)

WARD, W.A., *Egypt and the East Mediterranean World 2200-1900 BC* (American University, Beirut, 1971)

WARD-PERKINS, J. & CLARIDGE, A., *Pompeii AD 79* (Catalogue of 1976 Royal Academy Exhibition, London, 1976)

WARREN, P.M., 'The Miniature Fresco from the West House at Akrotiri, Thera, and its Aegean Setting' (*Journal of Hellenic Studies*, 1979, pp115-29)

WARREN, P.M. & HANKEY, V., 'The Absolute Chronology of the Aegean Late Bronze Age' (*Bulletin of the Institute of Classical Studies of the University of London* 21, 1974, pp142-52)

WEINSTEIN, J.M., 'The Egyptian Empire in Palestine: A Reassessment' (*Bulletin of the American Schools of Oriental Research* 241, 1981, pp1-18)

WENHAM, J.W., 'Large Numbers in the Old Testament' (*Tyndale Bulletin* 18, 1967, pp19-53)

WILSON, J.A., *The Burden of Egypt* (Chicago, 1951)

WRIGHT, G.E., *The Bible and the Ancient Near East, Essays in Honour of W.F. Albright* (Doubleday, New York, 1961)
Biblical Archaeology (Duckworth, London, 1962)
Shechem (Duckworth, London, 1965)

YADIN, Y., *The Art of Warfare in Biblical Lands in the Light of Archaeological Discovery* (Weidenfeld, London, 1963)
Hazor, The Rediscovery of a Great Citadel of the Bible (Weidenfeld, London, 1975)
'Is the Biblical Account of the Israelite Conquest of Canaan Historically Reliable?' (*Biblical Archaeology Review*, March/April 1982, pp25-35)

ZEUNER, F.E., 'Notes on the Bronze Age Tombs of Jericho' (*Palestine Exploration Quarterly* 87, 1955, pp118-28)
A History of Domesticated Animals (Hutchinson, London, 1963)

Acknowledgments

The publishers would like to thank the following for kindly supplying photographic material for reproduction:

© A.C.L. Brussels: 58T

Archives Photographiques, Paris (S.P.A.D.E.M.): 27T, 27B

BBC Hulton Picture Library: 111

Dr Manfred Bietak, Österreichisches Archaeologisches Institut, Cairo: 46B, 52, 53T & B, 54

Courtesy of the Trustees of the British Museum: 63, 68, 145, 173, 177

Cairo Museum: 26, 174

Dr Joseph A. Calloway: 38

Peter Clayton: 23, 72T

Daily Telegraph Colour Library (Photo Patrick Thurston): 184-5

Ekdotike Athenon: 104T & B, 107T & B, 91T

Dr Hans Goedicke: 130-1

David Harris: 11, 151T, 162-3, 169B

Hebrew University (Weidenfeld & Nicolson Archives): 160B

Hirmer Verlag: frontispiece, 78, 79, 82T

Michael Holford: 22, 69, 151B

John S. Holladay, University of Toronto (Wadi Tumilat Project): 66

Paul Jordan: 30

The Rev. Chris Kelley: 186T

Dame Kathleen Kenyon & the Jericho Excavation Fund: 33, 36T & B, 168, 169T

Kunsthistorisches Museum, Vienna: 58B

David Livingston: 164

Bildarchiv Foto Marburg: 84

Metropolitan Museum of Art, New York: 138

Middle East Photographic Archive: 17T, 172

N.A.S.A., Washington: 21

Yorgi Panayotidi: 102T

Josephine Powell, Rome: 140B

Ronald Sheridan's Photo Library: endpapers, 160T

Steve Small (*The Columbian*, Vancouver): 117

Uni-Dia Verlag: 17B, 72B, 76, 82B, 125B

University College of London: 180

University Museum, University of Pennsylvania: 87

Wide World Photos, New York: 124, 125T

Ian Wilson: 91B, 95, 98T & B, 101, 103B, 107C, 109, 114, 186B

Yale University Art Gallery/Dura Europos Collection: 13B

Zefa Picture Library: 109

Illustrations from Books

The Athenian, March 1980: pages 126-7

Magnusson, Magnus: *B.C. The Archaeology of the Bible Lands* (Bodley Head, 1977): page 29

Yadin, Yigael: *The Art of Warfare in Biblical Lands* (Weidenfeld & Nicolson, 1963): pages 182-3

Yadin, Yigael: *Hazor* (Weidenfeld & Nicolson, 1977): page 160

For the artwork on the following pages we would like to thank Swanston Graphics, Derby: 29, 34, 40, 46, 54, 84, 87, 94, 99, 102, 110, 113, 117, 118, 134, 155, 157, 172 and 186.

All other charts, tables and diagrams were supplied by the author.

Index